Housing for the Urban Poor in Developing Countries

Housing for the Urban Poor in Developing Countries

Edited by

Brian C. Aldrich
Ranvinder S. Sandhu

RAWAT PUBLICATIONS
Jaipur • New Delhi • Bangalore • Guwahati • Kolkata

ISBN 978-81-316-0713-8

Published by
Prem Rawat for **Rawat Publications**
Satyam Apts, Sector 3, Jawahar Nagar, Jaipur 302 004 (India)
Phone: 0141 265 1748 / 7006 Fax: 0141 265 1748
E-mail: info@rawatbooks.com
Website: www.rawatbooks.com

New Delhi Office
4858/24, Ansari Road, Daryaganj, New Delhi 110 002
Phone: 011 2326 3290

Also at *Bangalore, Guwahati* and *Kolkata*

Typeset by Rawat Computers, Jaipur

Printed at Chaman Enterprises, New Delhi

Dedicated to
the urban poor in the developing countries
who have been marginalized by neoliberal housing policies,
and to the NGOs who work unceasingly
to provide access to housing for them.

Contents

PART II
Societal-Level Housing Provision Policies

PART III
Comparative Housing Policies

PART IV
Conclusion: Challenges for the Future

Acknowledgements

The volume was envisaged as a sequel to our earlier book entitled *'Housing for Urban Poor: Policy and Practice in Developing Countries'* (1995). The intention was to find out what has happened in the area of housing for the urban poor in 20 years since the above volume was published. This volume is based on papers which were specially written by the contributors at our request. We thankfully acknowledge the cooperation and commitment extended by them in the form of their valuable papers. We express our heartiest gratitude to Professor Charles L. Choguill, Editor, *Habitat International* for writing the foreword. We are indebted to the Department of Sociology and Criminal Justice, the Dean of the Liberal Arts, Dr. Ralph Townsend, and the Administration of Winona State University for extending their moral and financial support to Professor Brian C. Aldrich to visit India for finalization of this anthology. We are also thankful to our family members; Lynn, Robert, Michael and Jasmeet and Sandeep for their unflinching support to complete this volume.

Finally, we are thankful to Mr. Pranit Rawat of Rawat Publications for bringing out the book in record time for the benefit of our readers across the world.

Brian C. Aldrich
Ranvinder Singh Sandhu

Contributors

Brian C. Aldrich received his PhD in sociology at the University of Wisconsin-Madison in 1972. He taught at the University of Minnesota and is currently a full professor in the Department of Sociology and Criminal Justice at Winona State University in the Minnesota State Colleges and Universities. He is the co-editor of two books with Ranvinder S. Sandhu: *Housing in Asia: Problems and Perspectives,* Jaipur: Rawat Publications, 1990 and *Housing the Urban Poor: Policy and Practice in Developing Countries,* New Delhi: Vistaar/Sage, 1995. He is the author of numerous research articles on housing in Asia. His recent papers and publications focus on transglobal computer games.

R.G. Ariyawansa is a professor attached to the Department of Estate Management and Valuation, Faculty of Management Studies and Commerce, University of Sri Jayewardenepura, Sri Lanka.

Johanna Brauch is an urban planner and specialist on informal settlements and has worked on land issues in Cambodia for more than five years. As an advisor from the German International Cooperation (GIZ), she established and supported partnerships between local government and NGOs, and strengthened their capacity to implement pilot projects for the regularization and upgrading of informal settlements in Battambang. For this work, she received a medal of honour from the Royal Government of Cambodia.

Belew Dagnew Bogale is Assistant Professor, Department of Transport Management for Masters Programme at Ethiopian Civil Service University, Addis Ababa. Earlier he taught at Addis Ababa University, Admas University College, and St Mary's University College. He has published many research papers in professional journals and books. He specializes in transport management and infrastructure. He is a permanent member of Ethiopian National Road Transport Advisory Committee.

Camila D'Ottaviano is an architect and urban planner with a masters in Urban Environmental Structures (2002) and PhD in Architecture and Urbanism at the University of Sao Paulo (2008) with an emphasis on housing, urban design, city history, habitat and population studies. She has been a professor at Faculty of Architecture and Urbanism of University of Sao Paulo since 2010 and a researcher of Sao Paulo Metropolis Observatory and Research Group on Contemporary Cities.

Julio Guadarrama is a geographer and researcher at the Regional Center for Multidisciplinary Research of the National Autonomous University of Mexico and a professor at the Faculty of Philosophy at the same university. His research interests are land management and urban development planning, as well as mobility in large cities.

On-Kwok Lai is a professor at the Graduate School of Policy Studies, Kwansei Gakuin University, Japan, Honorary Professor in Social Work and Social Administration at The University of Hong Kong and Visiting Professor at United Nations University – Institute of Advanced Studies (UNU-IAS).

Fernanda Magalhaes graduated in Architecture and Planning at the Universidade Federal Fluminense, Rio de Janeiro, Brazil (in 1985). She obtained a Graduate Diploma in Housing from the Architectural Association of London (in 1988), as M.Sc. in Architecture and Planning at the Bartlett School of the University College of London (in 1989) and a PhD in the same school (in 1992). She is visiting professor of UniversidadeLusófona in Lisbon, Portugal (since, 2009) and Universidade Mackenzie in Sao Paulo, Brazil (since, 2005). Since 2007, she is Senior Urban Specialist of the Inter-American Development Bank (IDB). She has recently published two books with the IDB.

Carla Narciso is a graduate in landscape architecture at the University of Lisbon, Portugal. She is currently a PhD student in urban planning at the National Autonomous University of Mexico. She is a specialist in housing and public space issues.

Guillermo Olivera is a social geographer and researcher at the Regional Center for Multidisciplinary Research of the National Autonomous University of Mexico, campus Morelos. He is a specialist in urban land and housing issues, metropolitan expansion, and urbanization of the ejido (communal farm lands) in Mexico.

Suzana Pasternak is an architect and urban planner, with a degree in Public Health, at the University of Sao Paulo (1970), specialization in Urban Planning at the Université Paris 1 (1968), Master in Public Health (1975) and PhD in Public Health (1983), both at the University of Sao Paulo. She retired as Full Professor at Faculty of Architecture and Urbanism of University of Sao Paulo (FAUUSP). She is the local coordinator of Sao Paulo Metropolis Observatory.

Sheela Patel is the founder director of Society for the Promotion of Area Resource Centres (SPARC) which works in partnership with National Slum Dwellers Federation (NSDF) and Mahila Milan, two community-based organizations that support informal slum dwellers to seek secure tenure and right to the city. She is also the chair of Slum Dwellers International.

M.A.N. Rasanjalee Perera is a senior lecturer attached to the Department of Sociology and Anthropology, Faculty of Humanities and Social Sciences, University of Sri Jayewardenepura, Sri Lanka.

Kiran Sandhu is Senior Lecturer, Guru Ramdas School of Planning, Guru Nanak Dev University, Amritsar, India. She has a Master's Degree in Urban and Regional Planning, a M.Sc. in Development Planning from University College London, and completed a two year academic assignment in Ethiopian Civil Service University, Addis Ababa, Ethiopia. She has published several articles and chapters on planning, housing, transportation, environmental planning and management.

Ranvinder Singh Sandhu is UGC Emeritus Fellow at Punjabi University Patiala. He retired as Professor of Sociology from Guru Nanak Dev University, Amritsar in 2009 and he has been Dean, Faculty of Arts and Social Sciences, Coordinator of UGC Special Assistance

Programme, UGC Visiting Fellow to The Netherlands (1998), Overseas Fellow of Human Science Research Council of South Africa (1995), Visiting Professor in Winona State University, Winona, Minnesota, USA (1991–1992), British Council Visiting Fellow (1990) and Head of the Department of Sociology (1989–1991). He has twelve books to his credit.

Ahmed M. Soliman is currently working as an Emeritus Professor of Urban Planning and Housing Studies and was formerly Chair of the Architecture Department in the Faculty of Engineering at Alexandria University (2007–2012). He has published widely on issues of urban planning, and informal housing settlements in several distinguished international journals and has contributed chapters in various books.

Manoj Kumar Teotia is Assistant Professor and HUDCO Chair Coordinator at the Centre for Research in Rural and Industrial Development, a national status institute under Indian Council of Social Science Research (ICSSR). He has more than 15 years research experience working on urban issues. He has published several articles on urban issues.

Asuman Türkün graduated from the Department of City and Regional Planning, Middle East Technical University in Ankara in 1980. She took her PhD degree on regional planning from the same department in 1998. She took her associate professor degree on 'Local Governments, Urban and Environmental Policy' in 2004. Her research areas include industrial geography, economic geography, urban restructuring, urban regeneration, housing policies, methodology in social sciences and gender studies.

Yap Kioe Sheng is an urban anthropologist who worked at the United Nations Centre for Human Settlements (Habitat) in Nairobi, and at the Asian Institute of Technology and the UN Economic and Social Commission for Asia and the Pacific (ESCAP) in Bangkok. He was a consultant in Cambodia, Laos, Pakistan, Sri Lanka, Thailand, and Vietnam. Currently, he is an honorary professor at Cardiff University and an advisor to the Government of Myanmar on housing policy.

Foreword

Housing policies have passed through many permutations over the last 60 years, based on differing, even conflicting, approaches that, if we were to be totally truthful, have not really solved the housing problems faced by the majority of the world's population. In fact, if we follow the lead of the United Nations Human Settlements Programme and refer to slums as the 'shelter dimension of urban poverty', we find that the number of slum dwellers increases year by year, suggesting that the demand for safe and healthy housing is increasing in tandem with this number.

If one examines closely the evolution of housing policy as applied to the developing world over the last half decade, the inevitable conclusion has to be that government's role in solving this problem is severely constrained by various factors. In the early years of the 'development effort', governments built residential units and rented them at full or subsidized rates, or gave them to those who needed them (or more accurately, perhaps, those who had the right connections to get them). As resources were in short supply, this set of policies inevitably failed.

Responding to this failure, a second approach was initiated in which the institutional approach to housing policy shifted to taking steps to lower the price of housing, making it more affordable to residents. Again, resource constraints came into effect and, although some benefitted, the approach came nowhere near meeting the demands that existed for housing.

Perhaps it was frustration with the failure of these interventionist approaches that led to revisions in which governments worked to improve the workings of the market to facilitate home ownership among those who needed it through steps as facilitating self-help, making mortgages and other home loans more readily available, or through improvements to the access to residential land. Housing policy is currently in this era of market promotion.

This book addresses the important question of whether or not this market-based policy really works, or whether another iteration is required if the housing shortages within the developing world are adequately addressed. The challenge is enormous and complete success of any single set of policies is, perhaps, unlikely. Yet, if sustainable policies with respect to housing can be derived and implemented, the poor in the developing world will experience a significant improvement in their living standards, and this is what development is all about.

It is through studies like those presented in this volume that progress toward finding a solution to the housing challenge can be made. The authors and editors are to be commended for their effort in examining once again the details of this frustrating policy problem. How nice it would be if these studies contributed to progress in this direction.

Charles L. Choguill
Habitat International, London

Introduction

Brian C. Aldrich and Ranvinder S. Sandhu

For the first time in human history, the majority of the world's population is living in urban areas and the urban population is growing at a higher rate than its counter part, the rural population (Chan, 2010). The global urban population has quadrupled since 1950, and cities of developing world now account for 90 per cent of the world urban growth (UN-Habitat, 2006). The developed countries of the world already have higher levels of urbanization. In the case of the developing countries, Latin America is the most urbanized with 77 per cent of its population – 433 million people living in cities. Although Asia has the largest urban population (with more than 1.5 billion people living in its cities), its level of urbanization is only 40 per cent. On the contrary, the developed region has only 1.3 billion urban population. Within the developing region, Asia and Africa are least urbanized with 39.9 per cent and 39.7 per cent of their population living in cities in 2005, respectively. By 2050, both regions will become predominantly urban: Asia with 65 per cent and Africa with 62 per cent. If predictions prove accurate, by 2050 nearly 5.2 billion people – 80 per cent of world's urban dwellers, will be living in cities of the developing countries (WHO and UN-Habitat, 2010). The chapters in this book cover a range of cases related to the latest generation of policies for providing housing for the urban poor. They represent different stages in this process in a variety of metropolitan or societal, as well as the limitations inherent in a liberalized or free market approach. The outcomes, in most cases, are yet to be seen.

One of the major consequences of this urbanization, particularly in the developing countries, has been the formation of urban slum housing or over urbanization, i.e. the influx of more new residents than the new cities and metropolitan areas can either integrate into their economies or provide housing and other urban services. According to Mike Davis (2003: 28) 'the slum remains the only fully franchised solution to the problem of warehousing the twenty-first century's surplus humanity'. Slums and other forms of low-income, informal housing have emerged as a dominant and distinct type of settlement in cities of the developing countries and one out of every three city dwellers, i.e. nearly one billion people, are living in slums. Slums are characterized by shelter deprivation; lack of sufficient living area; lack of access to improved water; lack of access to improved sanitation; and lack of secure tenure. Slums are not only manifestation of poor housing standards, lack of basic services and denial of human rights, these are also symptoms of dysfunction of urban societies where inequalities are not only tolerated but allowed to perpetuate (UN-Habitat, 2006: ix). There are some 860 million residents of slums in the developing countries, and the number is estimated to be growing by 6 million per year between 2000 and 2010 (UN-Habitat, 2012).

Urbanization has traditionally, i.e. in the 1950s and 1960s, been virtually synonymous with slum growth, especially in sub-Saharan Africa, Western Asia and Southern Asia, where annual growth rate of urban areas and slums were the same. But recent analysis by some economists has shown that this relationship no longer holds (Marx, Stoker and Suri, 2013). They show that the relationship between urbanization, poverty and slum housing no longer shows a consistent relationship across countries. Countries like India, for instance, are experiencing slower slum growth and higher GDP, while others, such as the Philippines, show the same traditional relationship between urbanization, poverty and slum housing (Marx, Stoker and Suri, 2013). Their explanation is that the growth of the world market has tempered the relationship between cities and their hinterlands. Some countries have profited by this, in the reduction of the growth of slums, while others, they conclude, have become 'poverty traps' (Marx, Stoker and Suri, 2013). The conclusion from these studies is that the source of variation is in the policies, institutions and strategies of the different countries (Glaeser, 2013). The reduction or expansion of slums in various cities and countries revolves, not around the straight forward effects of urbanization-population growth, but the nature of the policies and programmes employed by the various urban entities to deal with shortage of adequate housing for the population.

Whether slum housing is expanding or contracting in countries, metropolitan areas and cities, the UN-Habitat report describes an urban reality where slum dwellers die earlier, experience more hunger, have less education, have fewer chances of employment in the formal sector and suffer from ill-health than the rest of the urban population. Although they generally constitute one of the largest groups in developing countries, most of the time their existence in a city is not recognized (Sandhu and Sekhon, 2013). On the contrary, efforts are made to make them invisible within the city so that they may not damage the image of the city in the eyes of international visitors. The evidence suggests that despite the enormous potential of cities to bring prosperity, the wealth generated by cities does not automatically lead to poverty reduction or slum improvement. On the contrary, inequalities between the rich and poor continue in cities despite their economic development, and the number of slums and slum dwellers/urban poor has been consistently increasing. Although slums have a symbiotic relationship with the city, slums and informal settlements in most cities suffer from extreme inequalities and are deprived of basic services which are essential for human existence. Housing is predominantly a basic problem of the urban poor.

In his last clear statement of the theory and practice of housing in developing countries, Cedric Pugh* (2001) described the key shift in housing for the urban poor: the World Bank's move towards 'Whole Sector Housing Development'; better known as liberalized or free market housing, beginning in 1983. The Marx, et. al. analysis shows, however, that these market changes have not had uniform effects on housing and economic development. They did not find a consistent pattern in this regard. On the contrary, the case studies which follow describe a variety of different programmatic, policy and cultural factors which, the respective housing specialists argue, effect the provision of housing for the poor in each country.

The cases which follow describe, in the urbanized areas of the developing countries, the variety of policies, programmes, strategies and cultural orientations taking place in the way various developing countries are seeking to deal with slum housing. They illustrate the profound but varied transformation taking place in the social organization of societies in regard to housing in general and housing the urban poor, in particular. The chapters in the book are divided into three parts: programme-level cases, societal level cases and multiple-society cases. Part I shows examples of how this process is working at the project level. In Cambodia, Brazil, Turkey, Ethiopia and India, it shows how particular programmes are fairing and the kinds of successes or failures they have evidenced. Part II examines various policies and their effects at the societal level in China, India, Egypt, Brazil and Sri Lanka. Part III compares several societies at once in terms of their strategies and cultural orientations towards providing housing for the poor, including Lisbon and Porto, Portugal and Bogota, Colombia; Natal, Brazil and Mexico; Sri Lanka and Singapore; Bangkok, Thailand and Mumbai, India.

Part I
Programmes for Housing the Poor

Chapter 1, in Part I, 'The Struggle for the Right to Adequate Housing: Urban Poor Communities in Cambodia', by Yap Kioe Sheng and Johanna Brauch is a limiting case. Cambodia is only 20 per cent urban but almost 80 per cent of its urban housing, according to UN-Habitat, is sub-standard slum housing. The country's housing allocation process is still pre-market, with the Prime Minister and other elite members of the society making up the rules to their own advantage as they go along – but in no institutional capacity. The Boeung Kak Lake area in Phnom Penh is a prime example according to the researchers. When land ownership was first formalized, this area along the lake was declared State Park Land. Thus, it was disqualified from private ownership – or the receipt of land title by occupants under a 2001 law. The Regime, however, turned around and leased the land to a foreign commercial interest. The residents appealed to the World Bank Inspection Panel. Upon review by the World Bank (and support from a German NGO working with the group), the regime responded by issuing an ad hoc sub-decree granting title to 12.4 ha and 800 households in the area. As many as 500 families had received title by 2011. Cambodia, in this case, illustrates a 'pre-market' approach to the provision of housing for the urban poor. Negotiations around a particular project are carried on between the regime and various socio-economic and political groups. The housing market is not part of the process because that sector has not yet emerged.

Chapter 2, 'New Urban Policies and Radical Transformations in Historic Urban Centres and Squatter Housing Neighbourhoods in Istanbul, Turkey', describes the fate of squatter housing neighbourhoods in Istanbul, under the new, free market for housing. The assumption of the Turkish government, according to author Asuman Türkün, was that 'property rights and commodification of informal housing would integrate the poor ... into the formal real estate market by enabling market transactions'. Instead the new laws created support for large urban space projects similar to the United States in the early 1960s. The power for local municipalities to take land for various reasons, like conservation, cultural and natural heritage, eliminated the influence of the squatters who had been resettled in these areas. The chapter reports the results, with photos, of the outcomes for six low-income neighbourhoods which had developed under previous regimes. In the case of Istanbul, these housing projects for the urban poor, put in place much earlier, have fallen victim to the operation of an urban housing market with strong central government powers.

Chapter 3, by Sheela Patel, 'Perils of Policies to Produce Housing Without Community Participation: Jawaharlal Nehru National Urban Renewal Mission (JNNURM) and Basic Services for the Urban Poor (BSUP) Projects in India', recounts the conflict between community participation by the poor in the provision of housing and the bureaucratization of the new housing policies in Mumbai and other Indian cities. Patel lists a large number of problems facing the poor in their attempts to take advantage of the policies of the government, including flawed designs, poor financial estimates of project costs, project location problems, costly delays, late bureaucratic institutionalization, minimal community participation, negligible response to community resistance and lack of municipal knowledge and experience in setting up and executing the projects for low income residents. The process described in the Indian situation shows that the new legislation to support the provision of housing through broad sector and institutional processes was indifferent to the special needs – and participation – of the urban poor.

Fernanda Magalhaes, in Chapter 4, 'Housing the Poor in Brazil: The Slum Upgrading Experience', presents keys to rehousing and integrating the low income squatter settlements into urban life. It is based upon reports from nine case studies of housing projects for low-income residents in Brazil. These projects occur in the context of a society which has defined housing as a social right. Magalhaes lists nine critical factors for successful integration: preserving project continuity over time, enhanced degree of political commitment and participation, urban and architectural quality, pluri-sectoriality, local economic development, resettlement, adequate technical staff, support from social workers and institutional arrangements. Her mega-summary of lessons and challenges include: obtaining legitimacy and institutionalization, integrality and sustainability, quality and cost, and targeting and globalization. The study conclusions are the other limits of housing for the poor (compared to Cambodia): making certain that housing is a right, and its provision fully integrated into the institutional structure of the society.

Chapter 5 completes the presentation of programme-level studies of housing. The chapter, based on research in Ethiopia by Belew Dagnew Bogale and Kiran Sandhu, approaches the problem of housing for the urban poor from a more oblique angle. The work by Dagnew and Sandhu shows that in order for high levels of urbanization to be accommodated, there needs to be coordination between the transportation and the housing sector; especially with the level of informal housing occurring on the outskirts of Ethiopian cities (a fairly typical development). This thorough study shows precisely the problems of transportation for low income individuals – actually a range of different transportation users – and how their solution is tied to the larger issue of inter-sector coordination. They point out the difficulty of getting inter-sector integration under conditions of a weak, fragmented governmental authority.

Part II
Societal-Level Housing Provision Policies

In Chapter 6 in Part II, 'Housing Questions in Hyper-Modernizing (Post-) Socialist China: Enigma of Urban Contradictions and Dualism in Economic Miracle,' On-Kwok Lai examines the effects of the policy of market financing of housing on the Chinese population. He reports that at least 250 million people are without permanent housing as a result of urbanization from unprecedented market growth and new market-oriented housing policies. At the same time, the collapse of the housing registration system (*hukou*), the control of land policies by local municipalities and the Chinese Communist Party officials, housing speculation and increased costs have created a 'dualism'. Rural residents, unregistered new urban immigrants, newly educated members of the labour force, and increasingly, new members of the middle class are marginalized in regard to adequate housing. The result, Lai concludes, is increasing social conflict, segregation and social exclusion. Consequences spread to the surrounding countries who also suffer from the environmental pollution created by decades of economic expansion. China, in this case study, is an example of the housing market run amok; everyone in the society is dependent upon the operation of the market without any provision for social housing, i.e. government support of housing for the urban poor.

Chapter 7, 'The Crucible of Housing the Bottom of the Pyramid in Egypt' by Ahmed M. Soliman, describes the several previous attempts by the Egyptian government to provide adequate housing to its increasingly urbanized population. This case describes the absence of a private market sector for housing. Confounding the challenge of housing for the urban poor, he reports, is a huge expansion of informal settlements during the current transition in governments. Although Soliman recognizes the problems of land control and planning under the government, he calls for an 'implemental perspective' rather than a move to a finance-based urban land market for the benefit of the poor. He would prefer to see the development of a common ground among the major stakeholders in providing urban housing for the poor, i.e. a form of inclusive social housing.

Chapter 8, 'Intervention Policies and Practices Regarding Favelas and Other Precarious Dwellings: Brazil and The City of Sao Paulo' by Suzana Pasternak and Camila D'Ottaviano, presents a history of the modes of intervention in favelas and other irregular settlements. Their analysis leads up to the policies and provisions of the current regime in Brazil and the set of laws, policies and programmes which have been developed up to the present. They show that partial, non-integrated, low budget interventions were not only unsuccessful but also inherently unequal in social outcomes. The new, 'holistic' model, involves urban equality, land regulation, access to public services, facilities and green areas, as well as to social programmes. The Pasternak and D'Ottaviano analysis provides 'deep background' for the chapter in Part I by Fernanda Magalhaes.

Chapter 9, 'Review of State Role in Provision of Housing for Low Income Community in the City of Colombo, by R.G. Ariyawansa and M.A.N. Rasanjalee Perera, report a description of the housing situation in Sri Lanka. The emphasis is upon the districts of the metropolitan area around Colombo, the population growth, the condition of housing and the need for additional housing units. They describe the level of satisfaction of the residents of a major part of the metropolitan area. The main elements of the new, post-civil war housing programmes, resulting from new housing legislation in Sri Lanka, are described.

Chapter 10, 'Housing for the Urban Poor in India: Emerging Trends and Issues' by Manoj Kumar Teotia, displays an encyclopaedic knowledge of Indian policies and programmes for housing the urban poor. In the process, he directly examines the effects of the liberalization of housing programmes for the poor by the World Bank and other global institutions. First he shows the continuing relationship in India between urbanization, the low income population and access to adequate housing and related services. He reviews the liberalization of the housing market in India and its failure to solve the problem of housing for the urban poor. These problems include: lack of access to land, lack of security of tenure, problems with housing finance, and lack of affordability of market-built housing. The solution, he concludes, include greater allocation of money from the public sector for investment in housing for the poor, developments in material and technology to lower costs, stricter regulation of private builders and an increase in the repayment capacity of the poor.

Part III
Comparative Housing Policies

Chapter 11, 'Low-Income Housing and Market-Driven Urban Development in Asian Cities', by Yap Kioe Sheng compares current projects in several Southeast Asian cities: Singapore, Bangkok, Mumbai and Colombo. He reviews the ideas of Turner in the 1970s of sites-and-services which eventuated in a project-oriented approach to the provision of housing for the urban poor. By the late 1980s, this emphasis on special housing projects was judged a failure and the World Bank announced its 'enabling' approach. This calls for cities (and societies) to organize the housing sector into a market with an emphasis on housing exchange value. He reviews several approaches, including land buying and land sharing in Bangkok, Colombo, Phnom Penh and Mumbai. Each of these has had its weaknesses, resulting in negative outcomes for the poor original inhabitants. He reviews a project in Bangkok, *Suwan Prasid 2*, which follow-up studies indicated, had positive outcomes for its inhabitants. He puts his analysis within the current context of the competition between cities for world-class status and attractiveness.

Chapter 12, 'Urban Land Planning and Management for Affordable Housing: Experiences in Countries in Ibero-America and their Implications for Mexico' by Guillermo Olivera, Carla Narciso and Julio Guadarrama, compares the provision of social housing in Mexico with that of selected cities in Portugal, Brazil and Colombia. They present a case for the argument that Mexico has a weakened commitment to social housing through the '... weakness and neglect' of local governments and the '... character of the local property regime ...'. This has resulted, they conclude, in a '... limited and interrupted attention to the housing needs of the poor.' Portugal, Brazil and Colombia, have each developed its own version of a commitment to the provision of social housing for the poor, both in its constitution and in current master plans. Colombia, for instance, created a special public company for the production of social housing. The master plan for social housing takes into account sustainability, compact urban growth, urban ecology, facilities and the road system.

Part IV
Conclusion: Challenges for the Future

Some of the challenges facing the future of housing for the urban poor in developing countries are outlined in the following pages. An attempt has been made to summarize and spell out the implications of the World Bank's model shift to the privatization of housing for the poor. With slums and squatter settlements expanding as rapidly as the urban metropolitan population as a whole, what do these cases from around the developing world suggest needs to be done at the programme, societal and global level? The following conclusions emerge:

1. A free or liberalized market for housing, by itself, does not solve the problem of housing for the urban poor.
2. Some form of governmental support for social housing is necessary if the problem is to be dealt with effectively, including the recognition of special needs.
3. The implementation and institutionalization of all the 'conceptual points' listed by the World Bank is a difficult, ongoing task.
4. The 'use value' of housing for the urban poor is more important than its 'exchange value', i.e. housing for the poor is not just a lifestyle or status issue, but a matter of social and economic survival in the explosion of the metropolitan population in developing countries.

Large scale urbanization in developing countries continues to support squatting and informal settlement in large cities. While some urban regimes have been able to halt or reverse this process, it continues in most countries. The cases examined in this book illustrate the extent of the problem and the variety of efforts being made to mitigate it.

References

Aldrich, B. and R.S. Sandhu. (1995). *Housing the Urban Poor: Policy and Practice in Developing Countries,* New Delhi: Vistaar and London: Zed Books.

Chan, Margarat. (2010). 'Foreword', *Hidden Cities: Unmasking and Overcoming Health Inequalities in Urban Settings,* Switzerland: WHO and UN-Habitat.

Davis, M. (2004). 'The Urbanization of Empire: Megacities and the Laws of Chaos', *Social Text, Special Issue: Global Cities of the South.*

Glaeser, Edward L. (2013). 'A World of Cities: The Causes and Consequences of Urbanization in Poorer Countries', *NBER Working Paper No. 19745,* December.

Marx, Benjamin, Thomas Stoker, and Tavneet Suri. (2013). 'The Economics of Slums in the Developing World', *Journal of Economic Perspectives,* 27(4), pp. 187–210.

Pugh, Cedric. (2001). 'The Theory and Practice of Housing Sector Development for Developing Countries, 1950–99', *Housing Studies,* 16(4), pp. 399–423.

Sandhu, R.S. and B.S. Sekhon. (2013). 'Slums and Planning in Urban India: A Case Study of Amritsar City,' paper presented at International Seminar Shimla Retreat III on *'The Social Dynamics of the Urban'*, organized by Indian Institute of Advanced Study, Shimla, in collaboration with School of Advanced Study, University of London and South Asian Studies Council, Yale University, USA, 10–11 June.

UN-Habitat. (2000). *Global Strategy for Shelter to the Year,* 83rd Plenary Meeting, 20th December, New York.

UN-Habitat. (2003). *The Challenge of Slums: Global Report on Human Settlements,* London: Earthscan.

UN-Habitat. (2006). *State of the World's Cities 2006/7,* London: Earthscan.

UN-Habitat. (2011). *Housing for the Future: A New Global Housing Strategy to the Year 2025*, 23rd Session of the Governing Council, 14 April, New York.

UN-Habitat. (2012). *State of the World's Cities 2012/2013: Prosperity of Cities,* Nairobi: United Nations Human Settlements Programme.

World Health Organization and UN-Habitat. (2010). *Hidden Cities: Unmasking and Overcoming Health Inequalities in Urban Settings,* Switzerland.

PART I

Programmes for Housing the Poor

1

The Struggle for the Right to Adequate Housing

Urban Poor Communities in Cambodia

Yap Kioe Sheng and Johanna Brauch

In 2010, Cambodia had a population of 14.1 million; 2.8 million (or 19.8%) of them lived in urban areas, according to UNPD (2012). Although housing conditions have improved over the past two decades, they are still inadequate for many families in urban (and rural) areas. UN-Habitat (2010: 260) estimated that 78.9 per cent of the urban population in 2007 lived in 'slums', defined as houses lacking improved water, improved sanitation, durability and sufficient living area (see Table 1.1). Most households in urban areas still build their own house. There is a small but expanding private sector that builds houses for the upper middle class and the expatriate community. The government built public housing in the 1960s and 1970s, mainly for government staff, but has not done so since. The urban poor can build or buy only a rudimentary shelter with limited access to basic infrastructure services.

Table 1.1 *Urban population and slum population in Cambodia (1990–2007)*

Year	*Urban population (millions)*	*Slum* population (millions)*
1990	1.222	0.964
1995	1.613	1.273
2000	2.160	1.705
2005	2.750	2.172
2007	3.020	2.385

Source: UN-Habitat, 2010: 260.

Besides a limited access to basic infrastructure, a major problem faced by the urban poor is land tenure insecurity. Many urban families do not have a land title, although they are entitled to the plot they occupy, if they occupied it for at least five years prior to the adoption of the 2001 Land Law. However, as land prices increase due to a growing demand for urban land by middle and upper income households and local and foreign companies, those without a legal title (and even some with a legal title) face a serious threat of eviction. Forced eviction from land within the city has become a regular occurrence in the capital Phnom Penh and elsewhere. Some evictions go largely unnoticed; others cause international outrage with political implications, as shown by the following case.

The Boeung Kak Lake in Phnom Penh used to be a natural reservoir for excess drainage water during the rainy season. The first people probably began settling around the lake in the 1980s and many more arrived during the early 1990s. Eventually, some 4,250 families made it their home. They used the lake to grow vegetables and catch fish and snails. Foreign tourists frequented the lake-side restaurants and low-cost guesthouses. In 2006, the government started land registration in the area, but excluded most lake settlements, because it considered the area state public land which cannot be privately owned or leased. In 2007, the Phnom Penh Municipality nevertheless included the lake in a 99-year lease to a Cambodian-Chinese company with links to senior government officials. In 2008, the government retroactively converted the lake area into state private land to regularize the lease agreement.

When the company began to fill the lake, many lakeside houses were flooded. The company offered the residents three types of compensation: (a) a cash payment of US$ 8,500; (b) a core house and plot of land in a resettlement area 15–20 km from the city centre and US$500; or (c) resettlement on site at some undefined time in the future. For the residents these options were unsatisfactory, but most took the cash payment and left. In 2009, communities from the Boeung Kak area wrote, however, to the Inspection Panel of the World Bank, the major donor of the land registration programme, requesting a review of the programme's impact (Inspection Panel, 2009: 23–27).

The communities claimed to have been adversely affected by the programme which had failed to formalize their land tenure. It argued that if the status of the area was unclear, it could not have been leased to a private company; if it was state private land, the communities would be entitled to land titles; if it was state public land, it could not have been leased to a private company and the communities should have been resettled according to agreed guidelines, which require that their living standard and economic conditions are restored to pre-project levels. After assessing the situation, the Panel agreed that the Boeung Kak communities had been unfairly excluded from the land titling process.

In response, the World Bank requested the government to resettle the Boeung Kak residents according to its resettlement guidelines, but the government denied that the guidelines applied, as the lake area had not been part of the land registration programme. Instead, the government ended its agreement with the World Bank, citing the complexity of the conditions attached to the funds, and continued land registration on its own. Faced with an escalating controversy, the prime minister eventually intervened with a sub-decree granting titles for 12.4 ha of land in the project area to 800 remaining households, but by then 85 per cent of the population had been forcibly displaced. By the end of 2011, some 500 households had received a title.

Evictions occur in many countries, but they occur more often in Cambodia due to its rapid urbanization and economic growth from an extremely low base during a short period of time. Its outcomes are often more serious, because the government lacks the institutional capacity (including policies, laws, regulations and procedures) and the political will to regulate urban development, protect the population against its negative impact and enforce the law. An all-pervading culture of corruption further complicates the situation. The dominant political culture attaches little value to the rule of law or the protection of the poor, but allows the rich and powerful, in collusion with senior government officials, to grab land with impunity.

Seeing that the rich and powerful are above the law, some other persons try to seize every opportunity to take advantage of the poor and powerless. There are many stories about people who, with support from government officials, buy the identity of eviction victims to acquire their land, housing or cash compensation, or assume two or more identities to claim additional compensation or property. Many urban poor mistrust their leaders who deal with landowners and developers on their behalf, because private companies bribed community leaders in the past to betray the community and allow the company to grab its land.

The Boeung Kak Lake case is illustrative of the struggle by the urban poor for the right to adequate housing, where they face powerful political and economic interests. The Boeung Kak Lake case may also be important if it turns out to be a milestone in this arduous struggle. The following chapter takes the Boeung Kak Lake case as the watershed and consists of two major parts. The first part presents the factors in Cambodia's recent history that contributed to the current housing situation of the urban poor in Phnom Penh and elsewhere. It describes the work of NGOs, the United Nations (UN) and bilateral agencies to improve the living conditions of the urban poor and to develop a national housing policy.

The second part of the chapter traces the aftermath of the Boeung Kak Lake case which led to the introduction of several government measures that could improve the living conditions of the urban poor. It focuses on the opportunities which the measures generated in Battambang, a secondary city, for cooperation between the Municipality, NGOs and local communities to improve the housing of the urban poor. Despite these measures, realization of the right to adequate housing for the poor remains, however, difficult to achieve in Phnom Penh due to the high land development pressure.

Re-urbanization

In 1960, Phnom Penh had a population of 3,89,000 which represented 69.7 per cent of Cambodia's urban population. As the Vietnam War spilled over into Cambodia's countryside, refugees swelled its population to 9,00,000 in 1970 (UNPD, 2012), although some estimates put it at 2 million (see Table 1.2). Due to the war, urban infrastructure and housing were destroyed and hardly any urban development took place between 1965 and 1994. When the Khmer Rouge seized power in 1975, it moved the entire urban population to the countryside, leaving the urban centres virtually devoid of people. The goal of the Khmer Rouge was to destroy traditional and modern institutions and build a new egalitarian, agrarian society.

Cambodia's re-urbanization started with the overthrow of the Khmer Rouge in 1979. People fled the countryside where the civil war continued and sought refuge in urban areas. They occupied abandoned villas, apartments, offices, temples and cemeteries or built their shacks on vacant land and rooftops. Because most government records had been lost, there was no proof of land or building ownership: everyone was a squatter. The 1991 Peace Accord handed the United Nations the tasks of preparing national elections, demobilizing 1,90,000 soldiers and their families, resettling 1,80,000 internally displaced persons and repatriating 3,77,000 refugees from camps along the Thai border.

Table 1.2 *Population of Phnom Penh (1970–2010)*

Year	*Population*	*Year*	*Population*
1970	9,00,000	1990	6,15,000
1975	1,00,000	2,000	11,49,000
1980	2,38,000	2010	15,09,000

Many figures are estimates because no census was conducted for several decades.
Source: UNPD, 2012.

The authorities expected the returnees, demobilized soldiers and displaced persons to return to the rural areas, but many, particularly the younger ones, preferred to go to the urban areas as they had never farmed, cultivable land was scarce and much of it was mined. Phnom Penh and other urban centres were totally unprepared for this influx and lacked the capacity to look after even their resident population (Yap et al., 1992). Squatting was the only option, but many migrants had to buy 'the right to squat' from local leaders, municipal officials or the police. Buyers knew that the officials were selling state land for private profit, but still saw themselves as owner of their plot, as they had written contracts or a family book which gave them an urban status.

After the 1993 elections, the economy grew rapidly at an average annual rate of 7.8 per cent for the period 1994–2010. Per capita GDP (PPP, 2005) increased from \$740 in 1993 to \$ 1,968 in 2010. The percentage of persons below the international poverty line (\$1.25 a day) fell from 48.6 per cent in 1994 to 28.3 per cent in 2010 (World Bank, 2012). Due to a lack of other investment opportunities, many people with spare capital bought and developed land. Phnom Penh has also seen investment in real estate by Koreans, Chinese and other Asians. Prices for residential land rose from \$700 per m^2 in 2006 to \$ 1,600 per m^2 in 2007, but declined in 2008 due to the global financial crisis (Hong, 2010: 57).

As land values rose, evictions became more frequent (see Table 1.3). Previous land uses were restored and dilapidated structures were demolished and replaced by modern buildings. As the city needed more infrastructure, the houses of the urban poor had to give way. The rehabilitation of the railway system is expected to affect some 4,100 families nationwide (BABC, 2012: 3). The need for people to move is perhaps understandable, but most resettlements occur on an ad hoc basis, without timely warning or planning, without suitably located alternative sites and adequate economic and financial support. The land the urban poor used to occupy often remains vacant long after the eviction. Donors like the World Bank urged the government to introduce a modern land registration system to secure property rights and develop efficient land markets. Since most Cambodians live in the rural areas, attention was centred on rural land, although most land development pressure was in the urban areas.

Table 1.3 *Eviction threat by development type in Phnom Penh (2003)*

	Settlements	*Percentage*
Infrastructure	74	38
Beautification	22	11
Commercial	23	12
Other	22	12
Uncertain	56	27
Total	197	100

Source: ACHR, 2004: 16.

Security of Land Tenure

The Khmer Rouge had banned private property. After their fall, people occupied houses and land, and acquired use-rights on those properties. As the government tried to control migration to the city, properties were specifically allocated to state workers. In 1989, the government introduced limited private property with ownership rights in urban areas and possession rights in rural areas. All claims on pre-1979 ownership of land were made invalid. Houses could now be inherited.

In 1993, a new constitution replaced the centrally planned economy with a free-market economy, and gave citizens the right to own land. The 2001 Land Law (RGoC, 2001), recognizing the right of private landownership, stated that one cannot be deprived of landownership, unless it is in the public interest and in line with regulations, and compensation is paid. Land owned before the war could not be reclaimed, but anyone who had enjoyed uncontested possession of land that can be lawfully possessed for at least five years prior to the adoption of the law acquired the right to an ownership title.

The Land Law and a subsequent sub-decree (RGoC, 2003) introduced the concept of 'social land concession', a legal mechanism to transfer state private land to the poor who lack land for housing and/or farming. The recipient cannot sell, rent or donate such land for five years, but can apply for a land title after five years. Social land concessions do not apply in case of a *de facto* occupation of land (i.e. squatting), but can be used to resettle evicted urban poor households on state private land. As land rights were clarified, public functions related to land management were consolidated in the Ministry of Land Management, Urban Planning and Construction (MLMUPC).

As for housing, the MLMUPC was expected to: (a) develop policies, plans and measures to solve the problem of squatters and house building; (b) set rules and regulations regarding land tenure, urbanization, construction, expropriation and land reserves; and (c) plan urbanization by subdividing open land, developing zones and promoting housing development (RGoC, 1999). However, the Ministry has no unit responsible for housing and none of the above tasks received much attention; the focus was clearly on land registration.

In 2002, the MLMUPC launched the Land Management and Administration Project (LMAP) with support from Germany, Finland and the World Bank to register urban and rural land in the country. By September 2009, more than 1.58 million parcels had been surveyed and 1.24 million titles distributed, mainly in the rural areas (Inspection Panel, 2009: 48, 54). It had been agreed that LMAP would not title land in areas where disputes were likely or 'informal settlers or squatters' occupied state land. Titles could only be issued to informal settlers, after the government had decided to grant them land through land sharing or resettlement, or had taken steps to legalize their occupation (Inspection Panel, 2009: 52–53, 74, 115).

In reality, the authorities frequently excluded land from registration in order to deny the urban poor a title for land that they occupied, but was sought after by businessmen, politicians or foreign investors. They also prevented the urban poor from registering land by accusing them of illegal occupation of state land. They can do so because the land classification process is not transparent and a register of state land is not publicly accessible (Bugalski and Pred, 2010: 4–5). In fact, many urban poor never applied for a land title, because they did not know that they qualified or how to apply. Those who applied would be told to pay US$200–700 as informal fees (Bristol, 2007: 4).

Table 1.4 *Urban poor settlements in Phnom Penh (1997–2009)*

District	*Number of urban poor settlements*	
	1997	*2009*
Total inner districts	256	129
Total outer districts	123	281
Total	379	410

Source: STT, 2009: 2.

Due to evictions, 30,000 families in Phnom Penh(or around 10 per cent of the current population) have been displaced between 1990 and 2011 (STT, 2011). There are now more urban poor communities in the outer districts of the city than its inner districts (STT, 2009: 2; Table 1.4). Some communities have been resettled in a participatory and well-planned manner, but most households face hardship as a result of their forced resettlement. Sites lack adequate housing, potable water and sanitation (see Table 1.5). Access to jobs is difficult and costly due to the site's remoteness (Khemro and Payne, 2004: 193). This forces many households to return to the city, but finding alternative accommodation is not easy.

Some urban poor live in rental housing provided by private house owners. A 2008 study in Phnom Penh found that rental housing was often occupied by students and women factory workers. Most rental houses have wooden walls, corrugated-iron roofing and little ventilation. The rooms accommodate 2–8 persons and rents an average of US$ 15–20 per month. Piped water is available to only about a quarter of residents; over 90 per cent have access to electricity (with supply controlled by their landlord); 83 per cent have a shared toilet of which 60 per cent feel that it is in useable condition (STT, 2008: 1–2). Such conditions are not different from those in urban poor communities.

Table 1.5 *Infrastructure in urban poor communities in Phnom Penh (2009)*

	Inner-city districts		*Outer-city districts*		*Total*
	Coverage (%)	*Cost*	*Coverage (%)*	*Cost*	*Coverage (%)*
Water		(Riel/m3)		(Riel/m3)	
State	68	550–800	36	500–800	47
Private	32	1,500–3,000	53	2,000–4,000	45

Cont'd...

...Cont'd

Other (ponds etc.)	–	–	11	–	8
Total	100		100		100
Energy		(Riel/Kwh)		(Riel/Kwh)	
State (electricity)	60	350–750	41	350–750	47
Private (electricity)	40	1,000–2,200	49	1,200–3,000	47
Other (kerosene, wood)	–	–	10	–	6
Total	100		100		100

Riel: US$ 1.00 = Riel 4,100

Source: STT, 2009: 7

Capacity and Institutional Development

Since the late 1980s, NGOs have worked with urban poor communities to improve their living conditions. As the number of evictions increased, some NGOs shifted their attention to advocacy work, defending the right of the poor to live in the city. Other NGOs work primarily to build the capacity of urban poor communities to organize, improve their housing and economic conditions, resist eviction and negotiate a planned and participatory resettlement, when necessary. The Bangkok-based Asian Coalition for Housing Rights (ACHR) played a key role by helping establish the Solidarity for the Urban Poor Federation (SUPF), an urban poor community network (Boonyabancha, 2000: 10). In 1998, the Phnom Penh Municipality signed an agreement with SUPF and ACHR to establish the Urban Poor Development Fund (UPDF) whose activities include:

(a) organizing communities and savings groups, workshops, exchange visits and negotiations with government for land tenure and basic infrastructure;
(b) extending loans and grants to communities and community networks, provided they have a well-established savings group;
(c) developing partnerships between communities and local government to learn from each other in a productive relationship (Phonphakdee et al., 2009: 571–574).

From 1995 to 2006, UNCHS/UN-Habitat provided technical assistance to the Phnom Penh Municipality to draft and test upgrading and resettlement procedures and to build institutional capacity for its application. It also tried to forge partnerships between the Municipality, NGOs and urban poor communities. Jointly with NGOs, it upgraded informal settlements to show what can be achieved limited funding and people's participation. In order to establish a platform for district officials, community leaders and NGOs to work together, develop mutual trust and institutionalize public participation, the Municipality established community development management councils in each district (ACHR, 2001: 71).

In 2003, at the urging of ACHR, the Prime Minister launched a campaign in Phnom Penh to improve 500 urban poor settlements over five years. By 2008, almost 14,000 households in 122 communities had benefitted from infrastructure upgrading and house improvement loans from UPDF (UPDF, 2008: 10). However, land tenure security was often still lacking, and some upgraded settlements were later demolished and its community evicted. Moreover, upgrading was done on an *ad hoc* basis and communities needed to show their political allegiance to the government to be selected. Living conditions in the urban poor settlements improved, but a coherent low-income housing policy was still lacking.

In 2003, the UN agreed to provide technical assistance to the MLMUPC for the drafting of a national housing policy. Following studies and consultations with NGOs, community-based organizations, the private sector and ministries concerned, a draft policy was presented to the MLMUPC and a summary was prepared for submission to the Council of Ministers for approval. It was, however, never submitted, as the ministry was unsure about the practical implications of the policy and probably lacked the political will to defend it. Although part of the same ministry, LMAP did little to support the UN and NGOs working with informal settlers and squatters to enhance access to land, and provide adequate housing and basic services. It kept its focus on land registration, sometimes at the expense of the urban poor.

It is hard to say how effective the new policy would have been and if it would have put an end to land grabbing and involuntary evictions of the urban poor. Previously drafted procedures for the improvement or resettlement of urban poor communities had made little impact in practice, and upgrading programmes had been unable to withstand market forces and political machinations. Phnom Penh is the capital city, and much of the decision-making on its development is made at the national level. Despite attempts to build bridges, the gap between senior decision-makers and urban poor communities is very wide. Even senior municipal officials in Phnom Penh tend to be too far removed from the daily life of the urban poor to be much concerned.

It is at the level of the district and sub-district that the problems of the urban poor come into sight, but district and sub-district officials do not have the authority or willingness to intervene and risk the wrath of financially and politically powerful persons in case of land grabbing. In brief, Phnom Penh proved to be an extremely difficult place to realize the right to adequate housing for the urban poor. After the drafting of the national housing policy, the MLMUPC and the UN, therefore, agreed to continue their capacity development efforts, including a demonstration project, in a provincial capital.

Battambang: A Pilot for Good Governance

With 1,50,000 inhabitants, Battambang is Cambodia's fourth largest city. It was selected as the location for the testing of the national housing policy, because pressure on urban land is still low, although the economy is growing and tourist arrivals are increasing. In 2001, the Ministry of Interior had selected Battambang as a pilot district to promote decentralization and good governance, and to initiate projects on local self-administration, administrative reform, urban development planning and public participation. Since 2003, a team of the German Development Service (DED) had assisted Battambang with the formulation of spatial planning standards and procedures, and the drafting of a land-use plan involving local stakeholders. In 2008, the new decentralization law turned the district of Battambang into a municipality.

The land use planning process had increased awareness among local officials about the state of the urban poor settlements in the city. They hampered infrastructure development, but also showed the scale of urban poverty. A 2009 survey found 66 urban poor settlements with 2,250 households. Like in Phnom Penh, people had settled on land used or reserved for public facilities, in road corridors and above drainage canals, in temple compounds and cemeteries, and on railway reserves. The local government felt the need to take action and households felt the threat of eviction, but neither knew what to do.

The MLMUPC and the UN organized a series of workshops for local and provincial officials, representatives of NGOs and community leaders to show the options and the steps required to improve the housing conditions of the urban poor. Officials undertook trips to Phnom Penh, Thailand and Pakistan to visit actual upgrading and resettlement programmes. In 2005, Battambang's district governor formed a Technical Working Group (TWG) on Informal Settlements composed of representatives from concerned departments to ensure cooperation and coordination and institutionalize the activities. As most members had little expertise and experience, DED had to build its capacity and provide on-the-job training. With the support of the TWG, 13 urban poor communities in Battambang had set up savings groups and community-based organizations by 2006.

In 2006, the Battambang provincial governor selected the 'Garden Area', a long and narrow plot of state public land, reserved as a public garden in a 1981 city extension plan, as the site for a demonstration project. After the war, families had occupied part of the land and some 300 families lived there without security of tenure. The governor proposed to provide land tenure security, upgrade basic infrastructure and improve the houses, and to use any vacant land to resettle 200 poor households currently living in road corridors, above drainage canals and in a cemetery. The World Bank agreed to fund the project to test the applicability of social land concessions in urban areas, while Habitat for Humanity agreed to implement it.

The Garden Area in Battambang and the Boeung Kak Lake in Phnom Penh were both state public land occupied by the urban poor for many years, but that is where the similarities end. Leasing Boeung Kak Lake and converting state public land for private development proved easy. Making state public land available for the urban poor in the Garden Area proved very difficult as it had never been done before. Eventually, the authority of the provincial governor and his influence in the Ministry of Interior led to the signing of a note by the Prime Minister allowing the use of the area for housing the urban poor. This led to the preparation of a plan for the re-blocking of the settlement and for the upgrading of the infrastructure.

The difficulties of applying the sub-decree on social land concessions, the strict supervision by the MLMUPC, the terms and conditions of World Bank funding and the complexities of planning an existing settlement slowed implementation. Only in early 2012, the municipality invited the Garden Area residents to apply for occupancy certificates which allow them to apply for a title after 10 years. Within weeks, 279 families had submitted an application. By mid–2012, the demarcation of 113 plots had been completed, while landfill had finished for 80 plots; 50 families had already built a house on their newly demarcated plot. In November 2012, work on roads and drains will start.

In the meantime, the TWG, supported by DED, had drafted proposals for on-site upgrading of other urban poor settlements. Work on these proposals had, however, stalled, because of the reluctance of the Municipality to apply the arduous approach used for the Garden Area for the remaining settlements. Moreover, the Municipality did not feel it was authorized to take decisions on the use of state land, fearing it would infringe on the powers of national agencies. It saw resettlement as the only option within its remit, but it lacked the land and financial resources for resettlement and recognized the problems for affected families.

Decentralizing Responsibilities

After the Boeung Kak fiasco, Germany came under political pressure in the Bundestag and at a UN Human Rights meeting for its support to land registration in Cambodia. It was accused of having legitimized systematic inequality in the land sector and breached its obligation to respect and protect the human rights to food and housing. In response, Germany and Cambodia negotiated an agreement for continued German assistance in the land sector, but with an additional focus on urban low-income housing. With German support, the MLMUPC drafted a new housing policy, disregarding the policy prepared in 2003. International and local NGOs and other interested parties reviewed the draft, which is currently under consideration by the Council for Land Policy.

In addition, the Prime Minister signed Circular 03 '*Resolution on Temporary Settlements on Illegally Occupied Land in the Capital, Municipal and Urban Areas*' (RGoC, 2010), the first government directive opening the possibility of regularization and upgrading of informal settlements. In line with the decentralization policy, the Circular assigns local government the task of finding solutions for 'temporary settlements on illegally occupied land' through a series of steps: (a) data collection on the number of informal settlements; (b) identification, mapping and classification of their sites; (c) a census in their population; (d) identification of possible solutions (upgrading, resettlement or another option); (e) a decision on land tenure (usufruct, rental or ownership); (f) planning infrastructure and services provision; and (g) stakeholder participation in the project.

The Circular came at an opportune time for Battambang. The Municipality had already taken the first three steps but it could neither regularize informal settlements (because it had no control over the land) nor resettle the population (for which it did not have the resources). The Circular created the space for the Municipality to develop its own solutions for informal settlements. Until to date, it has focused its attention on settlements in road reserves, as local government has the authority to set the road width and convert road reserves without approval by the national government. Backed by the Circular, it is now willing to reduce the road width and give the land to informal settlers, provided they re-block their settlement to ensure adequate public access and contribute resources for settlement upgrading.

With the Municipality showing its commitment, communities made their commitment by increasing their savings and improving their settlement. In collaboration with NGOs, they tidied up their area, improved roads and cleaned drains. One community even built a new drainage canal, all using community resources. With the support of an NGO, Community Empowerment and Development Team, four communities are developing re-blocking plans, based on maps hand-drawn by the community. Two communities have completed their plan and are negotiating with local government for land tenure security. By contributing their own resources, communities are in a better position to claim tenure security. One community has received approval for tenure security from the provincial government, and started to plan house re-adjustments, minimizing costs through proper planning and reuse of materials.

Capacity development of urban poor communities is critical to expand Circular 03's impact throughout Battambang. Community Managed Development Partners, an NGO, helps organize monthly meetings of representatives from urban poor settlements that have established community-based organizations. In those meetings, communities can share knowledge and experience gained with the regularization and upgrading of informal settlements. Circular 03 is strengthening the relationship between urban poor communities, local government and NGOs who start to see each other as partners. It is opening a new field of cooperation between local government and the population for urban poverty reduction. The question remains whether this is sustainable.

Conclusions

During the past two decades, economic growth has lifted many people in Cambodia out of poverty and improved their housing conditions, but has bypassed many others in urban (and rural) areas. Despite years of work by NGOs to empower the poor through community-based organizations and years of efforts by multilateral and bilateral agencies to build government capacity for effective urban poverty reduction, progress has been disappointing. Without laws and policies that recognize the rights of all citizens to secure land tenure and adequate housing, and without the political will for their enforcement, the poor will continue to be the victims of rapid urban development, competition for urban land and land grabbing.

Some positive developments have emerged lately. The decentralization policy and Circular 03 have given local governments the responsibility to find solutions to the problems of informal settlements. Shatkin (2000: 2370) identified factors that determine the influence of community-based organizations and NGOs on local government with regard to informal settlements: intensity of land development pressure, access by local government to resources for the improvement of informal settlements, the nature of the relationship between powerful economic actors and local government, and the strength of community-based organizations.

Land development pressure and the collusion of government officials and powerful economic actors make it difficult to secure land for housing the poor in Phnom Penh, even if resources are available and communities are well organized. The conditions in Battambang are more favourable: land development pressure and land speculation are still limited; community organizations are gaining strength; regular meetings of officials, NGOs and representatives from urban poor communities reduce the distance between the parties; the contributions made by the communities, though small, help further enhance trust.

For Circular 03 to make a nationwide impact, the capacity of local governments needs to be developed. Although the Circular has not made much impact on informal settlements in large cities like Phnom Penh and Siem Reap, the experiences of Battambang can serve as good practices for other secondary cities and towns in Cambodia. Effective solutions from the secondary cities and towns may eventually find their way into a new national housing policy and make an impact in larger cities.

Circular 03 is a significant step forward, but there have been many false starts in the past and decisions based on merely a circular can be easily overturned. Also, the Circular does not give local government full control over informal settlements. For urban poor settlements on state land affiliated with a national Ministry, it can only propose solutions; the final decision about such land is made at the national level. There, the authorities do not always have the interests of the poor in mind, as the case of Boeung Kak Lake has shown.

Note

The authors would like to thank Erin Collins for her comments on an earlier draft of the chapter.

References

Asian Coalition for Housing Rights – ACHR. (2001). 'Building an Urban Poor People's Movement in Phnom Penh, Cambodia', *Environment and Urbanization,* 13(2), pp. 61–72.

——. (2004). 'Negotiating the Right to Stay in the City', *Environment and Urbanization*, 16(1), pp. 9–25.

Boonyabancha, Somsook. (2000). 'Bridging the Finance Gap in Housing and Infrastructure', *Cambodia: The Urban Poor Development Fund – A Case Study.* Coventry: Homeless International.

Bridges Across Borders Cambodia – BABC. (2012). *Derailed: A Study of the Resettlement Process and Impacts of the Rehabilitation of the Cambodian Railway*. Phnom Penh: Bridges Across Borders Cambodia.

Bristol, Graeme. (2007). *Cambodia: The Struggle for Tenure: Case Study Prepared for Enhancing Urban Safety and Security: Global Report on Human Settlements* 2007. Nairobi: UN-Habitat.

Bugalski, Natalie and David Pred. (2010). 'Land Titling in Cambodia: Formalizing Inequality', *Housing and ESC Rights Law Quarterly*, 7(2), pp. 1–8.

Hong, Phouma. (2010). 'Asset Price Bubbles and Challenges to Central Banks: The Case of Cambodia', in Kim Juhan (ed.) *Asset Price Bubbles and Challenges to Central Banks*, Kuala Lumpur: The Southeast Asian Central Banks (SEACEN), pp. 57–70.

Inspection Panel. (2009). *Report and Recommendation. Cambodia: Land Management and Administration Project (Credit No. 3650-KH)*, Washington DC: World Bank.

Khemro, Beng Hong Socheat and Geoffrey Payne. (2004). 'Improving Tenure Security for the Urban Poor in Phnom Penh, Cambodia: An Analytical Case Study', *Habitat International*, 28(2), pp. 181–201.

Phonphakdee, Somsak, Sok Visal and Gabriella Sauter. (2009). 'The Urban Poor Development Fund in Cambodia: Supporting Local and Citywide Development', *Environment and Urbanization*, 21(2), pp. 569–586.

Royal Government of Cambodia – RGoC. (1999). *Organization and Functioning of the Ministry of Land Management, Urbanization and Construction*. Phnom Penh: Royal Government of Cambodia.

——. (2001). *Land Law*. Phnom Penh: Royal Government of Cambodia.

——. (2003). *Sub Decree on Social Land Concessions*, Phnom Penh: Royal Government of Cambodia.

——. (2010). *Resolution on Temporary Settlements on Illegally Occupied Land in the Capital, Municipal and Urban Areas*. Phnom Penh: Royal Government of Cambodia.

Shatkin, Gavin. (2000). 'Obstacles to Empowerment: Local Politics and Civil Society in Metropolitan Manila, the Philippines', *Urban Studies*, 37(12), pp. 2357–2375.

Sahmakum Teang Tnaut – STT (2008). 'Living on the Edge: A Look at Three of the Groups Living in Phnom Penh's Informal Housing', *Facts & Figures*, Phnom Penh: Sahmakum Teang Tnaut.

——. (2009). 'The 8 Khan Survey: Urban Poor Settlements in Phnom Penh', *Facts & Figures*, Phnom Penh: Sahmakum Teang Tnaut.

——. (2011). 'Displaced Families Phnom Penh', *Facts & Figures*, Phnom Penh: Sahmakum Teang Tnaut.

UN-Habitat. (2010). *The State of Asian Cities 2010/11*, Fukuka: United Nations Human Settlements Programme.

United Nations Population Division – UNPD. (2012). *World Urbanization Prospects: The 2011 Revision*, New York: United Nations. <http://esa.un.org/unpd/wup/unup/ p2k0data.asp>.

Urban Poor Development Fund – UPDF. (2008). *Newsletter* May 2008. Phnom Penh: Urban Poor Development Fund.

World Bank. (2012). KHM_Country_MetaData_en_EXCEL. Washington DC: World Bank. < http://data.worldbank.org/country/cambodia>

Yap, Kioe Sheng, Terry Standley and Roberto Ottolenghi. (1992). *Report of the UNCHS (Habitat) Needs Assessment Mission in the Urban Sector in the Light of the Imminent Influx of Returnees in Cambodia*, 26 April – 24 May, Nairobi: United Nations Centre for Human Settlements (Habitat).

2

New Urban Policies and Radical Transformations in Historic Urban Centres and Squatter Housing Neighbourhoods in Istanbul, Turkey

Asuman Türkün

The Socio-Spatial Implications of Changing Urban Policies in Different Parts of the World

It is observed that under the waves of the dominant political and ideological form of capitalist globalization after 1980s, the flexible labour and production processes have diversified the spatial priorities of different types of economic activity, with varying socio-spatial implications in different parts of the world.[1] Despite contextual differences due to place-specific factors, it is possible to find surprisingly common economic and political measures as well as very similar urban policies in different countries. In the industrial core of the world, the majority of cities have started to be transformed into places of consumption from places of production, leading to the expansion of the service sector. In order to cope with the economic loss due to the deindustrialization of major industries, the new urban policy has been directed towards competitive efforts of raising the position of cities in the hierarchy of global cities by developing qualified services such as finance, insurance and real estate (FIRE) as well as 'cultural industries', so called 'creative industries', such as film-making, broadcasting, advertisement, art, fashion, and design.[2] According to this dominant urban policy, the investments made in these fields are expected to increase the competitive position of urban areas so as to take place as important nodes within the global economy by attracting capital investments as well as qualified labour.

It is also observed that the new urban policy attempts to transform cities into attraction centres at the global scale by means of urban regeneration projects or big urban projects as 'flagship projects', which poses generous investment opportunities for the national or international capital. Within this transformation, urban tourism has acquired an important role as an economic development strategy. Therefore, cities have started to search for some defined niches within the globalized circuits of tourism by investing in their underutilized assets or by 'manufacturing' new identities to become attractive. The areas with the potential of regeneration due to their locational or historical significance either gentrified or turned into tourist attraction nodes to attract higher income local or international visitors.[3] Consequently, investment on urban land has gained importance as the major means of capital accumulation in the new global order. There has always been a friction between the function of urban land as the arena of collective consumption and its importance as a means of capital accumulation; however, after 1990s, the second priority started to dominate urban policies and the 'exchange value' of urban land has gained importance at the expense of 'use value' by all means.

There has always been uneven development and segregation within urban areas with respect to unequal income levels and opportunities of different classes; however, parallel to the neoliberal economic policies, today we are faced with the reality of exclusion of increasing numbers of people from formal employment opportunities, decent living conditions and access to societal resources. Owing to the increasing importance of urban rent, the new transformations on urban space serve the function of redistributing this rent among capitalist classes and secure sustained economic growth through 'accumulation by dispossession'. Accordingly, it is an opportunity to rebuild urban areas so as to open new investment channels for 'surplus-capital' and to take the over-valued urban land from the hands of lcw-income people inhabiting those areas (Harvey, 2008). We can easily claim that after 1990s, this transformation took the form of 'state-led gentrification', which can be characterized by close direction and intervention of central and local governments in urban renewal and regeneration projects not only in the historic parts of the city but in almost all housing areas, including social housing areas. This type of transformation and gentrification can also be observed in all types of public spaces within urban areas by means of privatization. The criticisms on the negative implications of these spatial transformations on the disadvantaged segments of population are attempted to be guarded in the political discourse by the introduction of 'social mix policies' as well as the policies of minimizing the poverty problem through social aid mechanisms.[4]

The major legitimizing discourse in this process is that economic growth and developmental potential of the cities will increase the job opportunities and enlarge the labour market, leading to a decrease in socio-spatial inequality and segregation. However, as the majority of studies on globalizing cities clearly show, the increase in job opportunities in a growing economy does not guarantee an equal distribution of these opportunities for different segments of labour. As the new service sectors require a limited number of well-paid jobs for qualified labour, the need for a large number of poorly paid unskilled or semi-skilled service sector workers also increase. As a result, the number of the 'working poor' increases, leading to the intensification of segregation and exclusion tendencies within cities. Especially when economic growth depends on increasing productivity instead of increasing the employment opportunities of the labour force, no apparent improvement can be achieved for the masses of people. In other words, the economic growth encountered during the globalization process has been realized without creating sufficient job opportunities and the unemployment levels have continuously increased in the majority of the countries.[5]

On the other hand, in the developing part of the world two processes can be observed parallel to each other. As the major cities become the target of global production chains, they also become the nodes where qualified service sectors as well as urban tourism investments flourish. The global shift in the geography of industrial production has been manifested in those countries as the emergence of extraordinarily grown primate cities, due to lower labour costs and taxes as well as supportive governmental subsidies. The concentration of unemployed and underemployed cheap labour in major industrial areas hinders the decentralization tendencies of industrial establishments and leads to the polarization of capital in few, but frequently one primate city, which is the case in almost all developing countries. It can be claimed that with the introduction of economic globalization, i.e.

'globalization from above', this polarization tendency has intensified parallel to the preferences of international companies (Roberts, 2005; Türkün, 2009). It is observed that these companies tend to get located in central locations of developing countries owing to stronger networks between foreign and national political and economic elites in major cities and the ease of directing and controlling production in locations where specialized producer services, financial and professional services as well as craft and manufacturing industries are more developed and diversified. This preference is also related to the existence of an abundant labour force of various skills, which is ready to accept low wages and poor working conditions with no social security.

The second tendency in those cities, similar to the case in the developed part of the world, is the development of qualified producer services as well as real estate and construction sectors. These sectors are expected to sustain economic growth and provide a kind of guarantee in the face of economic crises. As a result, the scarce resources of those cities are directed to big urban projects, in the form of office blocks, financial centres, shopping malls and luxurious gated housing estates as well as tourism investments by means of the coalitions between central or local governments and local/international capital holders. These new urban policies have substantial implications for the housing areas in the developing part of the world. The scarcity of urban land in central locations has created a pressure on especially informally developed housing areas and dilapidated social housing estates located in rent-gaining areas, which have now become valuable urban land owing to urban sprawl (Türkün, 2011). In this process, the interest in the central historic areas has also increased, resulting in gentrified housing enclaves or tourist attraction zones. The common implication of these transformations appears to be zero-tolerance eviction practices in especially informally built squatter housing areas as well as the historic urban centres populated by the urban poor. This situation leads to severe problems especially in the big industrial cities of developing countries, where large numbers of people live under absolute poverty line (Türkün, 2009).

Istanbul has always been the most important city in Turkey owing to its location advantages and historical role in the national economy as well as its influential place in the region extending from Europe to the Middle East. The city has been highly affected by those radical restructuring attempts after 1990s. The effects of the process of deindustrialization, similar to that observed in western cities, can be observed in Istanbul (Turkish Statistical Institute, 2009). Since the mid-1990s, the vision of Istanbul as a centre of international finance, service and tourism guides the new urban policies, which are mainly based on encouraging the development of real-estate and construction sectors. The city is accepted to be the most important target of national and international capital for real-estate development due to its high rent-gaining potential. Therefore, development of big urban projects in the form of office blocks, hotels and shopping malls as well as luxurious housing estates has become the priority for municipalities, big construction firms, and development agencies. Consequently, the importance of urban areas with high rent-gaining potential has increased, leading to intensifying pressure on the housing areas of low-income working population that constitute the labour force of industrial establishments and the growing service sector in the city. It is intended to demolish these squatter housing areas especially in central locations and move the inhabitants to the housing blocks built by the powerful state institution, Housing Development Administration of Turkey (TOKI), in the peripheral locations of the city with the help of bank loans they are obliged to pay in 15 years. On the other hand, in the historic areas, regeneration projects are imposed, leading to the gentrification of these areas and eviction of the inhabitants.

In this paper it is aimed to put forward the spatial manifestations of these new urban policies in Istanbul, Turkey, with respect to the implications for the inhabitants with limited financial resources and almost no access to housing opportunities in the formal market. The findings of the research made in six low-income neighbourhoods, declared as 'urban renewal/regeneration/transformation areas', give an insight into the current and expected implications of these radical transformations in such areas.[6] These findings will be analysed so as to show the great gap between the objectives of the transformation projects and the ability of the people living in those housing areas to have an access and be included in this transformation. Our research project has stemmed from the observation that the new urban policies based on the transformation or renewal of informal settlements, social housing areas and historic urban centres, which are mainly legitimized on the basis of the 'earthquake threat' and the necessity of 'planned development', appear to ignore social policies. When we analyse the implementation processes and the outcomes of the completed projects, it is observed that the economic and social conditions of the inhabitants and the survival strategies established within those neighbourhoods are not taken into consideration. In addition, the mechanisms of including the inhabitants in decision-making processes have been neglected in almost all the cases. The common implication of all these transformations appears to be the displacement or eviction of almost all inhabitants in those areas. Therefore, it is aimed to discuss whether it is possible to attain a success story in terms of equality and the quality of life without considering the objective conditions of the inhabitants affected by those transformation projects. It is hoped to shed light on the new social problems and tensions this new urban policy is expected to create and bring into the agenda the ethical dimensions of urban transformation so as to suggest some alternative housing policies, which would take into account the present reality for a *fair and realistic* urban policy.

Implications of the Changing Urban and Housing Policies in Turkey: Socio-Spatial Transformation in Istanbul

Despite serious attempts in particular periods, there has never been a comprehensive and consistent housing policy in Turkey and the social dimension of those policies has been weak in all periods. There has neither been a policy of providing 'social housing' under public ownership nor 'cheap rental housing' and the housing policy has always been oriented towards owner-occupancy. This phenomenon can be observed in almost all late industrialized capitalist countries; the provision of housing is left to free market mechanisms and under these conditions, the only option for those people who cannot get an access to the authorized housing market is 'squatter housing'. Therefore, the shelter problem for low income segments of the population is still an unresolved issue. Because a high proportion of the people are excluded from the social security protection of the state, house ownership becomes the only means of security and the housing areas, where social networks and mutual help mechanisms are established within time, facilitate attachment to urban environment. Another housing option for low-income people is to settle in dilapidated historic housing areas in central locations of the city or in squatter housing areas as renters. Those housing areas, which had provided a temporary solution for the new migrants until 1990s, now tend to gain a permanent nature and transform into areas where urban poverty gathers.

In recent years, a powerful hegemonic coalition has emerged in Turkey, reflected in similar discourses shared by all the actors constituting this coalition. The major concern of these actors is focused on the 'necessity' and 'urgency' of urban renewal or transformation in the housing areas of the urban poor, which is expected to bring about economic growth through the proliferation of the construction sector. The most important means of enhancing the power of this coalition have been the changes in existing laws and the enactment of new laws, leading to an increase in the executive powers and financial resources of major state institutions. Key state institutions, especially the Housing Development Administration (TOKI) and the Privatization Administration, have been strengthened to enable the realization of big urban projects (Türkün, 2011). As a result, it can be claimed that most of the laws concerning urban areas in recent years have been intended to clear away the obstacles so as to enable the realization of a radical urban transformation process, targeting especially the housing areas of low-income working population and the urban poor. Therefore, in this part of the paper, first the attempts to solve the housing problem of low-income segments of population in Turkey and their socio-spatial outcomes will be evaluated in successive periods especially after 1950s. Then, the urban regeneration/renewal practices, which have become the major tool for urban policies after 2000s, will be explored together with the dense debates around this issue. The changes in the legal framework will also be put forward so as to discuss their crucial role during this radical transformation period.

The 1920–1990 Period: The Planned versus Informal Settlements

There has never been a comprehensive housing policy in Turkey due to financial and institutional weaknesses although high migration rates have generated a high demand for housing. Another important point is that housing policies have never been in favour of low-income population who are incapable of having an access to housing in the authorized housing market conditions. In general, owner-occupancy has been encouraged and rental social housing similar to those in European countries has never come to the agenda. Although there were some efforts to provide credits for housing cooperatives, only the housing demand of a limited number of urban residents with relatively higher income and social security coverage could be fulfilled. Considering the fact that almost half of the workers were devoid of such protection, the only option for the large number of migrants from rural areas and the urban poor was the construction of squatter houses (gecekondu) on state land or on divided parcels with no housing construction permit. First squatter housing development was experienced in Ankara due to high migration rates after it was declared as the capital city of Turkey in 1923 (Türkün, 2009). On the other hand, by the 1960s, squatter housing development had become widespread in major industrial cities of Turkey, such as Istanbul and Izmir, owing to the import-substitution industrialization policies in those years. As the data collected by the Ministry of Development and Resettlement indicates, in the 1960s, the share of squatter housing in the total housing stock in Ankara had reached 64 per cent; and this figure was 40 per cent in Istanbul and 24 per cent in Izmir. Especially in Istanbul, where the major industries of Turkey were located, the direct connection between the industrial areas and squatter housing districts were apparently observed (Tumertekin, 1997).

In those years, state officials or local governments had a sympathetic attitude towards those spontaneous developments. Although squatter housing was always acknowledged to be an important urban problem, it was tolerated as a temporary solution for the provision of low-cost housing for workers, who provided the necessary labour force for the flourishing industrial sector (Senyapili, 1992, 2006; Tekeli, 1982). In fact, in the first Development Plan of 1963, housing was one of the most important issues; the measures such as the provision of infrastructure to squatter housing areas, new houses for the ones living in desperate conditions, and the provision of credits for improvement were cited in detail. Due to the increasing number of migrants in metropolitan cities and their political power in affecting the elections, various measures were taken to integrate them into the system by giving their houses legal status especially during election periods. This was, in fact compatible with the sympathetic attitude of major international institutions towards squatter housing, which was considered to be a solution for the urgent housing problem in the developing part of the world (Turner, 1967, 1977; Mangin, 1967; Harris, 1998). In this respect, the *Law of Squatter Housing* (Law No. 775) enacted in 1966 was the basic law, which reflected the acceptance of the reality of informal housing in Turkey. This can also be considered to be an attempt to solve the housing problem of the urban poor in a realistic way by proposing different solutions for informal housing, including housing improvements and self-help methods supported by the state.

The liberalization attempts after 1980s were also reflected in the housing policies. Various laws were enacted to give those houses a legal status by distributing pre-title deeds, which would be converted into official title deeds after the completion of development plans. These measures were also in accord with the dominant neoliberal belief in increasing the volume and efficiency of free market transactions in the housing market, which was supported by World Bank and United Nations in that period. It was expected that the regularization of property rights and the commodification of informal housing would integrate the urban poor into the formal real estate market by enabling market transactions. This was, in turn, assumed to annihilate urban poverty by encouraging the use of credits in starting new businesses (De Soto, 1989, 2000). Other than these expectations, this also meant to be the allocation of urban rents among different segments of population, including the squatter housing residents, which also served the function of weakening the class conflicts under poorer work conditions. Consequently, the squatter housing residents were integrated into the system and this led to a new type of segmentation among the working classes by means of house-ownership. By strengthening the rent-gaining potential of these houses through regularization, the importance of house ownership increased at the expense of the claim for the right to affordable and livable housing. After 1980s, the squatter house owners started to convert their houses into low-quality apartment blocks, sometimes for the use of their children and sometimes to be rented for extra income (Senyapili, 1992).

Another important development in the 1980s was the foundation of Housing Development Administration (TOKI) to solve the housing problems of low-income people by encouraging the establishment of housing cooperatives supported by cheap credits. Although this aimed to fulfil the housing demands of the urban poor, in the end, mostly the middle-income residents benefitted from these funds and speculative investments in this respect undermined the expected returns. As will be mentioned in the following section, the importance and power of this institution has been expanded to become the most powerful state agent in the construction sector, especially after 2000.

The Period After 1990s: Neo-liberal Transformation in Urban Policies

Since the mid-1990s, although Istanbul is still the most important industrial city in Turkey, the vision of the city as a centre of international finance, service and tourism has guided the new urban policies. Parallel to these policies, especially big industrial establishments started to decentralize in the metropolitan region and the central urban spaces have been restructured to fulfil the demands of these new qualified service sectors, leading to the reinforcement of real-estate and construction sectors. This was also the period when big urban projects, including office blocks, hotels and gated housing estates started to replace comprehensive planning attitude and to abandon the notion of 'public interest' to a great extent. Under these conditions, Istanbul has become the most important city where all those projects could be realized with short return periods and high profit margins (Türkün, 2011). In the face of the scarcity of urban land and increasing land rents, renewal of the housing stock in squatter housing areas, historic urban centres and dilapidated social housing areas in central locations started to be considered as an opportunity. As can be expected, this urban policy has been supported by the actors of the central and local governments and the authorities of important state institutions as well as the private sector actors, such as developers, land-owners, advisors and professionals. This calls attention to the emergence of a powerful urban coalition and state support for these new urban policies, incomparable to previous periods.

Parallel to these developments, the discourse on squatter housing has started to change drastically and gained an exclusionary tone by claiming that the people living in squatter housing districts were 'invaders' and those districts were claimed to be the reason of increasing crime rates and separatist activities, associating it with the growing number of Kurdish migrants from southeast Anatolia (UNDP, 2006). Although the vote potential of large number of migrants is still very important in big metropolitan cities, increasing land rents through big urban development projects have become a higher priority for central and local governments. Both state officials and local authorities started to pronounce the 'necessity' and 'urgency' of transformation in squatter housing areas, dilapidated social housing areas and historic urban areas. The justification of these claims is built on the discourse of 'organized and planned development' or the danger of earthquake; on the other hand, the regeneration projects in the historic centre are legitimized on the basis of the necessity of preserving the historic sites. Parallel to this changing discourse, it is seen that the new laws and regulations have intended to prepare the legal framework for the restructuring of urban space by means of big urban projects. We can easily claim that this shift in discourses, laws and implementations mark the end of the policy of distributing urban rents as an important policy tool for maintaining social peace and stability (Türkün, 2011).

If we summarize the recent changes in the legal framework of transformation, especially after 2005, we can easily claim that there is a centralization of power on the behalf of the central and local governments and the citizens continuously get excluded from decision-making mechanisms. In July 2005, Article 73 of *Municipal Law* (Law No. 5393) gave the responsibility to take decisions on urban development and declare 'urban transformation/renewal areas' to local governments. With this law, it became possible to declare any urban area as 'urban transformation area', which restricts the rights of property owners and leads to double standards in this respect. In June 2010, the change made in the same article, with Law no. 5998, led to an increase in the executive power of greater municipalities at the expense of district municipalities, by giving the authority to declare 'transformation/renewal areas' and make development plans to greater municipalities. With this change, not only the citizens but also district municipalities become powerless and the citizens have lost the chance of negotiating with the district municipalities that would be expected to be more concerned about fulfilling the demands of citizens with vote expectations (Türkün and Yapici, 2009).

The other important attempt in this respect was the enactment of the *Law of Conservation of Deteriorating Historic and Cultural Property through Renewal and Re-use* (Law No. 5366) enacted in July 2005. With this law, municipalities were given the responsibility for 'the conservation and repair of cultural and natural heritage' and for the utilization of 'special planning tools' in these areas. With this law, it became possible to start regeneration or renewal projects in the important historic sites of Istanbul. The most important article in this law is related to the right given to special provincial administrations or municipalities to realize 'urgent expropriation', which had been a measure taken only in the case of natural disasters or for defense purposes. The threat and pressure of urgent expropriation make citizens powerless in negotiations and force them to sell their property to third persons who offer a higher price than the municipality. The implications of this threat were observed in Sulukule, which was one of the oldest districts of gypsies in Istanbul. Sulukule was the first neighbourhood where a renewal project was realized according to this law and the result was the demolishment of almost all the houses and displacement of all the inhabitants. The other historic area, declared as 'renewal area' was Tarlabasi, which will be mentioned in detail in the following section. In addition, with this law, a new special conservation council, Regional Council for Conservation of Cultural and Natural Heritage for Renewal Areas in Istanbul, was established to give decisions for the proposed projects in historic sites. The establishment of those special councils has served the function of bypassing the High and Regional Preservation Councils, which are claimed to have created obstacles for developments in historic areas.

The final step in these legal changes is enactment of the *Law of Transformation of Areas Under the Threat of Natural Disasters* (Law No. 6306) in May 2012. With this law, the power of taking all the decisions on urban transformations and implementation is given to the new Ministry of Urbanization and Environment together with Housing Development Administration (TOKI), which points to the 'centralization and concentration of power' in the hands of the central government at the expense of greater municipalities and district municipalities. In this law, the cost and burden of transformation is completely transferred to citizens: they have to get a report from particular institutions about the physical conditions of their buildings; if the building is found to be risky, they are obliged to have it demolished in 60 days time, paying the cost themselves. After the building is demolished, with the consent of two-third of the landowners, transformation project would be initiated with the permission of the ministry. In addition, it became impossible to stop the progress of any kind of transformation project by means of court decisions and the local governments became authorized to cut electricity and water facilities to force the inhabitants to leave the site. Consequently, it has become possible to trigger renewal projects everywhere by declaring 'risky areas' or 'risky buildings' using the threat of earthquake.

What is problematic about all these legal changes is the opportunity of using double standards in the transformation procedures in different parts of the city. When we analyse the transformations in Istanbul, we observe that different mechanisms are involved in particular urban spaces. In some of the transformations, the landowners have the right to direct the negotiation process with the developers in sharing the increasing rents. For example, transformation in historic urban areas with unique historic building stock with high rent-gaining potential is usually left to the market forces with the help of various triggering public investments and plan decisions. These regeneration areas are gentrified in a short time owing to the intense interest of developers in those areas. The historic buildings which can accommodate functions such as hotels, offices, headquarters of big companies and residences for high-income citizens are quickly renovated in market conditions, bringing excessive rents for land-owners as well as developers.

On the other hand, there are some urban areas whose transformation possibilities are somewhat 'locked' because of the characteristics of the building stock or the inhabitants' economic conditions. These areas are usually transformed by means of top-down decision mechanisms in declaring them 'urban transformation/renewal areas' on the basis of laws mentioned above. One of the examples of such areas is the historic urban areas with modest building stock. In such areas, radical and inappropriate renewal operations are made in the building stock to prepare the area for high-rent projects. For example the transformation project in Tarlabasi involves connecting the modest adjacent buildings from the inside by rebuilding them to make room for spacious shopping malls, hotels and residences for high-income people. This type of renewal practices enables the developers to maximize their rents in such areas.

Another example of transformation through top-down decisions can be observed in squatter housing areas located around urban areas with high-rent gaining potential. These areas are declared as 'urban transformation areas' or 'risky areas' so as to employ the new laws. In this process, the negotiation power of the landowners is restricted with laws and regulations, which enforce them to accept the disadvantageous terms of negotiation with the threat of 'urgent expropriation' and tenants are rarely considered in the negotiations. The procedure in those projects is almost the same everywhere: first, the central institutions estimate the value of the deteriorated flats or buildings and the newly constructed ones in the same housing area. Next, the property owners have to decide whether to sell their property at the estimated price to the construction company or accept to pay the difference between the price of the old and new properties by means of loans from banks. In most of the cases, the property owners cannot afford the dramatic rent increases in the luxurious housing projects constructed in the same location. Therefore, in the next step, they are offered to move to the housing estates for low-income people, built by TOKI in the peripheral locations. Even in those cases, low-income people have difficulties in making the regular monthly payments. This system appears to become very problematic when the timing and terms of transformation are decided on by central and local authorities, without the consent of the inhabitants.

Case Study on Six Low-Income Neighbourhoods in Istanbul

The urban renewal/transformation projects targeting the housing areas of low-income citizens are initiated with the claim of solving the housing problem of those people and improving the living standards in those neighbourhoods. However, the findings on the recently completed and on-going renewal projects in different housing areas have already shown that they are unable to meet those expectations. In order to understand the reasons of this failure, between July 2008 and October 2010, a research project was conducted in the housing areas of six districts of Istanbul. Five of these were chosen as examples of different types of housing areas which are declared as 'urban transformation/renewal/regeneration areas'. Bezirganbahçe has been included as the sixth housing area in the research as an example of a completed mass housing project where the inhabitants of two squatter housing areas (Ayazma and Tepeustu) were settled in 2006 and 2007. The present situation in Bezirganbahçe gives the opportunity of evaluating the different repercussions of urban renewal and displacement. The common characteristic of all these neighbourhoods is their being the housing areas of the disadvantaged segments of the labour market and the urban poor; the other common point is their being located within or around areas with high rent-gaining potential. When we analyse when and how these housing areas were established and the legal status of properties in those areas, it is possible to trace the history of urbanization in Istanbul and the housing policies in general. In this research, it is intended to evaluate whether the discourse, which tries to legitimize urban transformation practices in low-income neighbourhoods, is consistent with the objective realities in those areas. In addition, it is aimed to discuss whether it will solve the current housing problems of those people or magnify the housing problem by creating more destructive conditions.

During the research, first, the related literature as well as newspapers and journals have been studied to analyse the housing policies in different periods and the changing discourses related to the housing problem, including squatter housing. In second stage of the research, questionnaires were given to 8–10 per cent of the inhabitants to comprehend the establishment process of those neighbourhoods as well as the social and economic conditions of the households. It was also aimed to understand the meaning and importance of these neighbourhoods and houses for the inhabitants with reference to their work relations and daily social practices. As a result, information about 1,362 households and 6,100 household members was gathered. In order to get information about the perceptions about the transformation projects and the impact of growing social movements in those neighbourhoods, intensive interviews were made with the major actors with different interests. These people were chosen among long-term inhabitants, the owners of commercial establishments, the previous and current middle men, the neighbourhood associations, related civil society organizations as well as the present and previous representatives and responsible civil servants in the local municipality and greater Istanbul municipality.

Map 2.1 *Districts of Istanbul: The research is conducted in six districts: Maltepe, Sariyer, Tuzla, Beyoglu, Gungoren and Kucukcekmece*

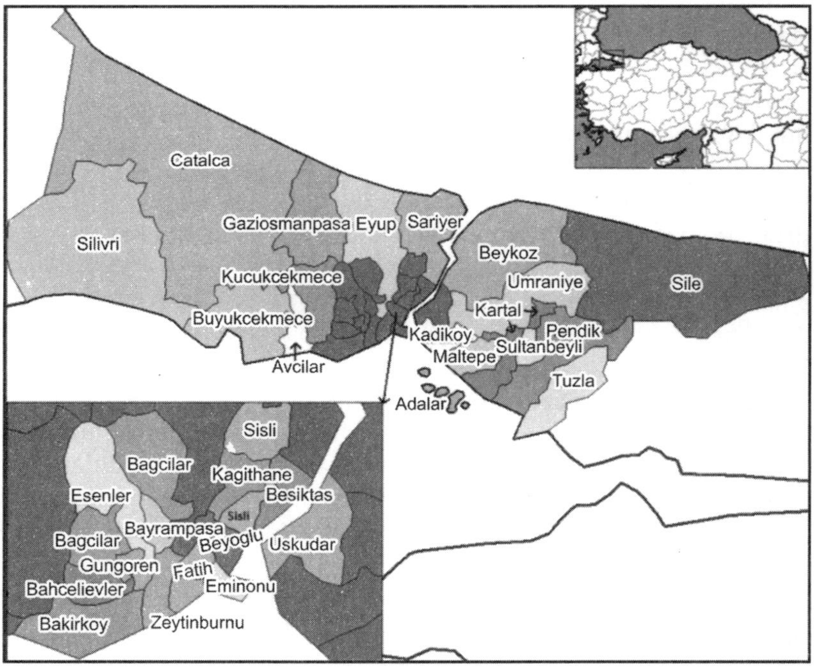

Source: www.ibb.gov.tr

Among these six housing areas, Tarlabasi (Beyoglu District) has been chosen as an example of a neighbourhood in the historic urban centre where the most disadvantaged segments of population live, including new Kurdish migrants from Southeast Anatolia, Roma population, foreign immigrants as well as gay and transsexual community. According to the law, which enables regeneration in historic areas, some parts of Tarlabasi were declared as 'urban renewal area'. The touristic developments in the surrounding areas have attracted the attention of the developers to the area; therefore, it is intended to convert the buildings into hotels, shopping spaces and residences by demolishing and rebuilding the adjacent historic buildings so as to connect them from the inside. This initial stimulus is expected to trigger a complete physical change and gentrification in Tarlabasi area. It can be claimed that the project aims to transform the area completely to be used by the richest segments of population and tourists to get the highest returns. The people living in the neighbourhood were forced to sell their properties to the local municipality or the construction company at very low prices with the threat of expropriation.

During this process, the inhabitants founded a neighbourhood association of house owners and tenants in order to defend their rights and they struggled hard to retain their rights to improve their properties themselves. However, the construction company did not want to share the profits with the property owners and owing to the law no. 5366, they used various tactics to oblige them to accept their terms. Some of the property owners took their cases to the court in Turkey and later on to European Court of Human Rights and they are still waiting for the final decision. On the other hand, some of the buildings are pulled down and construction started despite the objections of Chamber of Architects and City Planners and other civil society organizations related both to the inappropriate renewal practices in the historic area as well as the ethical problems of eviction.

Tozkoparan (Gungoren District) is chosen as an example of a social housing area where people are under the pressure of renewal and displacement. This neighbourhood was established in the 1960s as a 'squatter housing prevention area' and low-income people from

Picture 2.1 *Old and new Tarlabasi*

Source: www.beyoglu.bel.tr

different squatter housing areas as well as low-income people working in various state institutions, such as teachers and policemen, moved to the apartment blocks by getting loans from banks. This area can be considered to be one of the most successful implementations with respect to the provision of housing for low-income people in the 1960s by means of cheap housing credits. The people who moved to this mass housing site could pay their loans to the banks relatively more easily in those years owing to the abundant job opportunities in the industrial areas in the vicinity. The government also protected the people from high inflation rates by ensuring constant bank payments. After finishing their payments in 20 years, they got their authorized title deeds.

The urban renewal project in this neighbourhood now aims to transform this area, which is composed of dilapidated low-density housing stock, into high-density apartment blocks. The interesting situation in this housing area is related to the peculiar tenure structure; the inhabitants own only the flats but the land outside the buildings belongs to the state, which is transferred to Housing Development Administration (TOKI) to be used for new constructions. Therefore, TOKI has initiated this transformation project by claiming the right of utilizing the spacious open spaces used as parks, sports fields and playgrounds by the inhabitants. The renewal project is legitimized on the grounds of earthquake threat and the risky conditions of the building stock although it is possible to strengthen the buildings. Faced with the pressure of renewal, the inhabitants also founded a neighbourhood association to defend their rights. The flats in this area are quite small but this disadvantage is tolerated owing to the spacious public places within the neighbourhood. The people realize that

Picture 2.2 *Tozkoparan (Gungoren district): From low-density social housing neighbourhood to high-density TOKI blocks*

Source: http://tozder.net; www.gungorengundem.com

moving to high-density apartment blocks will mean to be a loss in their living standards. In addition, it is still not certain whether they will have to pay for this transformation.

Basibuyuk (Maltepe District), Derbent (Sariyer District) and Aydinli (Tuzla District) have been chosen as squatter housing (gecekondu) neighbourhoods, which were developed after 1960s, especially parallel to the development of industrial establishments in the close vicinity. These three neighbourhoods are under the pressure of transformation related to the excessively high rent opportunities for new investments owing to their location. The developments in those housing areas started by invading state land in the first place but after 1970s the common practice was buying pieces of land from landowners to build unauthorized houses on shared plots of land. The inhabitants got their pre-title deeds owing to the Law no 2981, enacted in March 1984, on *Procedures to be Applied to Buildings not Conforming to Development and Gecekondu Legislation* for the regularization of unlicensed buildings by paying 'occupancy duties' to the provincial administrations. After that date, the inhabitants started to build additional stories to their buildings before waiting for Improvement and Development Plans to be completed for these areas. On the other hand, these additional stories served the function of fulfilling the housing demand of the second generations or new low-income migrants of the 1990s, who do not have the opportunity of building squatter houses under stricter controls and prohibitions after mid-1980s.

Today, the squatter housing areas, which were located in peripheral areas around industrial establishments in the 1960s have become valuable land due to the urban sprawl in those directions in time. As the big industrial establishments in such locations decentralized within the Istanbul Metropolitan Area and the others were brought together in Organized Industrial Sites after 1990s, the abandoned industrial sites have generally been transformed into central business areas consisting of hotels, shopping malls and office blocks, depending on their location within the city. As a result, these areas, which were not preferred as housing areas by middle and high-income groups in the past, have now become valuable due to the scarcity of land in central locations and high increase in land values. Therefore, the pressure of transformation on squatter housing areas especially in advantageous locations has increased in time. It is observed that the increasing accessibility of these areas by means of public transportation as well as the new housing and service sector developments in the adjacent areas attracts the attention of developers in real estate and construction sectors. These new development opportunities also explain the current discourse on the 'urgency' and 'necessity' of transformation and the following laws, which facilitate the transformation process for the flourishing construction sector.

As mentioned earlier, owing to the laws which enable the declaration of squatter housing areas as 'transformation areas' or 'risky areas', it becomes possible to use different procedures in the transformation process, leading to direct or indirect displacement of the inhabitants. Therefore, it can be argued that the government has the

Picture 2.3 *Aydinli (Tuzla district): From squatter housing to TOKI mass housing blocks*

Source: Pictures taken by Asuman Türkün during the survey

Picture 2.4 *Basibuyuk (Maltepe district): TOKI blocks built in the neighbourhood park area*

Source: Pictures taken by Asuman Türkün during the survey

chance of bypassing property rights protected by the Constitution by treating some people's property rights as 'less sacred'. The use of different standards in urban transformation and the apparent inequality in the distribution of urban rents create discontent and anger among the citizens. Therefore, it is observed that the social movements against these transformations appear to get stronger in those neighbourhoods especially when their modest shelters and their livelihoods are threatened by these new urban policies.

Picture 2.5 *Derbent (Sariyer district): The street shared by two different worlds – squatter housing and a gated housing site*

Source: Pictures taken by Asuman Türkün during the survey

Bezirganbahce is the sixth research area where high-rise apartment blocks were constructed by Mass Housing Institution (TOKI) for people that would be displaced during the implementation of different renewal/transformation projects or for low-income people in need of affordable housing. This area has been included in the research as an example of a completed renewal project in which the inhabitants of two squatter housing areas (Ayazma and Tepeustu) were settled by means of mortgage arrangements. The current situation in Bezirganbahce gives the opportunity of evaluating the implications of urban transformation for low-income people who have to make regular monthly payments to the banks. Other than those bank payments, the people are faced with the increasing costs of living, such as maintenance costs of apartment houses and natural gas payments for heating.

The findings on Bezirganbahce have shown that there is a great gap between the optimistic expectations about renewal practices in low-income neighbourhoods and the current economic and social realities of inhabitants living in those areas. It has been found that 1,400 families moved to the area; however, more than half of the families, not being able to pay the bank loans, had to return back to the city as tenants or migrated to other cities, especially in the metropolitan area of Istanbul. In fact, during the displacement phase, 54.4 per cent of the workers lost their jobs. The other problem is related to the mismatch between the daily practices of inhabitants and the spatial organization of the new housing environment.

Picture 2.6 *Bezirganbahçe (Kucukcekmece district): From Ayazma and Tepeustu squatter housing areas to TOKI blocks*

Source: Pictures taken by Asuman Türkün during the survey

The Impact of Renewal/Regeneration Projects on the Urban Poor

The situation in Bezirganbahce gives a lot of insight on the expected repercussions of these transformation practices in the neighbourhoods inhabited by people with more or less similar conditions, in terms of economic and social resources, property rights, tenure structure, education levels, places of work and survival strategies in the city. Therefore, in this section the conditions and limited alternatives of the households will be evaluated with reference to the economic and social burden of urban renewal/transformation for these people. As noted above, the transformation projects in low-income neighbourhoods require paying the difference between the estimated value of new buildings and the old ones that will be demolished in this process. The problem here is considering the old buildings as a 'wreck' and, in turn, setting a very low value for those properties, while the value of the new buildings are assessed on the basis of the prices determined by the

Ministry of Development and Resettlement. When the new buildings planned for the demolished site are in luxurious category, the amount to be paid exceeds the financial means of low-income people and displacement occurs in almost all cases. Even if the new housing developments aim to accommodate low-income people in the same site, the moderate bank loans coupled with the new expenses in the apartment houses create serious problems for the majority of inhabitants, leading either to dispossession or increasing poverty.

The research findings point to the high rate of owner occupancy in these neighbourhoods, both in squatter housing areas and social housing areas. The rate of owner occupancy range between 63 per cent and 76 per cent. The only district with high rate of tenants is Tarlabasi (64.4%), which is mostly inhabited by the marginal segments of population and new migrants especially after 1990s as mentioned above. Within time, most of the squatter houses gained some kind of legal status, which is still ambiguous in many respects. Official title deed is still rare and there are a considerable number of houses with no legal documents. In Derbent, for example, the houses with no legal documents reach 25.5 per cent of the owner occupied houses. On the other hand, as noted above, the government took new measures after 1980s to regularize the squatter housing areas by giving them pre-title deeds, which means permit for settlement until the development plans are completed. In addition, in this regularization process, the users of those houses paid quite a sum of money to the state to get the pre-title deeds with the expectation of getting the official title deeds later on. On the other hand, today the property rights are still in an ambiguous state due to the delay in the realization of development plans in most of the squatter housing neighbourhoods. Today, during many of the renewal practices, pre-title deeds are not considered as official documents and different terms of negotiations are applied to those people although they have official documents showing real estate tax payments or documents showing payments they have made for garbage collection, electricity and water. This situation creates anger among inhabitants due to the fact that the promises given in the 1980s are not kept in the prevalent renewal operations.

When the findings on income levels of household members and total household incomes are considered, it can easily be claimed that only a small portion of the households are capable of making the regular payments dictated in this process. The subsistence wage was 280 dollars in 2009, while the monthly payment in those mass housing projects was around 110–220 dollars, which requires the employment of more than one family member to afford paying this amount. Although the amount that should be paid may seem reasonable in the first place and it is announced as 'low housing payments equal to rents' by TOKI, the realities of life do not fit this model (www.toki.gov.tr). It is known that especially in crisis periods, people experience difficulty in finding jobs and they have to accept wages lower than the subsistence level with no social security. Therefore, the sustainability of the system is arguably related to the strict obligation of regular payments. If the payment cannot be made for two months, the bank gives one more month to clear the debt; otherwise, the house is taken back by the bank. Within the 15-year payment period, there will most probably be two months for all households when they are unable to make this payment. As noted above, in the case of Bezirganbahce, almost half of the families lost their houses not being able to pay their debts; in other words, the families lost all their savings they had made since they migrated to the city. The interviews with the people who are struggling to pay for their houses have shown that young people at school age and women have started to work, accepting very low wages and poor working conditions.

According to the research findings, the household incomes are the lowest in Tarlabasi and Bezirganbahce, which are generally the housing areas of the new migrants from Southeast Anatolia and the most disadvantaged segments of population. In Bezirganbahce, the household income of 26.5 per cent of the families is less than the subsistence wage level; this figure is 19 per cent in Tarlabasi. The wage levels in other neighbourhoods are relatively higher but still, most of the households do not have enough income to be able to make the payments unless they accept severe poverty conditions. In those neighbourhoods, around one-third of the families earn less than 400 dollars a month and half of the households consist of only one wage earner. The number of wage earners is higher in Tarlabası due to the informal job opportunities in the touristic establishments in the surrounding areas, but this does not always guarantee higher family income because of the high number of 'working poor'. The interesting point here is that renewal projects have been initiated in the most disadvantageous neighbourhoods, consisting of people with very limited financial resources. This apparently reflects the unconcerned attitude towards the shelter problem of the urban poor.

The education levels also reflect the disadvantageous position of the people living in those neighbourhoods in the labour market. In general, education level is very low but the lowest education levels are observed in the neighbourhoods of new migrants, i.e. Tarlabasi and Bezirganbahce. The findings on education levels are surprising when 50–60 years of urban experience in the most developed city of Turkey is considered; the general education level is lower than the average of Istanbul and even Turkey. The most striking differences between neighbourhoods appear in the ratio of illiterate groups and the ones who have finished secondary school. In the neighbourhoods inhabited by the new migrants, Tarlabasi and Bezirganbahce, the rate of illiteracy is very high; in Tarlabasi, 31.6 per cent of the women and 8.5 per cent of men are illiterate, while these figures are 22.1 per cent and 5.1 per cent in Bezirganbahce, respectively (Figure 2.1). The illiteracy rates are the lowest in Derbent and Tozkoparan, where the oldest migrants live; however, they are still higher than Istanbul averages. When the secondary school graduates are considered, it is observed that only in Tozkoparan social housing area the share of people at this level of education reaches Istanbul averages. As can be observed in Figure 2.2, the share of people with secondary education in Bezirganbahce is only 1.9 per cent, both for women and men; these figures are 3.5 per cent for women and 5.3 per cent for men in Tarlabasi.

Figure 2.1 *The share of illiterate people: Comparison with Istanbul and Turkey averages*

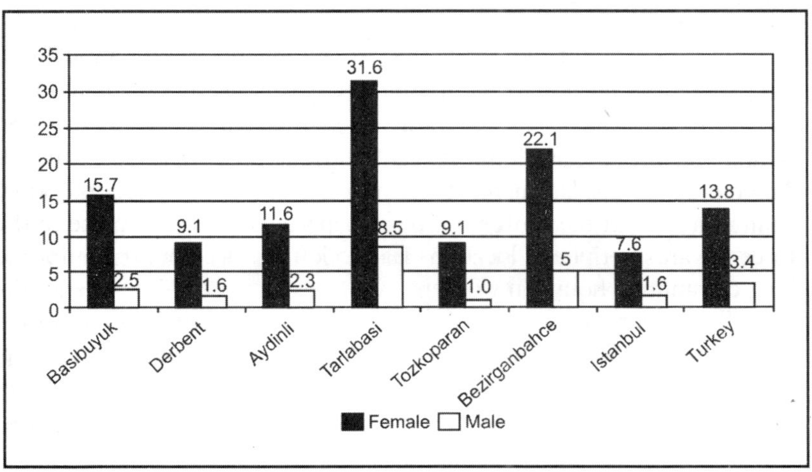

Figure 2.2 *Share of secondary school graduates: Comparison with Istanbul and Turkey averages*

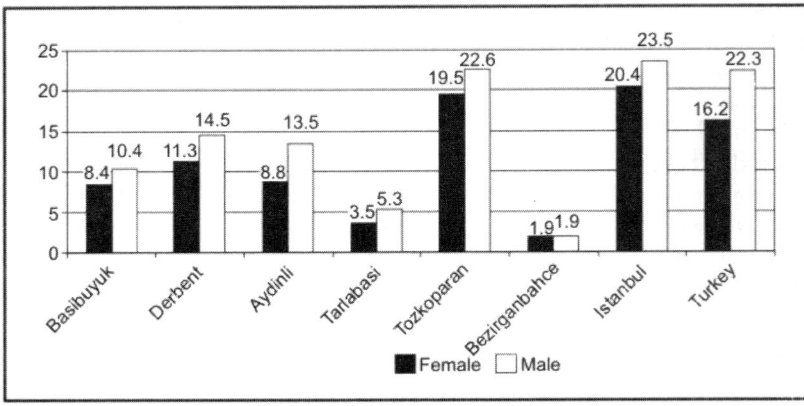

Statistics show that there is a close connection between the education and income levels; in fact, the share of people under poverty line decreases as the education level gets higher. This is related to the types of jobs and positions people can get based on their education and career opportunities. In the neighbourhoods, people are generally employed in jobs, which do not require special skills or education. They are generally involved in tasks, which can be learned through a short period of training or experience, either in industrial establishments or in the service sector. The share of such jobs is the highest in Tarlabasi (70.9%) and Bezirganbahce (82.9%). In other neighbourhoods, this figure is around 55–60 per cent within the working population. Although some of the big industrial establishments have decentralized within the Istanbul Metropolitan Region, there are still numerous small and medium sized firms close to the housing areas of low-income people. In addition, the second and third generation migrants now constitute the new labour force of the growing service sector in the central areas of the city and there is still a close connection between housing areas and work places. Therefore, the displacement of the people from the neighbourhoods in central areas and the movement of housing areas of low-income labour force towards peripheral locations lead to job losses or put the burden of long commuting hours on workers.

The other important information about working conditions is related to the low rates of social security protection among wage earners. In Tarlabasi, the rate of workers with no social security is 55 per cent and in Bezirganbahce, this figure is 51.3 per cent. In other neighbourhoods, the share of workers under social security protection is relatively higher, but still 20 per cent of the workers do not have any security; these figures are even higher among women. Considering the high rates of informal working conditions, the houses they own become the only source of security under the tough conditions of unemployment, low wages and poor working conditions. In fact, the unemployment rates are high in Turkey and this rate is even higher in Istanbul. When we analyse the unemployment rates in the neighbourhoods, it is seen that in 2009, when the people in Bezirganbahce were struggling to pay their debts to the banks, the unemployment rate was 29.6 per cent. In the same year, this rate was 16.8 per cent in Istanbul and 14 per cent in Turkey. In the other neighbourhoods, the unemployment levels were around Istanbul averages.

It should also be noted that these districts have served the function of providing the cheapest rental housing stock for the new migrants or the urban poor; especially among the young generations. The average rent paid for the houses in these neighbourhoods is found to be around 110–220 dollars, which is impossible to find in formal housing neighbourhoods. Although the price of rental houses appears to be the same as the amount paid to the banks for buying new houses, the difference is related to the informal relationship between land owners and tenants, which involves tolerance and solidarity relationships during the times of job and income losses. On the other hand, there are quite a large number of people who live in their parents' or relatives' houses without paying any rent. Therefore, the transformation in those low-income neighbourhoods is expected to bring about dramatic repercussions when the number of such people is concerned. The transformation projects are based on the assumption that everybody has the opportunity and will to buy houses in the formal market and unfortunately they have no concern for the tenants in these districts. Therefore, it can certainly be claimed that the cities are now transforming into 'spaces of hopelessness' for new migrants and new generations, who have lost the opportunity and means of integration into urban areas, both through housing and employment (Türkün, 2009).

When we analyse the other support mechanisms and financial resources of these households, it is seen that they are highly vulnerable in the face of any kind of interruption in the survival strategies they have adopted. The research findings show that around 90 per cent of the families do not have any properties other than the ones they live in; this increases the negative impacts of urban transformation. On the other hand, the support mechanisms of their families, who still live in rural areas, have also diminished in time. In fact, the findings show that more than half of the households do not have agricultural land in their home towns and even if they have some land, the contribution to the family budget is almost none. Therefore, the survival strategies are now based on employment relationships in the city and the social networks formed especially with family members or acquaintances sharing the same housing areas. As noted above, these housing areas also fulfill the housing demand of the young members of the families as well as low-income relatives as an important means of survival strategy. Another tendency observed in the neighbourhoods is related to the frequency of small commercial or industrial establishments opened by the inhabitants themselves in the first floors of the buildings or in the adjacent additional units. Those small establishments bring income to the owners; but at the same time, they serve the function of providing variety of goods and services for the inhabitants in those neighbourhoods. The relationships based on acquaintanceship enable the poor inhabitants to fulfil their daily needs from these shops by making the payments later on. During the interviews, people expressed their fears about living in housing areas where they cannot develop such survival strategies; on the other hand, the owners of those establishments were worried about losing their financial resources. Therefore, transformation in those neighbourhoods will not only create housing problems for the low-income people but also lead to a loss of income for many of the households.

When we analyse the daily lives of people, it is seen that people spend almost all their time in those housing areas. During the interviews, majority of the households stated that they spend their spare time in their homes; the activities such as going to the cinema or to picnic areas and the seaside are observed in a small proportion of households. The physical layout of squatter housing areas, consisting of a close interaction between the street, garden and the house enables social interaction and strengthens the solidarity relationships among people. In fact, during the interviews, majority of the people have expressed their satisfaction with their housing areas and the demand for transformation does not come from the inhabitants. The reasons of satisfaction are based on having close social relationships in neighbourhoods, being used to living in a house with a garden and living close to work places. This reflects the objective perception of their financial means and draws the limits of their expectations. On the other hand, the phyisical organization of mass housing areas is based on a clear separation of private and public domains, which, in fact, do not fit the daily routines and needs of those households. The flats in the apartment blocks are quite small when the average household size is considered and the outdoor spaces do not fulfil their needs for spending time with neighbours and friends. Therefore, people usually express their feelings about living in those areas as 'being locked in prison'. Although the mass housing estates of TOKI are being propagated as being the symbols of 'modernity' and 'high standard housing', the people complain about the quality of housing as well as the housing environment which does not meet their needs and demands.

Final Remarks

It is generally observed that the 'interventions from below', such as squatter housing and illegal housing constructions are mainly explored in many of the research made on housing provision for low-income people. On the other hand, there is a need to question the consequences of dominant neoliberal urban policies and the ways of 'intervention from above' through 'urban regeneration/renewal' projects especially in the developing part of the world. The new urban policy throughout the world appears to be based on encouraging the development of real-estate and construction sectors by increasing the urban rents. Consequently, the interest in the urban areas with high rent-gaining potential has increased, leading to the eviction or displacement of disadvantaged segments of population inhabiting those areas. It can be argued that the new urban policies, which are mainly put forward with economic considerations, invalidate the social policies and intensify the acute housing problem, especially for the urban poor. It is also observed that the decisions about urban transformation projects have been directed by the state and left to free market actors, who are directed by their short-term financial interests. As a result, most of the citizens get excluded from important decision-making mechanisms affecting their lives. The constant reality in all these cases is the transfer of valuable urban land to the well-to-do as a result of increasing rents and prices and the creation of gated urban spaces distanced from the urban poor. Although the practice of forced evictions and displacement of residents have been criticized by various governments and international organizations, it is observed that in many of the cities, the housing areas of the urban poor have become important targets of big urban projects, in accordance with the new urban policies.

In this respect, we can claim that the regeneration and renewal projects in the low-income housing areas, located in over-valued central urban areas, points to a radical change in the urban and housing policies of Turkey. The increasing importance of such policies in Istanbul is not surprising with respect to the changing vision of the city as the centre of finance, tourism and culture. The scarcity of urban land necessary for the development of these new sectors makes the housing areas in central locations the main target of real estate and construction sectors. Those areas include squatter housing areas, social housing areas and the historic housing stock in the city centre and they illustrate the urbanization history of Turkey by exemplifying different solutions found in successive periods to solve the shelter problem of low-income people. Today, the standard model of moving those people to high-rise mass housing estates built by TOKI extends the housing problem to all segments of population, who have solved their housing needs in some way or another since the 1950s. Although there is high housing demand for the growing low-income population in the city, this standard model imposes the renewal of all low-income housing areas that have been established in successive periods of massive migration. The discourse on the 'urgency' and 'necessity' of renewal, based on the threat of expected earthquake, conceals the possibility of different types of improvements that can easily be made in most of those neighbourhoods. This type of transformation, not only demolish the housing areas of the low-income people, but it also erases from our minds the meaning and function of these working-class housing areas in the industrialization and urbanization experience of Turkey. This policy is pursued as if the conditions of the working population or the urban poor have substantially improved, although we all know that the situation has become much harder for the majority of the people after 1980s.

It is observed that the regeneration efforts in the historic centre of Istanbul have led to dramatic rent increase and the current inhabitants are displaced through the dynamics of gentrification. On the other hand, the intended urban transformation in squatter housing areas and dilapidated social housing areas are realized by demolishing the existing building stock and replacing it with high-rise mass housing units built by the *Housing Development Administration* TOKI, either in the same location or in the periphery. On the other hand, during this process, the economic and social conditions of the residents that will be affected by these changes are not taken into consideration. Displacement usually leads to loss of jobs as well as supporting social relationships and survival strategies they have established within years within those neighbourhoods. Especially in high unemployment periods, it becomes extremely difficult to make the necessary regular payments to banks, leading to increasing poverty, if not dispossession. In Istanbul, these housing projects have been completed in a few cases but in all these cases it is observed that faced with job losses and financial difficulties, the households cannot survive in those new mass housing areas and come back to the city as tenants, having lost all the investments they have made since they migrated to the city. In sum, we can certainly claim that there is a great gap between the misguiding expectations about solving the housing problem of low-income citizens by means of regeneration and renewal policies and their actual economic and social conditions.

The relocation or forced eviction of the inhabitants in those districts is expected to lead to severe economic and social problems for the majority of low-income people who constitute the labour force in industrial establishments and the service sector. In this process, it is observed that the major decisions concerning the citizens and the city have been given in a top-down manner by a powerful elite coalition composed of the representatives of central and local governments, potential large-scale developers, landlords, and professionals, without any consent to public opinion. In addition, the leading media actors serve to diffuse the hegemonic discourse on the legitimization of those transformations, sometimes through disinformation and sometimes by using 'the second face of power', by not bringing into the agenda the important issues and decisions that would directly affect the daily lives of citizens. In addition, strict 'zero-tolerance' policies employed in the case of social movements and protests against these transformations also tend to discourage people from expressing their claims with respect to their rights to the city (Türkün, 2011). However, the protest movements related to the insistence of building a shopping mall in Taksim Gezi Park in Istanbul have shown that people are already fed up with the government's top-down decisions in every aspect of life, including the interventions on important public spaces of the city with rent expectations. The massive urban movements in almost all the cities of Turkey, with the participation of neighbourhood associations, chambers, trade unions and numerous civil society organizations have clearly reflected the discontent with the new urban policies mirroring the neoliberal economic and political agenda. It is hoped that these movements will open a way to more participatory and equitable urban policies on the basis of 'the right to the city'.

Notes

1. See Dicken, 1988; Brenner and Theodore, 2002; Fainstein, 1996; Harvey, 1989; Hirst and Zeitlin, 1991; Schoenberger, 1988; Massey, 1984; Marcuse and van Kempen, 2000.
2. See Florida, 2002 and 2005; Montgomery, 2003;Peck, 2005; Amin and Thrift, 2007; Pratt, 2008; Scott, 2006.

3. See Loftman and Nevin, 1995; Urry, 1995; Smith, 1986, 2002; Hackworth and Smith, 2001; Ley, 2002; Slater, 2006; Weber, 2002; Türkün-Erendil and Ulusoy, 2002; Fainstein, 2008; Fainstein and Judd, 1999; Judd, 1999; Beauregard, 1998; Swyngedouw, et al., 2002; Atkinson and Bridge, 2005; Mullins, 1999.
4. See Lees, 2003 and 2008; Smith, 2002; Bolt, Phillips and Van Kempen, 2010; Crump, 2002; Goetz, 2002 and 2010; Kleinhans and Varady, 2011; Van Kempen, et al., 2005.
5. See Davis, 2006; Lawson, 1992; Castells and Portes, 1989; Cawthorne, 1995; Benton, 1990; Sassen, 1991; Marcuse, 1993; Castells, 2003; Fainstein, Gordon and Harloe, 1992; Turok, 2004; Drakakis-Smith, 1996; Boratav, 2003; Eraydın, 2008; Pınarcıoðlu and Iþık, 2009; Eraydın and Erendil-Türkün, 1999 and 2005; Keyder, 2005.
6. This paper is based on the findings of the research project, 'Urban Transformation and Socio-spatial Change in Historic Urban Centers and Squatter Housing Neighborhoods in Istanbul', supported by TUBITAK (Turkey Institution of Scientific Research) and conducted in July 2008 – November 2010 in Istanbul. The developments after that date have been followed by the researchers to understand the further manifestations.

References

Amin, A. and N. Thrift. (2007). 'Cultural-economy and Cities', *Progress in Human Geography*, 3(2), pp. 143–161.

Atkinson, R. and G. Bridge. (2005). *Gentrification in a Global Context*, London: Routledge.

Beauregard, R. (1998). 'Tourism and Economic Development Policy', in *The Economic Geography of the Tourist Industry*, D. Ioannides and K.G. Debbage (eds), London: Routledge, pp. 220–234.

Benton, L. (1990). *Invisible Factories: The Informal Economy and Industrial Development in Spain*, Albany, NY: State University of New York Press.

Bolt, G., D. Phillips and R. Van Kempen. (2010). 'Housing Policy, (De)segregation and Social Mixing: An International Perspective', *Housing Studies*, 25(2), pp. 129–135.

Boratav, K. (2003). *Turkiye Iktisat Tarihi 1908–2002*, Ankara: Imge Yayinevi.

Brenner, N. and N. Theodore. (2002). 'Cities and Geographies of Actually Existing Neoliberalism', *Antipode*, 34(3), pp. 349–379.

Castells, M. and A. Portes. (1989). 'World Underneath: The Origins, Dynamics and Effects of the Informal Economy', in A. Portes, M. Castells and L. Benton (eds), *The Informal Economy Studies in Advanced and Less*

Developed Countries, Baltimore: The John Hopkins University Press, pp. 11–37.

Castells, M. (2003). 'The Rise of the Fourth World', in *The Global Transformation Reader,* Held, D. and A. McGrew, (eds), Cambridge: Polity, pp. 430–439.

Cawthorne, P.M. (1995). 'Of Networks and Markets: The Rise of a South Indian Town, the Example of Trippur's Cotton Knitwear Industry', *World Development*, 23(1), pp. 43–56.

Crump, J. (2002). 'Deconcentration by Demolition: Public Housing, Poverty and Urban Policy', *Environment and Planning D: Society and Space*, 20, pp. 581–596.

Davis, M. (2006). *Planet of Slums*, New York: Verso.

De Soto, H. (1989). *The Other Path: The Invisible Revolution in the Third World*, London: I.B. Taurus.

De Soto, H. (2000). *The Mystery of Capital: Why Capitalism Triumphs in the West and Fails Everywhere Else*, New York: Basic Books.

Dicken, P. (1988). *Global Shift: Industrial Change in a Turbulent World,* London: Paul Chapman.

Drakakis-Smith, D. (1996). 'Third World Cities: Sustainable Urban Development, Population, Labour and Poverty', *Urban Studies*, 33(4–5), pp. 673–99.

Eraydin, A. (1994). 'Changing Spatial Distribution and Structural Characteristics of the Turkish manufacturing Industry', in F. Senses (ed.) *Recent Industrialization Experience of Turkey in a Global Context,* London: Greenwood Press, pp. 155–174.

Eraydin, A. (2008). 'The Impact of Globalization on Different Social Groups: Competitiveness, Social Cohesion and Spatial Segregation in Istanbul', *Urban Studies*, 45, pp. 1663–1691.

Eraydin, A. and A. Erendil (Türkün). (1999). 'The Role of Female Labour in Industrial Restructuring: New Production Processes and Labour Market Relations in the Istanbul Clothing Industry', *Gender, Place and Culture*, 6(3), pp. 259–272.

Eraydin, A. and A. Türkün-Erendil. (2005). 'The Changing Roles of Female Labor in Economic Expansion and Decline: The Case of Istanbul Clothing Industry', in L. Nelson and J. Seager (eds), *A Companion to Feminist Geography,* Oxford: Blackwell, pp. 150–165.

Fainstein, S.S., I. Gordon, and M. Harloe. (eds). (1992). *Divided Cities, New York and London in the Contemporary World,* Oxford UK/Cambridge USA: Blackwell.

Fainstein, S.S. (1996). 'The Changing World Economy and Urban Restructuring', in Fainstein, S.S. and S. Campbell, (eds), *Readings in Urban Theory,* Oxford: Blackwell.

Fainstein, S.S. and D.R. Judd. (1999). 'Global Forces, Local Strategies and Urban Tourism', in D.R. Judd, and S.S. Fainstein (eds), *The Tourist City,* New Haven: Yale University Press, pp. 1–17.

Fainstein, S.S. (2008). 'Mega-projects in New York, London and Amsterdam', *International Journal of Urban and Regional Research*, pp. 768–785.

Florida, R. (2002). *The Rise of the Creative Class*, New York: Basic Books.

Florida, R. (2005). *Cities and the Creative Class*, London: Routledge.

Goetz, E.G. (2002). 'Forced Relocation vs. Voluntary Mobility: The Effects of Dispersal Programmes on Households', *Housing Studies,* 17(1), pp. 107–123.

Goetz, E.G. (2010). 'Desegregation in 3D: Displacement, Dispersal and Development in American Public Housing', *Housing Studies*, 25(2), pp. 137–158.

Harvey, D. (1989). *The Condition of Postmodernity,* Oxford: Basil Blackwell.

Harvey, D. (2008). 'The Right to the City', *New Left Review,* 53, pp. 23–40.

Harris, R. (1998). 'The Silence of the Experts: Aided Self-help Housing, 1939–1954', *Habitat International*, 22, pp. 165–189.

Hirst, P. and J. Zeitlin, (1991) 'Flexible Specialization versus Post-Fordism: Theory, Evidence and Policy Implications', *Economy and Society,* 20, pp. 1–54.

Judd, D.R. (1999). 'Constructing the Tourist Bubble', in D.R. Judd, and S. Fainstein, (eds), *The Tourist City,* New Haven: Yale University Press, pp. 35–53.

Keyder, C. (2005). 'Globalization and Social Exclusion in Istanbul', *International Journal of Urban and Regional Research*, 29(1), pp. 124–34.

Kleinhans, R. and D. Varady. (2011). 'Moving Out and Going Down? A Review of Recent Evidence on Negative Spillover Effects of Housing Restructuring Programmes in the United States and The Netherlands', *International Journal of Housing Policy,* 11(2), pp. 155–174.

Lawson, V.A. (1992). 'Industrial Subcontracting and Employment in Latin America: A Framework for Contextual Analysis', *Progress in Human Geography,* 16, pp. 1–23.

Lees, L. (2003). 'Policy (re)turns: Fentrification and Urban Policy: Urban Policy and Gentrification Research', *Environment and Planning A,* 35, pp. 571–574.

Lees, L. (2008). 'Gentrification and Social Mixing: Towards an Inclusive Urban Renaissance?', *Urban Studies*, 45(12), pp. 2449–2470.

Ley, D. (2002). 'Artists, Aestheticisation, and the Field of Gentrification', *Urban Studies*, 40, pp. 2525–2542.

Loftman and Nevin. (1995). 'Prestige Projects and Urban Regeneration in the 1980s and 1990s: A Review of Benefits and Limitations', *Planning Practice and Research*, 10(3–4), pp. 299–312.

Mangin, W. (1967). 'Latin American Squatter Settlements: A Problem and a Solution', *Latin American Research Review*, 2, pp. 65–98.

Marcuse, P. (1993), 'What's So New About Divided Cities?', *International Journal of Urban and Regional Research*, 17, pp. 355–365.

Marcuse, P. and R. van Kempen, (eds). (2000). *Globalizing Cities: A New Spatial Order?*, Oxford: Blackwell.

Massey, D. (1984). *Spatial Divisions of Labour: Social Structures and the Geography of Production*, London: Macmillan.

Montgomery, J. (2003). 'Cultural Quarters as Mechanisms for Urban Regeneration. Part 1: Conceptualizing Cultural Quarters', *Planning, Practice and Research*, 18(4), pp. 293–306.

Mullins, P. (1999). International Tourism and the Cities of Southeast Asia, in Judd, D.R. and S.S. Fainstein (eds), *The Tourist City*, Newhaven: Yale University Press, pp. 245–260.

Peck, J. (2005). 'Struggling with Creative Class', *International Journal of Urban and Regional Research*, 29(4), pp. 740–770.

Pınarcıoðlu, M. and O. Iþık. (2009). 'Segregation in Istanbul: Patterns and Processes', *Tijdschrift voor Economische en Sociale Geografie*, 110(4), pp. 469–484.

Pratt, A.C. (2008). 'Cultural Commodity Chains, Cultural Clusters, or Cultural Production Chains?', *Growth and Change*, 39(1), pp. 95–103.

Roberts, B.R. (2005). 'Globalization in Latin American Cities'. *International Journal of Urban and Regional Research*, 29(1), pp. 110–23.

Sassen, S. (1991). *The Global City*, Princeton N.J.: Princeton University Press.

Schoenberger, E. (1988). 'From Fordism to Flexible Accumulation: Technology, Competitive Strategies and International Location', *Environment and Planning D: Society and Space*, 6, pp. 252–262.

Scott, A.J. (2006). 'Creative Cities: Conceptual Issues and Policy Questions', *Journal of Urban Affairs*, 28(1), pp. 1–17.

Senyapili, T. (1992). 'A New Stage of Gecekondu Housing in Istanbul', in I. Tekeli, (ed.), *Development of Istanbul Metropolitan Area and Low Cost Housing*, Istanbul: Turkish Social Science Association, pp. 98–127.

Senyapili, T. (2006). *Baraka'dan Gecekonduya: Ankara'da Kentsel Makanin Donusumu 1923–1960,* Ýletisim.

Slater, T. (2006) 'The Eviction of Critical Perspectives from Gentrification Research', *International Journal of Urban and Regional Research*, 30(4), pp. 737–57.

Smith, N. (1986). 'Gentrification, he Frontier, and the Restructuring of Urban Space', in N. Smith, and P. Williams, (eds), *Gentrification of the City*, , London: Allen and Unwin, pp. 15–34.

Smith, N. (2002). 'New Globalism, New Urbanism: Gentrification as Global Urban Strategy', *Antipode*, 34, 427–450.

Swyngedouw, E., F. Moulaert, and A. Rodriguez, (2002). 'Neoliberal Urbanization in Europe: Large-Scale Urban Development Projects and the New Urban Policy', *Antipode*, 34, pp. 542–577.

Tekeli, I. (1982). *Turkiye'de Kentlesme Yazilari*. Ankara: Turhan Kitabevi.

Turkish Statistical Institute (TUIK). (2009). Regional Indicators www.tuik.gov.tr

Tumertekin, E. (1997). *Istanbul Insan Mekan*, Tarih Vakfi Yurt Yayinlari.

Turner, J.F.C. (1967). 'Barriers and Channels for Housing Development in Modernizing Countries', *Journal of American Institute of Planners*, 32, pp. 167–181.

Turner, J.F.C. (1977). *Housing by People: Towards Autonomy in Building Environments*, New York: Pantheon Books.

Türkün, A. (2009). The Manifestations of Voluntary and Involuntary Migration in Turkish Cities: From 'Spaces of Hope' to 'Spaces of Hopelessness', in R.S. Sandhu, J. Sandhu, and B. Arora, (eds), *Urban Poverty in Developing Countries: Issues and Strategies for Sustainable Cities*, New Delhi: Bookwell, pp. 57–100.

Türkün, A. (2011). 'Urban Regeneration and Hegemonic Power Relationships', *International Planning Studies*, 16(1), pp. 61–72.

Türkün, A., and M. Yapici. (2009) 'Kentsel Donusum ve Yasalarin Aracsallasan Rolu', *Iktisat Dergisi*, 499, pp. 48–58.

Türkün-Erendil, A. and Z. Ulusoy. (2002). 'The Re-invention of Tradition as an Urban Image', *Environment and Planning B – Planning and Design*, 29, pp. 655–672.

Turok, I. (2004). 'Cities, Regions, and Competitiveness', *Regional Studies*, 38(9), pp. 1061–75.

UNDP, Development Centre. (2006). *Forced Migration and its Effects in Diyarbakır*. Survey Paper, Development Research Center: Training, Research Implementation, Counseling, Production and Enterprise Cooperative.

Urry, J. (1995). *Consuming Places*, New York: Routledge.

Van Kempen, R., K. Dekker, S. Hall, and I. Tosics. (eds). (2005). *Restructuring Large Social Housing Estates in Europe*, Bristol: The Policy Press.

Weber, R. (2002). 'Extracting Value from the City: Neoliberalism and Urban Redevelopment', *Antipode*, 34, pp. 519–540.

3

Perils of Policies to Produce Housing Without Community Participation

Jawaharlal Nehru National Urban Renewal Mission (JNNURM) and Basic Services for the Urban Poor (BSUP) Projects in India

Sheela Patel

This chapter will briefly describe the experience of slum dwellers and organizations in Pune and other cities in India associated with The Society for the Promotion of Area Resource Centers (SPARC) as they sought to implement the Basic Services for the Urban Poor (BSUP) programme in 11 cities (see Appendix A). The chapter will report on elements that change the nature of design, participation of community resident households, execution of the project and its impact on the community and city. It will conclude with challenges that are evident for the next phase of whatever programme the government announces for the upgrading and redevelopment of housing for the urban poor in India. The study was commissioned by the National Technical Advisory Group (NTAG) and undertaken by SPARC to examine BSUP projects in general and community participation challenges in particular (see Appendix B).

In 2005, the Government of India announced the Jawaharlal Nehru National Urban Renewal Mission (JNNURM) scheme. Under the scheme are two submissions designed to meet the needs of the urban poor. Sub-Mission 1 is Urban Infrastructure and Governance (UI&G) formulated under the Ministry of Urban Development. Sub-Mission 2 is Basic Services to the Urban Poor (BSUP) formulated under the Ministry of Housing and Urban Poverty Alleviation. The main thrust of Sub-Mission 2 on BSUP was on integrated development of slums through projects for providing shelter, basic services and other related civic amenities with a view to provide utilities to the urban poor. The mission statement also emphasizes reforms driven, fast track, and planned development of identified cities with focus on efficiency in urban infrastructure/services delivery mechanism, community participation and accountability of Urban Local Bodies (ULBs) towards citizens.

BSUP was expected to run for 7 years from 2005–06. Sixty-three (63) cities identified under this scheme are further divided into three categories depending on population: greater than 1 million (7 cities), 1–4 million (28 cities) and special category (28 cities). The funding pattern also differs as per city population:

- 4 million plus and 1–4 million – Central: 50 per cent and Rest: 50 per cent;
- N-E cities and J&K – Central: 90 per cent and Rest: 10 per cent;
- Other cities – Central: 80 per cent and Rest: 20 per cent.

The community contribution must be a minimum of 10–12 per cent. For cities to access funding, a City Development Plan (CDP) has to be prepared and the ULBs/State governments are expected to undertake an agenda of reforms to meet the thrust of improving urban governance. Following this, detailed project reports for specific projects are required to be submitted for appraisal to the Government of India (GOI). It will then sanction final projects. A provision of 5 per cent of the central grant is kept for preparation of the Community Development Proposal (CDP), Detailed Project Reports (DPR), training and capacity building, community participation and information, education and communication. Although the urbanization of poverty is gradually being recognized by schemes such as JNNURM-BSUP, funds remain largely unutilized as projects have run into issues of procurement and execution. Yet, some cities have also shown innovative ways of using the subsidy and transformed processes by making them inclusive of communities.

The purpose of this study was to document a range of alternatives under BSUP explored by various cities across the country and draw lessons from it for the next phase, which is the extension of JNNURM-BSUP for another two years.

The main objectives of the study were:

- To understand how each city selected, designed and executed BSUP projects.
- To understand the manner in which communities were involved at each level and consequences of that.
- To what degree municipality, consultants and Non-Governmental Organizations(NGOs) were involved.
- To study how DPRs were made, contractors selected, structures designed; amenities provided and connectivity to the city ensured.
- To assess how cities would do this differently, issues they raise to the city, state and central leadership, BSUP and its strategy.

Observations and Challenges

Community Development Proposals (CDPs) and Project Linkages

Most of the CDPs were prepared by consultants and almost all reviews available suggest that BSUP-linked issues and reforms were not the area of focus. None of the much needed infrastructure investments in the same city had demonstrable linkages to amenities and services needed by slum dwellers. As can be seen in later discussions, in almost all locations, the subsidy-assisted houses had no water and sanitation and no transportation linkages.

Selection of Land, Slums, People

Poor levels of quality and accuracy of data from surveys, i.e. location and identification of slums and household surveys were an issue in most cities; poor justification of selection of a slum for subsidies and unclear selection criteria; landownership and/or litigation issues to make land available occurred in most cities; no de-notification process for slums.

Preparation of DPRs

In all cases, the DPRs were prepared by consultants or municipality engineers in a greater hurry than the CDPs and with little community input. For example, several DPRs were made without ascertaining availability and access to land for construction.

There were three variations of DPRs with most projects. The DPR has no relation to the projects in target population, location, design (few instances); the DPR designs have been insisted on even when communities have revolted against them. In one example, the DPR was redone because communities and NGOs demanded it. However, the city did not absorb the cost. Milestones essential in preparing DPRs were not undertaken in most DPRs: surveys to select vulnerable slums, household surveys to select eligible households, study of land availability, access to bulk infrastructure for amenities and addressing design issues for DPR preparation. In several DPRs there was a disconnect between actual needs and amenities and housing provided. There was little or no discussion and acceptance by communities of these designs.

Appraisal Process

In some cities, projects were approved, after which land was found to be inadequate or falling under (CRZ) guidelines which made the project a nonstarter.

Procurement and Tendering

DPRs have to prepare the basis of procurement. In most instances, it is evident that routine and standard procurement used by the state and city were applied. Upgrading was seen as contractor-built housing to replace the units where slum populations live.

Cities began by either seeking project execution from other public sector or large consulting agencies(with deep financial pockets) who did not find these projects profitable enough. Few cities changed their procurement strategies(Pune, Bhubaneswar) but there were no support directives from the Ministry of Housing and Poverty Alleviation (MoHUPA) or state(SLNAs). Most cities had to tender several times to find a willing contractor to work at very low rates. Except Madurai, Bhubaneswar and Puri, self-construction was not considered. However, the poorest households could not take part in the process.

Project Design and Planning

Relocation Sites

All locations were chosen on land far from the city and not linked to livelihoods or transport. All designs were ground plus three or four and similar in design. Most had no infrastructure installed as yet and remain unoccupied. Most projects did not select the eligible households prior to DPR preparation or construction and, thus, faced resistance from communities who were not consulted beforehand.

In Situ

The general strategy was to break existing houses and build uniform new ones. Most people who had *pucca* houses protested and in some instances resisted. Most designs of the in situ houses are also uniformly designed without much cultural or community inputs. For example, there is no design consideration for those who use *chullahs* and firewood for cooking.

Incremental Upgrading

This was manifested in three forms. *First*, subsidy was given to households to use the way they wished; second, although a contractor executed the project, only 269 square feet was upgraded. And third, households built a second dwelling in addition to their existing homes.

Financial Issues

Communities were not prepared/not aware of need to make their contribution. In most instances they were not encouraged to save for their contribution nor were they given loan possibilities to make that contribution. As a result, most cities are finding it difficult to collect substantial community contributions at this stage. No provision has been made at any level to factor in cost escalations resulting or causing delays as contractors are not paid in time. In cities that did allow for cost escalation, the increased costs had to be borne by the state, ULB and eligible households.

Transit Housing

Most projects have extended beyond the projected completion time. As a result, most households had to pay additional rentals for transit which often was not supplemented by city municipalities. State housing agencies have a weak trust quotient among the poor of ever leaving transit areas, so most have resisted being moved if they could.

Project Implementation

Most projects had not begun, the cycle of delays due to land or delayed payments had led to price escalation, thus creating a growing crisis. Delays have also made the survey and eligible household lists out of date which, if updated, are at the cost of the NGO/contractor. Often a project was considered complete although it had no basic infrastructure in place. Despite most cities showing a high percentage of ongoing or completed work, few houses were occupied. Construction quality is mostly not acceptable to everyone. Yet delays, lack of supervision and very low costs have all added to this situation.

Institutional Capacity

State and Local Government Level

Institutions and measures (accountability, governance)that support BSUP are not in place. In some cities, the project implementation units were set up only recently, much after projects began. There was a high attrition rate and poor institutional memory due to weak record management or documentation. There was also poor horizontal and vertical coordination, negotiation and trust between departments. Finally, there was a lack of planning for the BSUP to overlap with other schemes.

Central Government Level

There was no real capacity other than drawing down money. Those who implement projects need different capacity building than those who are commissioners. No timely support to provide flexibility or to make changes.

Monitoring and Supervision

Almost all periodic engineering inspections need staff, coordination and management systems. Most of the processes have not been in the system and have produced huge problems of billing, quality, and course correction.

Land Linked Issues

Central Government Level

There is no support being provided by the central governments to assist the state with slums on central government lands.

State Government Level

Different state level ministries have stopped work on projects and no arbitration has been undertaken by the state to address this issue.

City Level

Lands chosen for upgrading or relocation are mainly from a pool that belonged to the corporation or the city. Here in too many instances the court has placed a stay after work orders were given by the central government. This clearly indicates that issues of reform necessary for this process have not been taken seriously and have not been addressed by state leadership. The MoHUPA has not been able to assist, support or reprimand states for this remission.

Finance Management

Non-usage of funds has not drawn any red flags for interventions at any level. At the central government level disbursals have not been substantial, as most projects were abandoned.

State Government Level

The State-level nodal agencies have not sorted out these glaring issues. Cities and states have only dealt with CDPs and DPRs to get funds allocated to their cities but have not addressed ground realities which include seeking the consultation and partnership of slum dwellers. With most projects now abandoned and most cities not even having begun projects means that allocations made centrally have not been fully used. Most cost escalations have not been considered by the centre, state or city in a decade resulting in both poor quality and unfinished work. All projects re-initiated have either had the number of eligible households reduced, the contractors have absorbed losses or the community contribution was increased. Cities have pending payments to be made to contractors but have not addressed this issue.

Community Participation

The project provided ample opportunity to let people make their own decisions and for local governments to forge a relationship with communities. Yet, in most if not all the cities, there was little awareness or participation in the scheme. There is a lack of awareness about the benefits of community participation at city as well as community level. Government views participation as rhetoric and not in practical terms of engagement. Slum upgrading is seen mostly as moving 'slum dwellers' to contractor built housing – sometimes in situ, usually elsewhere. For almost all municipalities, participation was viewed as simply providing information to communities about the project in order to obtain consent for implementation of the scheme. Participation remains an unclear and misunderstood term in all cities.

Even though some DPRs recognize the importance of community participation and there is an expressed will of local authorities to involve communities, there are no mechanisms on the ground to guarantee community involvement at all stages of the projects: planning, implementation, monitoring, maintenance and evaluation of outcomes. In practice, while communities were aware of the schemes, they did not understand the connection between conducting the surveys and implementing the projects. Communities were not involved in any decision about the selection of slums for subsidies, selection of eligible households, design or planning decisions, construction, terms and conditions of repayment and also their contribution towards housing. Also, the realities on the ground such as the size of families living under one roof, their investment in their homes, livelihood, capacity to contribute financially, etc. were not recognized by cities. The connection between the proposed projects and reality is often too distant to understand and the cities provide little support to communities undergoing changes as a result of the scheme. For example, there is no provision under BSUP guidelines for capacity building or livelihoods.

Consequences of No Participation

The lack of awareness amongst people to be affected by the projects often led to public protests and community resistance which consequently affected any mobilization efforts thereafter. Despite much resistance from community, most construction choice was contractor-built ground plus 3 or walk-up houses which do not meet community choice.

Relocation Projects

These were resisted strongly by communities because of the distance between site and livelihoods. Yet these remained the main preference of cities. Projects were mostly located outside the city with no transport or amenities.

Design of Units

There was no acknowledgement of the special needs of women and children in design in most instances. Issues such as cooking fuels, home based livelihoods and internal space usage was not considered. Most designs across cities were uniform without consideration of environment or usage.

Construction

Most households had no involvement at all in supervision of construction; most did not know which would be their home. Almost all projects are contractor managed.

Community Resistance

It was rarely seen as a necessary feedback. Instead it was seen as lack of cooperation. For almost all the sites, although the whole point of slum upgrading is to benefit the residents, the residents were dissatisfied with the initiatives and often in conflict with the authorities. Also, there is no provision in most initiatives for redressing grievance.

Concerns Raised by Eligible Households

High rise housing did not work for communities. The quality of construction of existing *pattas,*[1] which were larger, were ignored. Livelihood issues were not addressed, e.g. distance to/from relocation sites to work, capacity to pay contribution, pay or manage services and maintenance, and increases in living and transition costs (such as shifting) to the new housing.

Concern About Consultants Chosen for DPR Preparation

Projects were designed, including procurement by consultants, with little ownership by the city. Typically non-local and/or large scale consultants were used to prepare DPRs. There was no accountability of consultants chosen for DPRs and no understanding of what is needed. Consultants were unaware of local realities. House designs were by engineers with no awareness of how spaces are used by women and the poor.

Concerns Stated by Municipalities

Most ULB officials do not have the knowledge or experience of implementing upgrading initiatives and the capacity to get the required agreements from different agencies. With most PMUs being in place more recently, most staff had no history of the development of projects and very little documentation to create institutional history. There was little support for crisis resolution on the problems and challenges faced by the staff. This led to a lowering of morale amongst some of the more enthusiastic staff. There was a thirst to find out what other cities were doing and compare and explore how it would work in their city. Almost none of the staff had participated in capacity building events at city state or central level. Every group wanted a follow-up meeting and opportunity to discuss or visit other projects and share challenges with other PMUs. Everyone felt they had learned a great deal, and given an opportunity to do more, would help make valuable changes.

Reflections

BSUP announcements produce a deep sense of excitement amongst activist and policy-makers seeking ways to integrate slums into the city.

Fifty per cent of the JNNURM funds were to be allocated to the Ministry of Housing and Urban Poverty to provide improved housing and amenities to JNNURM cities and smaller towns. There are many areas for reflection of what can be learnt from this experience, and we highlight the following.

Crisis of Absorption of Funds for Subsidies

The institutional arrangements of state institutions produce a strange paradox, in which monies that the national state allocates to social issues, such as health, education and welfare in general, and in development, are the first to be cut if the national budget faces deficits. In almost all instances the amount allocated is rarely adequate in percentage terms or in actual amount to address the quantified amount needed to address the needs of that particular constituency. Or, decade after decade, the funds lie unutilized.

The national and provincial or state and even cities are trapped in a fiscal arrangement that allocated budgets have to be utilized in the specified time, otherwise they 'lapse'. Even if in a particular scheme money did not lapse, leading to the allocations being protected for the coming year, their lack of absorption allows for cuts in subsequent budgets on the basis that there seems to be no urgent need for the funds that can be best utilized elsewhere.

State governments and cities hastily prepare DPRs to secure central government allocations of units for slum upgrading which are clearly flawed but which the ministry accepts to place on record demand for the scheme. Apart from the design flaws, there were deep financial planning flaws as well. The scheme sought to leverage state and city funds and also sought community participation through a 10 per cent financial contribution.

While seeking to extract subsidies from the central government, many cities and states did not examine their own fiscal situation to address the challenge of matching funds. In some instances states and cities had no funds to match this allocation leading to non-absorption. In other instances, many ongoing slum upgrading projects of the state which were already ongoing, although very much low key, were stopped to ensure allocations to leverage central funds. An even more critical element was the inability to anticipate the impact of delays in taking up projects and the cost increases due to the increased time needed to obtain cement, steel and sand. In many instances the projects took off almost five years after the project was sanctioned and cost escalations were not accepted by the central scheme. In our own experience of BSUP, and our own experiences with the execution of the projects, NGOs got contracted simply because no private contractor could work at costs that the city wanted the housing to be constructed. We know that this was the main reason for finally involving communities and NGOs in the process. Paradoxically, participation of slum dwellers in a project was the last resort rather than the first choice in upgrading slums.

Capacity Building in Development Projects

Anyone involved in development projects knows about the constant dilemmas of allocation of funds for actual costs of project versus resources to facilitate delivery. In almost all projects (like BSUP and JNNURM in general), there were funds allocated for capacity building. But in my observations, as part of both the National Technical Advisory Group (NTAG) and as a part of the organization seeking to engage state and city administrations to facilitate community participation in BSUP projects, these resources were used to build momentum for getting states and cities to prepare proposals to obtain funding, and to get mayors and administrators to see this as a vital city project. While many vital and important aspects, such as setting aside 25 per cent budget in a separate budget allocation for slums, were also mooted in such discussions, those who actually designed proposals, and had to execute them, somehow did not benefit from this process. It reflects on defining what capacity building means. Capacity to undertake what? To those of us who work in this field with slum dwellers, we believe that the capacity to engage communities of the slum dwellers, to arbitrate between norms of the city and what is possible in slum localities, to facilitate architects and planners to work with communities of slum dwellers to produce technical strategies that work for the poor and to manage and execute project delivery, are just some of the capacities that have to be mainstreamed.

Government officials at ward levels are essentially engineers whose engagement with slums has been minimal and whose whole professional career seeks to uphold norms of the city to which slums do not adhere. Almost all slum upgrading programmes end up needing cities to lower these norms, which only very senior administrators and state administration can take on. Architects and planners do not study slum upgrading in a serious sense in their university training and most practices do not undertake working in slums unless asked by the state.

In almost all instances in the BSUP study, DPRs were prepared without creating an information base of the location and the needs of the residents. As a result, projects, if they were initiated, had to have their design redrafted for which these consultants had already been paid.

The Value of Participation

Development projects usually have a lot of rhetoric about participation. Seeking to engage the beneficiary of the project is always written in the project design as critical. However, in the actual execution of the project, no time lines, or inadequate time lines are developed to facilitate real buy in from communities of the poor. In some instances what the poor are 'told' what they can benefit from the project is counted as constituting participation. In some others their financial contribution is deemed to symbolize participation. Often, genuine attempts to facilitate participation are short changed because what communities want may not 'fit' into the already finalized project. In other instances, even when communities are consulted, they may seek changes halfway through which completely destroys time lines and project design investments.

Cities have a history of being in a constant war of attrition with communities in slum neighbourhoods in India. This kind of intervention comes on the back of many negative encounters and often viewed by communities with suspicion and distrust. Cities often claim not to have time or energy to deal with it. If it is left to politicians to address this challenge, communities then accept what is 'given' but show their antipathy by non-contribution of their money, selling away the asset created or just not moving to the new location.

About Co-Production

C.K. Prahalad, who gave us the well-used concept of the 'Bottom of the Pyramid', spoke about coproduction. It is a process that seeks to develop strategies for projects and products in collaboration with the end user. If the concept is applied to the slum upgrading process, it would mean that cities and residents of informal settlements work together to develop solutions that work for the city and themselves. These in turn form the basis of the projects to be financed and executed. However, to date such protocols have neither been acknowledged nor undertaken by state institutions. They form some of the foundational reasons for non-delivery of slum upgrading. A few NGOs working in this field in India, like SPARC, sought to develop this strategy only to find that the scale at which such a process needs to be undertaken requires governmental investments in finance, legitimacy and learning the ethics necessary to examine some global rituals with local adaptability.

About Procurement Strategies and What They Miss

How a policy is delivered is as much dependent of its procurement policy as it is on the other aspects discussed in this paper. In India and in the context of this BSUP programme, this process has completely excluded NGOS and community-based organizations. The initial DPRs were undertaken by consultants who did their other routine projects or who were referred to this project by a government agency. Almost all DPRs studied in the 11 cities have absolutely no relationship to projects on the ground. No city or HUPA has challenged these inaccuracies or created any culpability for taking government funds to produce such reports. Procurement for construction projects was again given to contractors already registered with the city, most of whom abandoned the projects due to cost increases in materials. Most were not blacklisted. In retrospect, given the volume of slum upgrading that cities and towns had to undertake, here was a chance to produce a whole new set of technical, administrative and facilitative actors who could have developed skills and capacities to scale up this project at city levels. They could also have created new curriculum in universities for engineering, architecture, planning and community organizing. Building NGO and community capacities to participate in such processes and gradually standardizing the process and transforming investments in informal settlements to benefit cities and residents would also have been important.

Challenges to Learn from Mistakes

Government agencies are in perpetual denial of the possibility of mistakes, often inflating targets achieved and losing sight of the reality that dealing with habitat issues is complex and difficult to change. Mistakes are viewed as milestones for accepting failure and failure means the project gets less allocations and personnel in charge get reprimanded. In reality, processes which require many stakeholders to work together, to explore possibilities that are not yet standardized to deliver robust and timely solutions, need experimentation; an embracing of risk and innovation. Failure is often an outcome of some omission and its acceptance and consequent change can produce a pathway for a robust, scalable and sustainable strategy. In the case of BSUP cities, professionals and communities are still a long way from developing protocols to work together, reformulating systems and procedures to adapt a national scheme to local realities and a very long way from universalizing slum upgrading as a citywide process. Failures have to produce a response of learning and changing of the processes and protocols of action.

About Addressing Informality and Poverty in General in Cities

Nation-states, international development and cities are in complete denial about the inability to reverse urbanization. In Latin America, the urbanization which began in 1970s has more or less stabilized at 80 per cent urban populations with very large numbers now residing in informal settlements. More recent democratic governments like Brazil are making huge investments in addressing issues of slum upgrading and redevelopment. They are deepening the investments in health and education and projecting this as a national investment in human resource development. In Asia and Africa, which are now facing urbanization, there is still denial about the irreversibility of the urbanization trend. Urban investments are seen as competing with rural investment in development rather than being on a continuum to address challenges of poverty.

Cities seeking to compete against each other for national and global investments want cheap labour. As a result, they produce informal settlements through their consistent inability to produce spaces for the poor to live and work. Evictions and punitive measure of confiscation and constant insecurity besiege the urban poor who continue to survive this and live in cities. They see no viable option to go back to the countryside. In many instances, their locations turn urban as cities grow and expand to encompass rural habitats on their periphery.

The very section of the city's most vulnerable and most in need of state support and assistance are the ones that face the wrath of the city. The foundational value of habitat security and basic amenities as the critical safety net for the urban poor has generally not been recognized by the government. Large parts of the cities in Asia have people living in informal settlements for several generations.

Ecological Aspects

The poor, who are kept 'invisible' in the city plan, often end up living and inhabiting low level flood zones, hill slopes or sea and riversides. As cities gear up to developing plans to deal with disasters the poor are often 'evicted' for their own safety, with no alternatives as a result of which most often they go back to the same locations. In other instances such households, devastated by the disaster, remain without help and assistance as their settlement is not 'recognized' or 'notified'. Many discussions in the adaptation debate suggest that cities with overall universally provided infrastructures are better placed to deal with disasters.

Value of Post-MDG Discussions

Like the MDG target of provision of housing for slum dwellers, and many national programmes to address issues of slums, the challenge is adopted at a superficial level. It does not deal with the deep political and legal impediments that create slums in the first place. It denies the reasons why poor people come to cities. It does not accept the reality that urbanization is going to accelerate not reduce in the present decade. Inherent exclusion from the city without land and basic amenities almost ensures the proliferation of slums and production of housing without engagement with the city, its safety norms and support. On a foundation like this, envisaging a city being driven and managing slum upgrading redevelopment or development investment possibilities without the participation of the residents and their association seems doomed before it starts.

The general discussion about poverty, its measurement, and how it should be addressed, make objects of the lives of those trapped in these circumstances. It denies the reality of their survival strategies which are critically essential to be understood and built on to produce sustainable and scalable solutions. Professionals, be they policy makers, technical advisors or managers of projects that address these challenges, seek solutions 'despite' their poor participation, and they clearly have not produced robust solutions that have the potential to scale.

Post-MDG discussion related to urbanization in general and with reference to informal settlements and slum dwellers, is beset with lack of voice and agency of the poor themselves. It is flawed because it only demonstrates the weaknesses of cities, nation states and international development. It has hardly been acknowledged how global capital investing in high end real estate in cities may have accelerated urbanization, increased disparity of incomes in cities and produced more exclusionary habitat policies at the cost of universal access to decent habitat for all.

Appendix A

The Alliance of SPARC, MM, NSDF and SSNS

Society for the Promotion of Area Resource Centers (SPARC) was set up in 1984 to create institutional mechanisms for professionals who wanted to work in partnership with communities of the urban poor to seek citizenship and equity. The focus today is towards securing tenure, fighting evictions without relocation and accessing affordable housing and sanitation for all. These are issues that small communities and their organizations cannot obtain themselves as city and state institutions have not responded to such expectations in the last several decades. Through trial and error, the Alliance has developed horizontal exchanges, peer learning, surveys and enumerations as core activities. These are used as a means of developing collective priorities, using data, negotiating with government institutions and demonstrating solutions that work for them as a means to collaborate with state to find scalable solutions for issues impacting the urban poor.

SPARC is part of the process of creating these solutions with the National Slum Dwellers Federation (NSDF) and Mahila Milan (MM) and the legal holder of all contracts and projects that the Alliance takes on. SPARC's relationship with NSDF and MM is symbiotic and all strategies, risks and explorations emerge from a consensus to explore solutions and face challenges together.

Mahila Milan (Women Together) was the name that the women pavement dwellers gave themselves when SPARC began to work with them to help explore the power of association through getting to know other women and their networks on pavements. It was this engagement that helped SPARC innovate its first enumeration, WE THE INVISIBLE, when women from pavements sought the support of SPARC staff to seek dialogue and negotiation with the city of Mumbai rather than be confrontational when facing demolitions. The survey sought to help communities and cites acknowledge that those who lived on pavements came from the poorest districts of Maharashtra and India, worked at very low wages and had no assets in the village when they left. The savings network also began in the pavement settlements and it was women from Byculla who developed the house model exhibition to demonstrate the kind of houses and solutions the women themselves could design.

NSDF was set up in 1975 by men defending their settlements against evictions and feeling betrayed and angry at the inability of the

NGOs working in their neighbourhoods to support this struggle. Over time, their explorations produced city-based associations and their networks linked communities across cities. In 1986, having observed SPARC and the Pavement dwellers address demolitions through data collection and negotiation with the city, NSDF sought collaboration with SPARC and the then nascent Mahila Milan. This engagement initiated SPARC into the trajectory of real partnership with NSDF who began to assist the pavement dwellers as well and who were to eventually become a part of the larger federation. In turn, Mahila Milan moved from being a collective of pavement dwellers to becoming a sister organization of NSDF through which women in more traditional NSDF linked slums began to get an opportunity to work in partnership with men. NSDF committed to Mahila Milan and SPARC that gradually, as women developed their capacities, NSDF has created space in the leadership structure for women and today 65 per cent of national leadership of NSDF is women.

Sparc Samudaya Nirman Sahayak (SSNS) which translates to 'SPARC support to community construction' was set up in 1997. By this time, SPARC, NSDF and Mahila Milan had begun to develop a deeper understanding of the construction, design and financing of habitats. However, SPARC as a registered charitable trust in the Indian context was legally unable to take on construction and seek finances for these projects. Thus, the Alliance together created SSNS, which is a not-for-profit company that supports communities to take on construction projects. It trains communities to design projects, assists them to work with professionals, provides them management support to apply for project bids and puts together project finances. SSNS serves to demonstrate alternate forms of construction practices that are driven by communities and provides opportunities for men and women and the possibility to set up small businesses in construction as they serve their communities.

Together, the Alliance explores community driven collective solutions towards affordable housing and sanitation in over 70 cities and nine states in India. The four organizations are accountable to each other and their unique qualities are needed for the processes and the strategies to work.

The Indian Alliance is also a founding member of Slum/Shack Dwellers International (SDI), a transnational network of the urban poor in over 30 countries, set up in 1996. SDI was founded by several other Alliances like the Indian Alliance and seeks to expand the possibilities for horizontal exchanges, learning and advocacy for the right of slum dwellers to adequate habitats and identity at national and global levels.

Developing solutions for the poor often means breaching existing rules and creating a new process – precedents – of negotiation to demonstrate the validity of these choices. Creating processes and products are all what we consider precedent-setting. Before involving the city or the state, first the community must agree on the solution. Once the community finds it acceptable, then it is presented to government representatives at different levels. When a precedent is acceptable in one place, it becomes a tool for advocacy for other cities and eventually in other countries, to be explored with some modifications. (Taken from SPARC annual report, 2011–12)

Appendix B

An Alliance Initiative in Pune Taken Up by Communities to Reinterpret How Communities can Design and Execute a BSDP Project

In Pune, the Alliance is represented by Pune Mahila Milan which has worked to build women's collectives in over 45 settlements in Pune, has built their capacity to undertake surveys, negotiate against evictions, seek water sanitation and provide livelihood loans to men and women seeking employment. In 2000, having learnt about the government subsidies for upgrading housing, Pune Mahila Milan built five demonstration houses in Yerawada. They designed a house with incremental expansions based on discussions with the residents and blending subsides with additional contributions by the residents. However, since the local construction businesses saw this as an opportunity, later contracts did not come to Mahila Milan. Yet, the design quality and value for money they represented as evidence of a new form of design and construction for the residents.

Over the years, they have designed and constructed toilets, helped a settlement get land and build their own houses with loans, and through negotiations, created a precedent where households whose homes were to be demolished for road widening would be rehoused rather than evicted. They rehoused the displaced on land on which they and two other NGOs had built tenements using community contribution and subsidies in a location called Hadapsar.

Some years after Pune got an allocation of over 20,000 units of subsidy for housing, and having initiated 7,000 units of ground plus 7 building away from the city to clear slums, the resistance of both residents and politicians to move people to the new location along with a realization that Pune had many slums which had some well-constructed homes and others side-by-side with tin sheds and recycled materials, a dynamic municipal commissioner explored the possibility to commission NGOs and CBOs to take on upgrading these settlements through a unique and innovative procurement strategy. He announced that NGOs who could get residents associations and their local municipally elected representative agreeable to upgrade the informal settlement would be awarded the BSUP projects. As many as 4,000 units were up for bidding in that tender. The only criterion was they should be on municipal lands. The alliance supported Pune Mahila Milan to apply for 1,500 units in the Yerawada area where residents welcomed them after their demolition of houses.

Since the original allocation for subsidy was made with a DPR that was almost 'fictitious', the entire process of creating a new plan for the project had to begin from scratch. Working with resident communities, PMM first mapped all the settlements and surveyed the structures and households. A criterion for which households would be selected for upgrading and accessing subsides was done with the resident and these structures were identified on a map. Those with houses which were *'pucca'* (a term in Hindi which means built from cement and bricks) and measuring 275 sq feet or more were excluded. The *pucca* houses were to be given money to build a toilet inside their homes, and connected to bulk infrastructure. A long and interesting series of negotiations with the city engineers produced a range of planning norms to ensure that everyone whose houses did not fit the existing rules had a solution. For example, all houses needed to be 275 sq feet, but almost all those selected for upgrading has 100 sq feet or less foot print. In many other projects the existing houses were demolished and row houses were built regardless of investments made by residents on their own homes. Here the outcome of the negotiation was that all those households who had 100 sq. feet footprint could have a additional floor on top for the rest of the area, and those with less than 100 sq. feet would pool their spaces and get 275 sq. feet in a ground plus two floors in the structure. Architects involved in this have fascinating stories about debates, negotiations and multiple plans to work with each household.

Preparing documentation to obtain the subsidy had to be done for every household. They had to open a bank account and agree to save 10 per cent of the construction cost. That was their contribution. Clusters of households had to agree to participate in managing supervision of their homes while they rented a place when their houses were demolished for reconstruction. The construction itself was seen as a means to circulate money in the neighbourhoods. All those who wanted to work on the job were encouraged to do so. PMM helped those who were masons or women in Mahila Milan who had construction backgrounds to set up a construction business and take up 10–15 houses to build. In the end, the process took double the time of other projects, but every household has a home they are proud of, and the project sets a precedent demonstrating how communities and NGOs can produce scalable and robust slum upgrading solutions. Many other federations of the Alliance, inspired by this example, sought dialogue with their cities to take on similar projects and in many instances got the projects; not so much because the city believed they were a good strategy, but because the private developers had either not responded to the tender, or because many abandoned these projects because of cost escalations. Issues of unfinished projects, many BSUP projects and cities facing inabilities to complete what they had started so enthusiastically, let SPARC undertake this NTAG[2] commissioned study to examine BSUP projects in general and community participation challenges in particular.

Notes

1. Pattas are land security offered to a household or person by the government that measures the foot print of the existing dwelling.
2. NTAG is the National Technical Advisory Group for JNNURM set up to advise both ministries.

References

Almansi, Florencia. (2009). 'Regularizing Land Tenure within Upgrading, Programmes in Argentina: The Cases of Promeba and Rosario Hábitat', *Environment and Urbanization*, 21(2), pp. 389–414.

Anzorena, E.J. (1988). 'The Incremental Development Scheme of Hyderabad', *SELAVIP Newsletter* (Journal of Low-Income Housing in Asia and the World), March.

Arputham, Jockin. (2012). 'How Community-based Enumerations Started and Developed in India', *Environment and Urbanization,* 24(1), pp. 27–30.

Boonyabancha, Somsook. (2005). 'Baan Mankong: Going to Scale with 'Slum' and Squatter Upgrading in Thailand', *Environment and Urbanization*, 17(1), pp. 21–46.

Cohen, Michael A. (1983). *Learning by Doing: World Bank Lending for Urban Development, 1972–82*, Washington DC: World Bank.

D'Cruz, Celine and Diana, Mitlin. (2007). 'Shack/Slum Dwellers International: One Experience of the Contribution of Membership Organizations to Pro-poor Urban Development', R. Kanbur, M. Chen, R. Jhabvala, and C. Richards. (eds). *Membership Based Organizations of the Poor*, Abingdon: Routledge. pp. 221–239.

Fernandes, Leela. (2004). 'The Politics of Forgetting: Class Politics, State Power and the Restructuring of Urban Space in India, *Urban Studies* 41(12): pp. 2415–2430.

Hardoy, Jorge E. and David Satterthwaite. (1989). *Squatter Citizen: Life in the Urban Third World*, London, Earthscan Publications.

McFarlane, Colin. (2004). Geographical Imaginations and Spaces of Political Engagements: Examples From the Indian Alliance, *Antipode* 36(5), pp. 890–916

Mitlin, Diana, David, Satterthwaite and Sheridan, Bartlett. (2011). 'Capital, Capacities and Collaboration: The Multiple Roles of Community Savings in Addressing Urban Poverty', *IIED Poverty Reduction in Urban Areas, Working Paper 34,* London: International Institute for Environment and Development.

Patel, Sheela. (2013). 'Upgrade, Rehouse or Resettle? An Assessment of the Indian Government's Basic Services for the Urban Poor (BSUP) Programme', *Environment and Urbanization,* 25(1), pp. 177–188.

Patel, Sheela, Carrie Baptist, and Celine D'Cruz. (2012). 'Knowledge is Power – Informal Communities Assert Their Right to the City Through SDI and Community-led Enumerations', *Environment and Urbanization,* 24(1), pp. 13–26; see also other case studies of community-driven enumeration in this issue.

Prahalad, C.K. 'The Fortune at Bottom of the Pyramid', www.cs.berkeley.edu/-brewer/ict4b/fortune-BOP.pdf.

Sivaramakrishnan, K.C. (2011). *Re-visioning Indian Cities: The Urban Renewal Mission*, New Delhi: Sage Publications, pp. 278.

SPARC. (2012). BSUP 11 Cities NTAG Study of BSUP Projects to Examine Potential for Community Participation.

SPARC (Society for the Promotion of Area Resource Centres). (2011). Annual Review, Mumbai: SPARC.

SPARC. (1985). We the Invisible: A Census of Pavement Dwellers, Mumbai: SPARC

UN Habitat. (2005). *Global Report on Human Settlements 2005: Shelter Finance*, London: Earthscan Publications Ltd.

Vaquier, Damien. (2010). The Impact of Slum Resettlement in Urban Integration in Mumbai: the Case of the Chandivali Project, *CSH Occasional Paper no. 26.*

4

Housing the Poor in Brazil

The Slum Upgrading Experience

Fernanda Magalhaes

Urban neighbourhoods in Brazil are plagued by inadequate housing and land-titling irregularities: tenements, favelas, irregular land divisions, or even residential blocks that, although built by the government, are often in a deteriorated state. Until the 1990s, the government actively promoted income-concentrating policies, exacerbating social and urban segregation and the housing deficit. At this time the housing deficit was estimated to have mounted to 7.2 million units (Ministério das Cidades, 2005), and during this decade the number of households in favelas grow four times the annual growth rate of housing provision, which was 1 per cent (Marques, E. et al., 2007).

The massive presence of slums in the Brazilian metropolis is the result of a dynamic that historically constrained access to urbanized land, and reflects, in spatial terms, its extremely unequal economic and social structure. These settlements are diverse, varying in location, size, density, building quality, illegality, risk situation, and level of consolidation and integration. However, some characteristics that they all share are illegality in land titling or property, the precariousness of dwelling conditions, the lack of urban infrastructure, and segregation from the formal town. This variety makes the design of public policies and actions more difficult.

The opinions expressed in this publication are those of the author and do not necessarily reflect the views of the Inter-American Development Bank, its Board of Directors, or the Technical Advisors.

Knowledge about slums in Brazil is still recent. The idea that urbanization[1] and regularization are needed is also quite new, dating back no more than two decades. The history of Brazilian urbanization has itself been much more about repeated attempts to eradicate tenements than the pursuit of solutions to improve in situ living conditions.

At the beginning of the 20th century, tenements and favelas were seen as provisional and illegal solutions and, for this reason, 'ignored' by public policy (Abreu, 1994 and Lira, 1994). Eradication actions intensified in the 1940s, as in the case of the mocambos settlements in Recife and eradication of favelas in Rio de Janeiro (Melo, 1985 and Burgos, 2006). An intensive Brazilian urbanization process that began in the 1950s was marked in the main cities by the expansion of favelas and the irregular occupation of the peripheries – similar to other Latin American countries, the urbanization rate in Brazil grew from 35 per cent in 1950s to 80 per cent in 2000.

In the mid-1960s, some specific mitigating actions were carried out. The pioneering experience of favela Brás de Pina, carried out by the Community Development Company – CODESCO (Companhia de Desenvolvimento Comunitario), in Rio de Janeiro, urbanized as a result of popular mobilization against its removal, dates back to this period. Until the 1990s, public policies were, paradoxically, complacent about the growth of squatter settlements, while simultaneously promoting systematic actions of favela eradication[2] (Bueno, 2000 and Denaldi, 2003).

This contributed to a relentless rise of informal settlements on Brazilian cities – from 1980 to 1991, this population raised from 2.2 to 5 million, reaching 11.4 million people in 2010 according to Census Data. In 2000, informal housing amounts to between 40 and 50 per cent of the population in large Brazilian cities (Pasternak, 2003). It is estimated that half of the 1.5 million housing units built annually are informal (Hereda, 2011) and only 30 per cent of the urban population can afford a house in the formal market (Maricato, 2006).

Through this flawed logic, slums were viewed as merely an urban problem, an anomaly to be resolved through 'cleansing' actions of a purely physical kind. Many urban slums were demolished and the population resettled in new housing blocks along the distant periphery.

The problem of slums was not seen comprehensively through an approach that would examine their economic and social dimensions and their connections with the country's high-income concentration development model, which exacerbated urban poverty (Ferreira, 2007). As a result of pressure by this excluded population, during the 1970s the first slum upgrading urbanization policies emerged, bringing infrastructure solutions, such as paved streets, electricity, basic sanitation, and solutions to traditional demands. This mobilization would intensify, leading in 1979 to Law No. 6766, which regulated land parcelling and penalized promoters of irregular plots. Those large-scale peripheral irregular land subdivisions played a key role in accommodating rural-urban migrants.

The return to democracy in the late 1980s redirected public policies to consider slums as worthy of being integrated into the city and widening the scope of interventions to include an inter-sectoral perspective along with infrastructure improvements. Several municipalities, such as Rio de Janeiro, Recife, Diadema, and Belo Horizonte, adopted this approach (Ferreira and Motisuke, 2007).

The 'Estatuto da Cidade' (City Statute), a chapter on Urban Policy (articles 182 and 183) in the Federal Constitution of 1988, addresses a crucial aspect of the social function of both the city and property: access to land by the poor in the urbanization process. Though the Article 9 of the City Statute states: 'an individual possessing an area or urban construction measuring up to 250 square metres or up to 50 hectares in rural areas for a period of five years, uninterruptedly and unopposed, using it as a place for him and his family to live, acquires dominion of such a place provided the individual does not own another urban or rural property' (Special Urban Usucapiao – a form of adverse possession on private land), entitling municipalities to regularize occupied land.[3]

But the City Statute, 'deals with much more than urban land. With its holistic approach, the law covers the following areas: guidelines and precepts concerned with urban planning and plans; urban management; state, fiscal and legal regulation (particularly referring to landed property and real estate); tenure regularization of informal properties; and social participation in the elaboration of plans, budgets, complementary laws and urban management, Public and Private Partnerships (PPPs) etc (Carvalho and Rossbach, 2010).

Above all, the Statute reinforced the role of municipalities to undertake urban development and gave them the opportunity for executing the policy set forth in the Constitution to achieve the social function of property through the need to combat property speculation and to find just distribution of the costs and benefits of urbanization and capture urban value generated by public authority interventions.

It created a new legal framework which gave rise to a number of urban policy instruments: compulsory land parcelling, utilization and building, progressive property tax, and expropriation-sanction arrangements, through the application in their Master Plan of constitutionally approved instruments to combat property speculation was explicitly acknowledged with the creation of a set of new legal instruments: progressive property tax, and expropriation-sanction arrangements such as compulsory parcelling and building, ZEIS (Special Social Interest Zones), progressive urban property and land taxes (IPTU), expropriation set against public debt bonds, Onerous Grant on the Right to Build ('waiver of building rights'), Consortiated Urban Operation, Transfer of Development and Pre-emption Rights, Special Urban Usucapiao and the Special Use Concession. Designed to have a direct impact on slum policies, these instruments offered the possibility of dealing with land titling, a complex problem still far from being resolved. However, the good intentions contained in those instruments were frequently barred by court decisions resulting from lawsuits by property owners and investors (Sousa, S., 2009).

Particularly at the municipal level, experiences with slum upgrading began to accumulate during the 1990s, allowing for a slow process of local public policy institutionalization (Denaldi, 2009a). Although this coincided in practice with a withdrawal of the national government from housing policies, local administrations were seriously constrained of financial and technical resources to implement initiatives in the housing and urban sectors (Valença, 1999). In the absence of public low income housing provision and with the private market unable to respond with affordable prices, informal housing was the only alternative to the poor. Ironically, early in 2000 the introduction of a Constitutional Amendment confirmed housing as a social right, conferring upon it the same status as education, health, employment, leisure, security, social welfare, maternal and child protection and assistance to the homeless.

In spite of the weak financial and institutional capacities of municipalities to respond the demand for housing and slum upgrading, more assessments and plans were developed at the local level, and project design and execution procedures were given greater importance.[4] Specific technical solutions begin to emerge, although in general they remained isolated experiences, limited to a few municipalities.

Presently, important federal financing policies for slum upgrading have placed the issue squarely on the political agenda.[5] Between 2002 and 2009, investments in housing have grown from 2 to 62 billion BRL (1.08 to 33.5 billion USD), and an increasing proportion has been allocated to social-oriented housing programmes (IPEA, 2011). In the period between 2007 and 2010, 23.4 billion BRL (12.65 billion USD) were invested in slum upgrading, though PAC Slum Upgrading, the largest ever programme in Brazil, implemented in favelas. There is a growing body of empirical knowledge on how to develop and execute integrated urbanization programmes.

Upgrading Slums in Brazil: More can be Done Efficiently

Over the 1990s, Brazil has made important progress in legitimizing illegal settlements in big cities. There is a body of empirical knowledge on how to develop and execute integrated urbanization programmes. The analysis in this chapter is based on a new study[6] for the Inter-American Development Bank (IDB), Cities Alliance, the Ministry of Cities, and the CaixaEconômica Federal (CEF o CAIXA).

The lessons learned from the study of urban development and favela urbanization operations in Brazil are summarized here to underpin the recommendations for the design of future public policies on the subject and improve the efficiency of specific programmes.

According to this study, the technical capabilities of Brazilian municipal governments need to be strengthened if improvements are to be integrated into housing and urban policies that can be implemented in the city as a whole. Those recommendations might be particularly relevant to urban development professionals and decision-makers involved in the design of urban development and favela urbanization policies and programmes, offering also an opportunity for other countries to learn from this experience.

The concepts of programme integrality and inter-sectorality, fundamental dimensions in favela urbanization operations figuring prominently in this analysis, are viewed as:

- Factors that connect the physical aspects to other programme dimensions, such a health care, education, economic development, and others.
- Process of change in the programmes' objectives, so as to include more ambitious and far-reaching goals, such as social and economic development.
- Changes in the contents of the components of operations financed by the government or funding agencies.

Four main research questions structure the study:

1. What factors contributed – positively or negatively – to achieve the objectives of programmes?
2. What are the best strategies for maximizing the advantages of an integrated approach and, simultaneously, for diminishing the hurdles imposed by institutional constraints and the growing complexity of intersectoral management?
3. Is it possible to institutionalize a public policy for the urbanization of favelas while at the same time enabling it to scale up and be sustainable?
4. What is the role of governments and financing agencies in this process?

The focus of the analysis shifts back and forth between the programme and the policy level and studies the relationship between them. This resulted in the inclusion of a fifth question: How can an action emanating from slum urbanization programmes and projects be institutionalized as public policy, gaining scale and continuity?

The nine cases, selected to ensure diversity in life cycle and geographic location are located in seven cities: Manaus, Belém, Aracaju, Vitória, Rio de Janeiro, Sao Paulo, Curitiba, and in a region on the periphery of Río de Janeiro – the Baixada Fluminense. It includes programmes financed by the IDB, the Federal Government of Brazil (PAC – Programa de Aceleracao do Crescimento (Programme for Growth Acceleration) and HBB Habitar Brasil, and municipal operations (Terra MaisIgual, in Vitória; Favela-Bairro, in Rio de Janeiro) and state projects (COHAB-Paraná).[7]

All of these operations have, in varying combinations and proportions, components of infrastructure, housing, local economic development, social inclusion, environmental protection, and rehabilitation of historical centres, among others. As a whole, the cases represent a powerful example of the diversity of strategies that Brazilian cities have developed to meet the challenges of urbanization.

Critical Factors in Urban Housing Policies: What Works?

Unsuitable dwellings of uncertain legal status continue to dominate the landscape in Brazilian cities. Scale is still a critical factor in urbanization and housing policies. The study shows that slum upgrading policies, when integrated into a municipal urban plan, ensures economies of scale and ensures the continuity of actions, enabling municipalities to obtain the maximum return in terms of development and well-being from investments.

The key to success in slum upgrading programmes depends on a number of factors. The study has identified nine critical factors: project continuity over time; degree of political commitment and community participation; urban and architectural quality; pluri-sectoriality and integrality; local economic development; resettlement; technical staff; social work, and institutional arrangements.

Project Continuity Over Time

The greater the degree of involvement by public actors, and more mature the social demand, the greater the chances are that slum upgrading programmes will be continued, even if political administrations change. In this context, the catalyzing role that the governor or mayor assumes is vital in establishing programme guidelines, while actions to strengthen institutions increase the possibility that a lasting legacy will be achieved.

Degree of Political Commitment and Community Participation

Often urbanization and housing programmes span several administrations, frequently each new administration changes the direction and main actions' focus, adjusting to emerging interests. This practice, often found in Brazil, turn out to be very counterproductive.

The priority given to a programme by state or municipal authorities, as well as the commitment on the part of different agencies involved (and the ability to build bridges with other government entities and navigate political-administrative differences) is crucial. Political commitment also brings more autonomy to the public administration in defining its policies and the ability to negotiate with financing bodies. Also, the influence of external funding is less when it complements broader municipal policy.

In the cases studied, the support given by each mayor was contingent on modifications that meant changes in scope and objectives. Some of those interviewed think that the changes were made so that the programme would be identified with the incumbent. Such modifications, including changes in the leadership, generated instability, which hindered the development of processes. This is not about validating the merit of any one proposal. It merely underscores the importance of the leading role performed by the staff in charge of the process, as contrasted with the institutional structure.

Fostering participation, seeking to strengthen the community's ability to make decisions or to influence decisions is essential. Social work in support of infrastructure interventions of favela urbanization programmes is the only area, from an institutional learning standpoint, partially organized and consolidated. The degree of influence of communities in decision-making regarding infrastructure investments varies and depends on regional conditions, such as the quality of the local team, which could be positively influenced through proper selection and training, and the degree of maturity and organization of the community representatives. The ability to participate in project design and implementation decisions can be considered a relatively consolidated outcome of social work.

A participatory approach, which involves and takes into account the role of the programme's beneficiaries, is essential to ensure the quality of projects. The residents are the ultimate beneficiaries and evaluators. A house that is too small and stifling embodies physical-architectural elements that undermine the beneficiaries' quality of life.

The gradual opening to an increasing number of social sectors contribute to strengthening governance. Furthermore, it is advisable to start on a relatively small scale, in the places, issues, and sectors where the chances for success are greater. As a consequence of that success, progressively enlarging the scope of public participation and support appears to be a correct strategy to follow.

Ideally, the goal of giving an effective voice to, or empowering, the community and their representatives should go beyond the scope of the favela urbanization programme and have a more explicit political goal of transforming the structure of power, promoting citizenship, transparency, and social control, and boosting the potential and the autonomy of civil society. Joint pressure from the community and from the financing side can expand the community's sphere of influence over the design of interventions. Despite that, interventions seldom extend beyond the project's time horizon, nor would they automatically translate into empowerment or democratization in a broader sense.

The more integrated the favela urbanization programmes become, the higher the expectations are for them to work as entry points for social inclusiveness and poverty reduction policies. The typical strategy is to include in the programmes the actions in various social sectors that focus on the same geographic area. Programme's social actions must be incorporated into social policies established by local governments. Specific resources for urbanization programmes (mainly through the institutional strengthening component) should be available so as to work as incentives for social departments to prioritize and accelerate the satisfaction of the community's demands (Koga, 2009).

Social actions in favela urbanization programmes need to be simultaneously localized (targeted to a given territory where the infrastructure project is located) and connected to public policies and to the city. Consequently, there is an intrinsic tension between the social interventions of a given programme in a given territory and the broader social policies of the municipality or the state. In operational terms, concentrating social interventions in the same area where the physical intervention takes place (and eventually in the surrounding areas) is a necessary condition for linkage between programme activities and municipal or state social policies to occur. The use or strengthening of geographic targeting instruments with resources from the urbanization programme itself can represent an incentive to intersectoral coordination.

In adverse contexts, the geographic targeting strategy needs to be complemented by upgrading and by progressive social investment accumulation criteria. The targeted groups of a project or an action must be identified based on the spatial concentration of specific relevant characteristics. Geographic information systems, incorporating various spatial, social, infrastructure, and facility indicators, are helpful in supporting geographic targeting.

Integrated, intersectoral programmes for favela urbanization almost always present a dilemma of reach versus governance: how far should the inclusion of social actions be extended within the programme? The answer clearly depends on various elements, among them the arrangements or processes previously discussed. A good dose of pragmatism is recommended: at the end of the day, from the social point of view, a favela urbanization programme cannot meet every need in its intervention area.

It is customary that the participatory organizations linked to a given programme cease their activities when the programme ends, unless they are covered with permanent, institutionalized municipal participatory arrangements. Actions that aim to guarantee the sustainability of local social organizations must be implemented from a truly operational standpoint, not through the typical training on project development and fund-raising. The actions should help in a practical way to identify possible funding sources (including in the private market), while linking and negotiating with them, as well as to manage new projects thus financed.

The promotion of collective action based on the strengthening of civil society and participatory organizations needs a scope that goes beyond a programme's time line. Participatory organizations, as well as community organizations fostered by the programmes, tend to become weak or even dissolve after the programmes are implemented. Actions designed to strengthen civil society organizations should be incorporated into programmes and linked with similar long-term local public policy initiatives. When those initiatives do not exist, they should be encouraged through actions to strengthen the programme institutionally.

Broad and unrestricted access to relevant and non-confidential information and guaranteeing the establishment of transparent and democratic proceedings of selection/election of the members of the organizations should be promoted. Respecting established term limits and elections, making the rotation of elected representatives compulsory, and securing effective and equal participation of all elected representatives in decision-making should be ensured. While supervision of implementation activities by elected representatives must be allowed, presenting periodic status report, not limited by electoral timetables, from the representatives to the people represented should be made mandatory.

The merits of the methods for selecting the community representatives or the decision-making mechanisms are rarely addressed in the programme's design. The absence in the programme's format of institutionally defined participatory parametres, or benchmarks, means that in unfavourable contexts for genuine participation, behaviours predominate that are incompatible with the exercise of citizenship, civic engagement, and education for democracy. To overcome these limitations, national and international funding organizations must support the organization, normalization, and, especially, inclusion of operational principles in the procedures to guarantee minimal conditions for authentic participation. An example of this normalization is the compulsory application of the safeguard on involuntary resettlement in international programmes.

Actions designed to strengthen civil society organizations should be incorporated into programmes and linked with similar long-term local public policy initiatives. When those initiatives do not exist, they should be encouraged through actions to strengthen the programme institutionally. In contexts unfavourable to the strengthening of genuine participation, it should be expected that a programme, regardless of the source of its funding, requires minimum standards of transparency, representation, and democracy as part of its conditionality. These include respect for term limits and elections, rotation of elected members, broad participation in decision-making, and control of the elected by the electors.

Joint actions by the programmes designed to create participatory organizations and foster local associations produce synergies, mainly by (i) training existing leaders after they have been selected as members of participatory organizations; (ii) promoting new leaders to staff the new participatory organizations; (iii) encouraging the formation of new associations to increase participation; and (iv) strengthening the capacity to attract members of the community to the associations because of the new role they assume within the newly created participatory organizations, including dialogue with the public sector (to facilitate its access to the communities or follow up on the demands by communities with the appropriate authorities).

The more the programme design is based on a prior collective agreement, the greater are its possibilities for success. Projects or programmes are successful when they respond to a 'collective desire' to solve a problem or an issue, that is, society and governments, and can be established as a consensus. Society's support for the design contributes to the creation of a framework that is favourable to its continuity. Social support inhibits dismantling or interruptions due to political-administrative changes, and sustains a certain degree of political engagement with the project that helps to preserve corporate memory and execution of the actions.

Urban and Architectural Quality

The quality of an urban programme relies on its ability to deliver good technical conditions, as well as other conveniences, such as public transportation, the availability of infrastructure, social facilities, sanitation, and commerce. These but those conditions are strongly dependent to governments' political and programmatic decision-making. Therefore, the technical character of adopted solutions is also conditioned by the political, institutional, and decision-making context, which is specific to each programme or each urban planning policy. Often, technical decisions are impacted from management changes and with discontinuity.

Urban development programmes, in particular those oriented to favela urbanization, generally devote substantial attention to problems of a physical-urban planning and architectural character. Various factors directly affect the quality of the urban and architectural project's technical options. In addition to the technical aspects of the project itself, other factors include urban infrastructure (water, electricity, sewage systems, road access, and street paving); urban integration and accessibility; dwellings site location; and the architectural project's technological options (quality and consistency of the construction and materials used, functional qualities of the units, among others).

There are also general and structural factors related to aspects, such as the priority levels in defining policies and negotiating for financing within the different governmental spheres; resident's engagement, and the skills of the technical staff, influence the final physical-urban and architectural quality of the programmes. These factors also impact the initial scope, its endurance and smoothness, the consistency of the procedures among government levels, its inter-sectorality, the choice of area, the balance between cost and quality of the architectural projects, and the operational effectiveness and maintenance of investments.

The local dimension of a project's technical decisions is also important. This is because decision-making involves a considerable number of variables, all of them unpredictable, for example – an unexpected shift in the number of dwellers per unit, the growth of informal occupation in the settlement during the course of the urbanization project, or because of internal political strife within the communities.

There is also a final factor worth considering, which has to do with the balance between the feasibility of financing and the quality of the urban and architectural projects. The projects' lack of quality is not only a consequence of local technical decisions, design, or materials selection. Overall, it arises from a contradiction commonly found in architectural activity: the project's quality depends on larger usable areas within the units and on higher quality construction materials that would generate good thermo-acoustic conditions for environmental well-being and lower maintenance costs. However, these conditions tend to be more expensive, namely when certain aspects are not considered, such as rapid depreciation and the need for maintenance stemming from the use of low-quality materials. Similarly, the more diverse the projects are, the more difficult it is to standardize the projects, which makes them more expensive. This issue implies a host of other aspects, such as variation in the cost of building materials in each region, the availability and training of the labour force, the mastery of technology, the reduction of wasted material, and others.

Additionally, one of the most significant items in the project's final cost is the land value. The price of land and construction is almost always the main consideration in the design of the projects, with quality being a secondary focus even though it is vital to the success of urban policies. Using budgetary arguments to justify a reduction in the quality of the buildings risks undermining programme objectives and increasing maintenance costs. Programmes should avoid building dwellings that are too small, that do not allow for the control of temperature and acoustics, and that cannot be expanded.

A higher quality of dwelling often increases costs and, consequently, reduces the number of units produced, conflicting with the quantitative proportions of the Brazilian housing deficit and generating obvious political costs because of the decrease in housing units supplied. Often, the importance of quality in a housing unit project design is not fully appreciated in slum urbanization programmes. This is conditioned by the requirements of variety of housing unit types and the quality of execution, size, and flexibility (at all levels: neighbourhood, building, and immediate dwelling surroundings).

Technological and design solutions should consider the local context and culture. In many of the cases analysed, solutions could be studied that take advantage of and complement informal networks. For example, in light of the state sanitation companies' lack of a culture for dealing with sewage in a decentralized way, plus the absence of comprehensive sewage collection and treatment systems, financing agencies should encourage the study of centralized treatment alternatives. This should include, eventually, a single drainage and sewer system, an option found in European countries. In more comprehensive areas, spillways and treatment stations with a subsequent connection to the city's collection network should be considered.

Also the type of building must be able to adapt to local environmental conditions and the topography, among other aspects. This reduces project costs, specifically those related to soil movement, and maintenance. The importance of this issue has often been disregarded in Brazil.

The need to scale up production must not result in excessive repetition of dwellings and blocks. The projects must be flexible in order to adapt to the needs of future dwellers. Maintenance aspects are also decisive in terms of the sustainability of the dwellings, which explains the importance of post-occupation routines, without which important amounts of public investment could very easily be completely wasted.

Even among programmes where the quality of urbanization was quite satisfactory, unit design quality did not follow the same standards. Mass production in programmes often implies the construction of identical houses or apartment blocks, which creates a monotonous urban landscape. This landscape visually stands out from the more diversified pattern of the city as a whole and leads to segregation. As suggested by Bonduki (1998) the use of typologies typical of the 1980s in Brazil of peripheral developments with four or five-storey identical apartments, installed by the hundreds, should be avoided. With respect to dwelling typologies, all of the programmes studied considered extending the units to meet the possible future needs of their users. This issue, generally known as the project's 'evolution', seems to be a current trend of high-quality interventions.

Urbanized neighbourhoods must undergo systematic and well-coordinated maintenance of buildings, infrastructure, and facilities, and they must foster social monitoring by providing incentives to community and condominium organizations that participate. After implementation, the quality can quickly decrease if insufficient attention is paid to post-occupancy routine maintenance. Due to their living habits, beneficiaries may have a difficult time adapting to the condominium lifestyle. Moreover, obtaining a house does not ensure that its inhabitants will derive economic and social benefits, obtain a job, or resolve personal or domestic strife. Finally, hurdles in programmatic decision-making processes can often lead to the deterioration of social facilities.

It is not unusual for lower government levels – states or municipalities – to resist having to assume the operation and maintenance of social infrastructure built and equipped with resources from favela urbanization programmes. Effective linkage with local social policies presupposes fulfilment of commitments related to the operation, maintenance, or expansion of social infrastructure. Sometimes, failure to assume responsibility for the operation, maintenance, or expansion of social investment is due not only to low institutional, technical, or financial capacity of the sector involved, but also to managerial errors.

The size of the units is a decisive factor in terms of architectural quality. It underscores the need to balance the permanent search for cost savings with the need to allow for expansion and maintenance. Given the diversity of possible situations, there is no way to fix the size of dwelling units in cost-controlled projects. However, there is a full discussion around the notion of 'decent housing', which considers the issue of minimal area requirements for good conditions of social coexistence, family integration, and, ultimately, human development.

Housing interventions that aim to provide good conditions for coexistence must consider a more generous minimal threshold than the one currently in use, of 40 m^2 to 45 m^2 per unit. This area is less than the 60 m^2 used more than 20 years ago by the Banco Nacional de Habitação[8], when the standard was a minimal area per inhabitant of 12 m^2, multiplied by the average size of the Brazilian family at the time (five people).

Pluri-sectoriality and Integrality: Integration and Diversity

Having an integrated scope must be a priority for all government levels, which call for the adoption of an intersectoral, urban socio-environmental integrated approach, and offer diversity in the type of housing, in accordance with the local context. A consensus already exists among specialists that adopting a holistic approach to all sectoral aspects is key for well-designed infrastructure and urban planning components of slum urbanization programmes. The scope should integrate sectors such as transportation, mobility, sanitation, land titling regularization, environmental, and social. Although each of these sectors belongs to independent policies, they should be thought of in an integrated way.

The concept of integration into the urban network relates to the ability to create a built environment able to link itself to the existing infrastructure of the city, in terms of roads, access to public transportation, and other available infrastructure. This depends, most of all, on the chosen programme's scope and area. Interventions in peripheral areas lacking infrastructure will be by definition more complex than in areas nearer to, or integrated into, the formal city. The intervention should not stand out from the surrounding environment in order to avoid stigmatization. Instead it should be integrated into the surrounding neighbourhoods.

Additionally, it is important to transcend the project's boundaries, which tend to be specific, so as to benefit not only the settlement but also its immediate surroundings. This is even more important when dealing with interventions in areas lacking urban infrastructure.

Integration into the urban fabric, transforming a slum into a neighbourhood within the city, is so significant for achieving quality that it became the central pillar of one of the programmes studied, Favela-Bairro, whose own name embodies this concern. The inhabitants remained close to their jobs and, given the mixed use, were also able to engage in commercial activities and to benefit directly from the new recreational facilities (parks, sports fields, etc.). The installation of these facilities also had the advantage of preventing reclamation of the area or its development.

Slum urbanization projects presuppose the adoption of specific urban parametres, adapted to the particular conditions of these settlements, which are generally very dense (around 1,000 inhabitants per hectare). It is important to bring in urban and aesthetic solutions, infrastructure, pavement, and public spaces of a quality comparable to what is customarily found in the formal city, either to achieve harmonious integration in the surrounding environment or to reduce the precariousness of the more peripheral areas.

A better design monitoring system would show the advantages in quality achieved by the smaller-scale development as well as its ability to integrate into the surroundings. This could lead to a preference for urban design layouts more human in scale made up of smaller neighbourhoods, or, at the very least, more variety in unit typologies.

As a general rule, urban slum projects must be appropriate to the context in which they are developed; it is not possible to use universal technical parametres. For this reason, a simple verification of indicators or numbers, taken generically, seldom allows for an appropriate qualitative analysis. But some technical aspects are determinants for interventions to be properly adapted to local conditions.

Context in urban planning determines variety in policy. Adaptation might be shaped through devising specific technical solutions or by actions of a more social nature (allowances for provisional dwellings, removal for new ensembles, etc.). For example, a favela located in a flood-prone area must be dealt with differently than one that is built beneath a viaduct or where there is a risk of fire. In both cases the solution will be different from those for a favela established decades ago in a consolidated area and integrated into the urban fabric.

Holistic focus on the provision of dwellings is essential. A consistent urban policy should combine the urbanization of precarious settlements with the production of new dwellings and support for progressive construction, especially for the lowest-income population. In turn, the increase in the supply of housing units is dependent on an ownership and urban planning policy that expands access to low-cost urbanized tracts of land and promotes the real estate market for the low and middle-income population.

Local Economic Development

In slum areas, creating space for businesses brings about greater urban vitality, the continuation of activities at night, more public safety, and better conditions for generating income and job opportunities for the community. Until recently, federally financed housing programmes in Brazil did not often include mixed-use structures. As a result, developments looked like 'bedroom towns', which in turn made social life more difficult. A growing awareness of the importance of creating mixed uses to guarantee urban quality and dynamism has enabled this prohibition to be overturned.

A consensus in this study has emerged that the best strategy for boosting economic development in areas where informality predominates is its insertion into the formal economy, that is, the city's market. In order to promote this kind of insertion, a well-coordinated strategy needs to be implemented, which often depends on local economic development policies. Employment and income-generation initiatives need to be incorporated into local economic development strategies, linking them to diverse agents and productive strategies. A minimum level of basic education is a precondition for any employment and income-generation action. Linkage with programmes from the education sector is highly advisable.

Employment and income is a current and problematic issue in favela urbanization programmes. Most programmes have an employment and income-generation component, but their frequency is a function of: (i) the urgency of the problem of unemployment or sub-employment and the low level of income of the population, and (ii) the fact that the funders and executors of the programmes have an interest in the population being able to assume expenses that they did not have before (house payments, utility bills, etc.). But this frequency does not translate into more success stories. What is observed is a multiplicity of individual initiatives that are not sustainable. There is a sense that after much trial and error, little knowledge and experience has been accumulated, and that the issue is addressed, in most programmes, as an aside and without sufficient emphasis or scale.

Income-generation projects need to identify local vocations and potential markets and, on that basis, to promote ad hoc initiatives rather than implementing generic packages. It is essential to establish effective processes for evaluating employment and income-generation initiatives, their outputs, and outcomes. If this is not done, there is a risk of continuing to design, finance, and execute employment and income-generation actions based on subjective considerations.

Employment and income-generation components must be provided with sufficient technical, financial, and institutional resources to tackle the complexities of this task. Generic packages, or specific and unlinked actions, produce limited results. The component must (i) be planned based on in-depth assessments conducted by specialists; (ii) finance actions compatible with vocations and previously identified markets; (iii) seek linkages with the formal market; and (iv) be subject to rigorous evaluation.

Resettlement

When the scope of the intervention implies resettlement of families, the choice of the resettlement area must be carefully considered. A programme in a correctly defined resettlement area will have a higher potential for success and will be a more rational funding option. The selection of areas with good possibilities for improvement of one aspect, but not others, can lead to the total inefficacy of the policy, once the negative aspects nullify the positive ones. Acting partially in large, deprived peripheral regions with infrastructure problems, creating disconnected 'islands' (Hübner, 2002) with better infrastructure (in the midst of large tracts of slum areas) might be a fiasco. The preference should be for locations integrated into the urban infrastructure network, with good access to public transportation, diversity of use, and appropriate sanitation, which transcend projects' boundaries in order to benefit not only the settlements but also their immediate surroundings (Denaldi, 2009a), are elements of what we call the projects' urban parametres.

The resettlement of slum dwellers in areas far from their original settlements, driving them away from their jobs and neighbourhoods and causing them to have to commute long distances, is one of the worst features of favela urbanization policies. Inserting proximity criteria into programme selection, as stipulated in IDB and World Bank-financed operations, is fundamental. Consolidating urbanized slums into the formal city should not, however, be considered a simple option: generally, its a political decision that goes against the established practice of moving the poor from central to peripheral areas.

The prospect of integrating slums into the city, seeking solutions focused on the settlement and its surroundings, strengthens the recognition of the broader right to live in the city (Denaldi, 2009b). This integrated perspective of slums should departure from a broad understanding of the city and its working, and the inter-dynamics generated between its different territories.

The involvement of the population and its community organizations in resettlement is essential, and the more involved, the better, if possible starting in the programme preparation phase. A good registration is a key instrument for a smooth resettlement process and must be done properly; registration should be performed by multidisciplinary teams of social specialists and architects/urban designers, and should be frequently updated.

Social work in resettlement requires a considerable investment of time (person-hours) and intensive training. Monitoring of families individually is especially important, and technical assistance should be permanent. It is also necessary to support the reconstruction of the resettled families' businesses and a local market to allow for their steady return, particularly in programmes that involve non-voluntary resettlement. Sufficient time should be allotted for the post-occupation phase, particularly in situations of physical decay of buildings and infrastructure, difficulties related to coexistence, and high default rates.

Technical Staff

The ability to promote the continuous training and permanent education of technical staff and to spread knowledge that enables replication of experiences in new programmes is a success factor.

Participation and motivation of the technical staff are essential elements for the success of social projects. Procedures for selecting and training the social teams working in the field should be established in all favela urbanization programmes. Skilled, highly motivated, and multidisciplinary field-based social teams, consisting of technical staff from various organizations, are key to the success of the social work. It is essential to boost the capacity and autonomy of these teams and local organizations in order to resolve the greatest possible number of social demands.

The composition of the multidisciplinary, intersectoral, extended field teams favour linkages with sectors, as the specific demands can be more easily identified by the technical staff and routed to the appropriate sectors for action. Challenges tend to increase when the demands from the community wind their way through the municipal bureaucracy causing delays and inefficiencies.

Problem solving, such as active conflict mediation, should be decentralized: it is better to identify and resolve problems in the field so that solutions can be swift, effective, and non-bureaucratic. For this to occur, local teams need to have the appropriate technical support. Crisis Management Commissions are also important asset for conflict resolution.

Social Work

Social and participatory components were gradually introduced and incorporated into slum upgrading programmes as part of their evolution. Since the early 1990s, in the context of Brazil's redemocratization, the Inter-American Development Bank and the World Bank have played an important role in promoting an integrated approach to slum upgrading. This has allowed for the development of more consistent and professional social components, as well as the incorporation of formal requirements for participation and popular consultation. The establishment and consolidation (both methodological and operational) of the social and participatory aspects have played a comparatively larger role in infrastructure interventions. Despite some limitations, there is now a corpus of procedures that works well when properly applied.

Social work and the universalization of social policies, in addition to support provided during the construction of the dwellings, help to generate long-term developments impacts – social inclusiveness, civic empowerment, and democracy. Urban housing programmes should strengthen social components of operations so as to include before and post-delivery experiences, while constructing housing units. Post-occupancy is the phase that presents more weaknesses – a great number of projects have had problems, such as poor use of public spaces, inadequate trash disposal facilities for residents, and problems with relationships among neighbours. Post-occupancy social work should be well designed with sufficient length and resources proportional to the tasks to be accomplished.

It is relatively secondary, from the point of view of effectiveness of coordination with the social sectors, that the programme be incorporated into institutional arrangements that promote coordination or that the programme itself is its promoter. In either case, the outcome is the same, and the programme manages to become a catalyst for social actions in the project area. From this perspective, it is important that coordination, as well as monitoring of the budget, be done by the managing body of the programme, rather than being diluted among the social sectors that, supposedly, must coordinate with it. Main risk factors are inadequate partnerships management, particularly between social and community organizations, the promotion of social inclusiveness and expanded participation, beyond their dependency on public sector strengthening (Denaldi, 2009b; Paz, 2009).

Institutional Arrangements

Institutional arrangements should not be mere cabinet products; they should be the product of experience and lessons learned, and they should be a priority for governments. They should be incorporated into the mayor's or the governor's planning process. It is generally thought that good management of a project or a programme's execution can be assured through strong institutional organization. However, it is people who essentially determine such processes. It is a dual condition. While institutional support compatible with the challenges that are being faced is essential, it is not sufficient to ensure success. Experiences of successful programmes and projects show that, concomitant with good operational structures, success is a function of the people involved in decision-making and the leaders engaged in the process, combined with the capacity of the technical staff that executes them. The players determine the actions when the organizations are appropriately structured. Among the biggest problems are institutional linkage and coordination as well as communication and conflict resolution between the public sector, the leadership, and the population (IBAM, 2002).

Empirical evidence has shown that institutional strengthening hardly occurs, limited sometimes to the purchase of a variety of service goods. However, to increase the possibility that the projects will be continued regardless of changes in political administrations it is of paramount importance to strengthen technical staff resources of implementing agencies. This will ensure that an intra-institutional legacy brought about by the qualified staff will remain viable.

The success of a programme or project is conditioned by the capacity for managing intersectoral connections that may emerge, with specific political timetables and responsibilities. Understanding the need to act together and to work to achieve the same goal is fundamental for the action's success. While the role of technical and political staff becomes relevant in leading processes, it is particularly decisive in the execution of intersectoral actions. There are institutional mechanisms that can aid in the difficult task of guaranteeing inter-sectorality. Centralizing resource management is one of them. When a project includes different sectors and levels from the public sector, multiple institutions, and inter-dependent sectoral actions, the effective management of processes is the key. It is also essential to clarify the respective responsibilities, to observe specific political timetables, to secure the commitment of institutional players, and to adhere to the initially defined paths, regardless of changes in the political leadership and administration.

Oversight is necessary because developing the integration needed to face the challenge of inter-sectorality is not easy. Agreements are reached but sometimes are not met. There are several reasons for that, and that is why negotiations must be permanent. These negotiations help build possibilities at each level of power; they occur at each level as problems emerge, until they are settled. In order for a true intersectoral dialogue in government to exist, it is essential that middle management and the local manager also understand the process. Senior management must be involved, as well as to impart to everyone the knowledge that the policy can be more effective if there is an understanding of what is being done and of how each entity's actions affect those of others.

Final Lessons and Challenges

The main lessons and challenges that emerge deserve to be highlighted for their potential contribution to the formulation of urban development policies; those might be grouped in eight or four pairs of interrelated issues: legitimacy and institutionalism, integrality and sustainability, quality and costs, and targeting and globalization.

Legitimacy and Institutionality

The two preconditions essential for good performance of any programme are legitimacy, based on mature social demand, and a favourable political-institutional climate. The commitment of the executive agency, the governor or the mayor, is a fundamental catalyst for programme success. Citizen participation and support of the main players is key to guaranteeing effective commitment on the part of the government. This influences the degree of engagement of the public players and is decisive for the political continuity of the actions implemented. A qualified staff and committed leaders, within a management structure able to carry out programmes in an intersectoral and effective way are success factors.

Integrality and Sustainability

The objective of urban policies for the sector must be integral and sustainable. Programmes that aim to tackle problems of urban poverty must also be conceived holistically, internalizing to the utmost the variables that impact on the problem. That especially implies that they are intersectoral and socially inclusive. Such an approach is critical for the sustainability of these initiatives, because it solves, simultaneously, their main problems of insalubrity and habitability, and helps to effectively strengthen the social capital of the beneficiary communities.

Another vital factor for sustainability is the continuity of the services delivered to the beneficiary population. Urbanization and housing programmes must make arrangements for the maintenance of existing works and services, and for the post-occupation of low-income housing projects, at the risk of jeopardizing the final results. The presence of urban monitoring on the ground, for a reasonable period of time after the completion of the works, to guide the construction and the expansion of buildings and enforce control over the use of the land, is essential for the environmental sustainability of operations.

The failure to maintain social facilities and continue urban services is another element that jeopardizes the physical incorporation of the favela into the city. The necessary and gradual reconstruction of the decayed social fabric is almost as important as the programmes themselves. Maintenance is almost as important as the execution of operations, since without it results in the short term might be reduced to nothing.

Quality and Cost

Quality – both urban and architectural – is a very important issue in terms of public policy. The monotype units, very small houses with no room to evolve or expand, scant lighting, and materials of low thermal-acoustic comfort and limited durability, are to be avoided. However, frequent cost constraints in projects for social housing means that quality aspects are often overlooked. In many construction aspects, such as the selection of materials, the less the need for future maintenance or the cheap, the better it will be for the residents. This is the most relevant issue for low-income residents, who have few resources available for this purpose.

Housing policies and programmes in general, and those for favela urbanization in particular, especially those that receive external financing, should serve as a reference point to foster improvement in the quality of low-income housing projects. To increase project quality, the incorporation of architects specialized in social-interest buildings in the teams that prepare and execute the operations should be encouraged as a way to stimulate the development of new models. Another way to foster innovation and improve the quality of projects is through public tenders for architectural ideas or projects.

Standardization can also be an efficient way to improve quality. In this sense, the development of standards and the requirement to respect patterns or parameters (for example, to guarantee better architectural and urban quality), would represent a considerable advance. It is not acceptable to require, monitor, measure, and judge standards by considering cost aspects only, or to adhere to them only in certain specialized or highly technical components.

Targeting and Globalization

Territorially targeted social work, especially in areas directly related to the core business of the favela urbanization programmes, has been institutionalized as a local operating procedure. This is because social work has its own body of knowledge and methodological procedures, accumulated from programmes and projects financed with the support of multilateral agencies and incorporated into government programmes.

The big hurdle arises from the difficulty in moving from the specific to the global. Social policies should be globalized through social work. In addition to supporting infrastructure execution, they can contribute to solving social problems and generate development, social inclusiveness, citizenship, and democracy.

This raises a critical and central issue. To what extent can operations (specific, territorially focused projects and programmes) sustainably achieve broader objectives, such as human development, participation, and civil society strengthening, without being supported by an integrated and institutionalized social policy? The scope of programmes for executing social actions is limited and depends not only on its place on the government's agenda, but also on the existence of government policies. In situations where these public policies already exist (at the federal, state and/or municipal levels), the difficulty is globalizing, integrating the programme or project into the policy.

The evidence points to the need to create appropriate incentives so that the competent government sectors can expand their responsibilities through intersectoral, social, and social capital-strengthening actions to be integrated into the specific actions of programmes and projects. One strategy may be to gradually link social sectors, beginning with those whose actions have greater chances of success, and consecutively enlarging the sphere of governance or influence, based on the gains made from greater credibility and visibility. Effective integration also requires institutional strengthening of the respective sectors. Therefore, integrated designed programmes must include strengthening of the sectors responsible for specific components.

Looking Ahead: Difficulties in Scaling Up

The Brazilian experience has shown that the evolution of public policy in the sector was clearly gradual and incremental, revealing a number of positive outcomes. Many key challenges persist and need to be overcome before broad integrated, efficient, and decent urban and housing policies can come to fruition.

The adoption of integrated urban policies at different levels of government can be influenced by good examples of successful projects. In many cases, however, it is necessary to transcend specific activities in order to link the intervention projects with a housing and urban policy conceived for the city as a whole (and not only for the irregular settlements). There are difficulties in scaling up, assuring continuity, and securing sustainability of processes, mostly because of technical deficiencies in the municipalities.

There have been a number of positive results, but it is still difficult to institutionalize at the political level the procedures and dynamics that led to specific outcomes at the programme and project levels. This is the case both for specific sectors (for example, the housing supply integrated into municipal housing policy, sanitation integrated into the citywide network, or improved access to public transportation not only for the settlements but also for all the surrounding neighbourhoods), and for intersectoral actions.

A comprehensive urban policy needs to combine favela urbanization with the construction of new houses and support to incremental construction, especially for the lowest-income groups. This increase in the supply of houses depends, in turn, on the establishment of a land and urban planning policy that expands access to low-cost, urbanized land and creates a housing market for middle and low-income segments. The availability of urbanized land is necessary not only to foster the expansion of the market to these segments but also, when needed, to resettle families living in the favelas that benefitted from the programmes.

Brazil has reached a level of maturity at which it is necessary to think about reducing the housing deficit without sacrificing the sustainability and quality of its cities. Public policies must pay special attention to the general aspects of durability and integrated responses, with particular emphasis on location, construction patterns, environmental impacts, efficiency in the use of natural resources, coherence with the city general plan, and others, so that the solutions proposed for urban and housing problems are compatible with the objective of raising the overall quality of life and the environment in the cities.

Notes

1. 'Favela urbanization' is used in this work to designate the various forms of interventions in urban agglomerations in situation of inadequate housing and land-titling irregularity.
2. According to Denaldi (2003), from 1968 to 1971, Rio de Janeiro had, simultaneously, a company that removed favelas, the Low-Income Housing Coordinator for the Rio de Janeiro Metropolitan Area (Coordinaçao de Habitação de Interesse Social da ÁreaMetropolitana do Rio de Janeiro, or CHISAM), and another that promoted their urbanization, the Community Development Company (Companhia de Desenvolvimento de Comunidades, or CODESCO).
3. The City Statute – Brazilian Federal Law no. 10.257 enacted in 2001 – gave regulatory form to Articles 182 and 183 of the 1988 Constitution provided a new legal basis for addressing the problem of urban property, establishing general urban policy guidelines. City Statute, in Article 39, stipulates that: 'Urban property fulfill its social function when it meets the fundamental requirements of organizing urban city growth which are set forth in the Master Plan, ensuring that the needs of citizens are met with regard to quality of life, social justice and the development of economic activities, under the aegis of the guidelines foreshadowed in Article 2 of this law'.
4. According to Fernandes (2007), 'Brazilian federalism is considered to be one of the most decentralized in the world, with Brazilian municipalities being compared to Swiss cantons in terms of political autonomy'.
5. Slum urbanization was incorporated into the objectives of the federal programme launched in 2007, through PAC Slum Upgrading (Programme for Acceleration of Growth). PAC goal is to encourage public and private investments in large-scale infrastructure projects restoring investment in the housing and public sanitation areas, which had been abandoned for almost 25 years. Under the PAC, investments of BRL$106 billion (104.12 billion USD) were earmarked for housing and BRL$40 billion for the provision of sanitation facilities (water and sewage) between 2007 and 2010.
6. Published in the format of a book in 2012 by the Inter-American Development Bank and other partners with the title *Slum Upgrading: Lessons Learned from Brazil* by Fernanda Magalhaes and Francisco di Villarosa, editors. Available at http://www.iadb.org/en/publications and at http://www.citiesalliance.org/sites/citiesalliance.org/files/Slum-Upgrading-Lessons-from-Brazil.pdf
7. The cases studied are the following: Social and Environmental Programme for the Igarapés of Manaus – Prosamim (Manaus, Amazonas); ProBelém Program– Bacia do Una (Belém, Para); Programme for the Rehabilitation of the Central Area in São Paulo – Procentro; Programme for the Improvement of Favelas in São Paulo – Cingapura/PROVER; Programme for the

Integrated Urbanization of Neighborhoods of the BaixadaFluminense – Nova Baixada (BaixadaFluminense, Rio deJaneiro); Programme for the Urbanization of Popular Settlements in Rio de Janeiro – Favela-Bairro; Procidades/Aracaju or PAC (Aracaju, Sergipe); Procidades/Vitória Program or Terra MaisIgual (Vitória, Espirito Santo) and Procidades/Curitiba Program or Favelas Urbanization Programme of COHAB-Paraná (Curitiba, Parana).

8. The BNH operated for 22 years (1964–1986) as the main agent of urban and housing policies in Brazil and financed between 4 to 5 million housing units, representing 25 per cent of the total market operations during the period. (Bolaffi, G., 1992 and Arretche, M., 1990).

References

Abreu, M. (1994). 'Reconstruindo uma Historia Esquecida.' *Revista Espaço e Debates*, 34.

Arretche, M. (1990).'Intervenção do Estado e Setor Privado: o Modelo Brasileiro de Política Habitacional'. *Revista Espaço e Debates*, 31.

Bueno, L.M.M. (2000). 'Projeto e Favela: Metodologia Para Projetos de Urbanizacao'. PhD thesis presented to FAU – USP. Sao Paulo, Brazil.

Bonduki, N. (ed.) (1998). *Origèns da habitação social no Brasil.* Sao Paulo: *Estação Liberdade.*

Bolaffi, G. (1992). 'Urban Planning in Brazil: Past Experience, Current Trends'. *Habitat International.* 16(2), pp. 99–111.

Burgos, M.B. (2006). 'Dos Parques Proletarios ao Favela-Bairro: as Politicas Publicas Nas Favelas do Rio de Janeiro.' In Zaluar, A. and A. Alvito. (eds), *Um Século de Favela.* Rio de Janeiro: Editora FGV.

Carvalho, C. and A. Rossbach. (2010). *The City Statute: A Commentary,* Sao Paulo: Cities Alliance and Ministry of Cities.

Denaldi, R. (2003). Politicas de Urbanizacao de Favelas: Evolucao e Impasses.' PhD thesis presented to FAU – USP. Sao Paulo, Brazil.

——. (2009a). 'Estrategias de Enfrentamento do Problema: Favela.' In *Política Habitacional e a Integração Urbana de Assentamentos Precários: Parâmetros Conceituais, Técnicos e Metodológicos*, Brasilia: Ministério das Cidades.

——. (2009b). 'Habitacao e Trabalho Social'. Apresentacao na Oficina de Trabalho Tecnico Social em Habitacao, São Bernardo do Campo.

Fernandes, E. (2007). 'Constructing the Right to the City in Brazil.' *Social and Legal Studies*, 16(2), pp. 201–219.

Ferreira, J.S.W. (2007). *O Mito da Cidade Global: o Papel da Ideologia na Produçãodo Espaço Urbano,* Petropolis: Vozes.

Ferreira, J.S.W. and D. Motisuke (2007). 'A efetividade da implementacao de Zonas Especiais de Interesse Social no Quadro Habitacional Brasileiro: uma avaliacao inicial,' In Bueno, L.M. and R. Cymbalista (eds), *Planos*

Diretores Municipais: Novos Conceitos de Planejamento. Sao Paulo: Annablume.

Hereda, J. (2011). Interview wirh Jorge Hereda, President of CAIXA. Available at http://noticias.r7.com/economia/noticias/brasil-precisa-fazer-30-mi-de-casas-em-20-anos-para-zerar-falta-de-lares-20100727.html [access 01.20.2013]

Hubner, C.F. (2002). Intervencoes Urbanas na Periferia: uma Analise do Programa Baixada Viva/Nova Baixada e da Proposta de Urbanizacao Integrada. Dissertacao Apresentado ao IPPUR – UFRJ. Rio de Janeiro: Brazil.

IBAM (Instituto Brasileiro de Administracao Municipal). (2002). Estudo de Avaliacao da Experiencia Brasileira sobre Urbanizacao de Favelas e Regularizacao Fundiaria, Rio de Janeiro: IBAM.

IPEA. (2011). O Planejamento da Habitação de Interesse Social no Brasil: Desafios e Perspectivas, *Comunicados do Ipea*, 118. Available at http://www.ipea.gov.br/portal/images/stories/PDFs/comunicado/111025_comunicadoipea118.pdf [access 01.19.2013]

Koga, D. (2009). 'Territorio, Intersetorialidade, Politicas Publicas Integradas e Trabalho Social em HIS.' Apresentacao na Oficina de Trabalho Tecnico Social em Habitacao, São Bernardo do Campo.

Lira, J.T.C. (1994). 'A Romantizacao e a Erradicacao do Mocambo, ou de como a Casa Popular Ganha Nome: Recife, Decada de 1930.' *Revista Espaçoe Debates*, 37, pp. 47–60.

Maricato, E. (2006). 'Posfácio'. In Davis, M. (ed.). *Planeta favela*. Sao Paulo: Boitempo, pp. 209–224.

Marques, E. et al. (2007). 'Assentamentos Precários no Brasil Urbano'. Brasília: Ministério das Cidades-Centro de Estudos da Metrópole/CEBRAP.

Melo, M.A. (1985). 'A Cidade dos Mocambos: Estado, Habitacao e Luta de Classes no Recife.' *Revista Espaço e Debates*, 14, pp. 45–66.

Ministério das Cidades. (2005). Déficit Habitacional no Brasil. Municípios Selecionados e Microrregiões Geográficas. Belo Horizonte: Ministério das Cidades-SNH- Fundação João Pinheiro.

Pasternak, S. (2003). 'O Brasil e suas favelas' In Abramo, P. (ed.). *A cidade da informalidade. O desafio das cidades latino-americanas.* Rio de Janeiro: Livraria Sette Letras, FAPERJ, Lincoln Institute of Land Policy.

Paz, R. (2009). Participacao, Cidadania, Pluralidade dos Sujeitos em HIS. Apresentacao na Oficina de Trabalho Tecnico Social em Habitacao, São Bernardo do Campo, Brazil.

Sousa, S. (2009). 'A Função Social da Propriedade no Estatuto da Cidade.' *Jus Navigandi*, 2182. Available at http://jus.com.br/revista/texto/13028 [access 01.20.2013]

Valença, F. (1999). 'The Lost Decade and the Brazilian Government's Response in the 1990s'. *Journal of Developing Areas*, 33(1), pp. 1–52.

5

Urban Transport and Poverty Mitigation Dynamics in African Cities

The Case of Addis Ababa, Ethiopia

Belew Dagnew Bogale and Kiran Sandhu

It is now a well known fact that the global future is largely and discreetly urban. The proportion of the population that is urban is expected to rise from the current figure of 50.5 per cent to 67 per cent by 2050 and more alarming is that almost all of the expected growth in the population will be concentrated in urban areas of the developing countries, whose population is projected to increase from 2.7 billion in 2011 to 5.1 billion in 2050 (United Nations, 2012: 3). The growth in the urban population shall continue to rise and is projected to reach almost 5 billion in 2030. Much of this urbanization is expected to take place in the developing the countries, with Asia and Africa having the largest urban populations. This phenomenal growth is attributed to both natural population growth, and rural to urban migration.

On the one hand, urbanization contributes to sustained economic growth which is critical to poverty eradication. The economies of scale in cities attract investors and entrepreneurs which is beneficial for overall economic growth. Cities also provide opportunities for many, particularly the poor who are attracted by greater job prospects and the availability of services. While on the dark side, urban living also presents conditions of overcrowding, congestion, unemployment, lack of social and community networks, acute inequalities, and severe social problems such as crime and violence. While some migrants benefit from the opportunities in urban areas, there are those that assume the face of stark urban poverty, concentrating in marginalized areas and informal settlements in the city crevices and peri-urban spaces, left to fend for themselves and struggle with the day to day challenges of surviving in harsh urban environs with poor access to even the most basic facilities such as water, sanitation and equitable transport. The urban poor are concentrated in peripheral and unattractive housing locations which do not offer potential for income-generating activities and service provision.

Thus, the rapid growth of urbanization has led to, among other things, a growing mobility and demand for transportation. Steadily rising car fleets have been increasing congestion, number of accidents and environmental deterioration in African cities and Ethiopia is no exception while at the same time alienating the poor completely from the formal transportation systems. Moreover, the marginal and peripheral informal housing areas located in adverse and disadvantageous geographical locations at the city edges are devoid or poorly served by public transportation systems leaving the poor with no choice but that of immobilization if they did not walk or use alternative transit modes as the non-motorized transport (NMT) or the paratransit (provided they too are accessible and available). Poorly developed public transportation systems isolate the poor while the paratransit, that is so vital to the transportation systems of African cities, create possibilities for both employment and travel for the poor. Efficient urban transportation systems create higher mobility at a lower financial and environmental cost. As such, an integrated public transportation network can be an important instrument to reduce poverty and to enhance sustainable socio-economic development. The main objective of this study is to make analysis of transportation for sustainable socio-economic development in African context, Ethiopia in particular to contribute in minimizing poverty.

This paper, therefore, investigates the dimensions of poverty in relation to access to transportation and suggests interventions for transport provision towards achieving the larger objectives of social-economic development and poverty alleviation. It attempts to highlight the vital interface between transport and urban poverty alleviation by focusing on five variables namely, mobility, accessibility, affordability, urban morphological structure and employment generation in the transport sector. All the listed variables are analysed in relation to the locational attributes of the urban poor in marginalized and peripheral settlements that have a serious consequence for the outcomes of the five variables under study. In doing so, the authors employ the case study method of research and use the city of Addis Ababa in Ethiopia to underpin the research focus. The study is conducted with the dual objective of establishing a generic link between transport and poverty alleviation and most specifically to address the issues of transport equity in Addis Ababa, the primate city of Africa and the capital of Ethiopia.

Research Methods

Following a pragmatic research approach, the study relies on both qualitative and quantitative methods to investigate and interpret the transport poverty interface, employing random sample survey as well as qualitative interviewing methodology to evaluate travel behaviour and capture related issues. A major reference is also made to secondary data sources to investigate the interface. A descriptive and exploratory narrative is adopted towards constructing lucid and clear interpretations emerging from the research. The research rests on a framework of criterion and indicators built from a methodological review of literature and employs five criterion to analyse the issue under question.

The Dehumanizing Face of Urban Poverty

The decades post 1960s have seen the focus on poverty debates like never before. The focus of international organizations like the UN-Habitat and the World Bank on poverty has ensured it its rightful place at the centre stage and at the heart of international summits, agendas and conventions. Researchers, institutions and policy makers have been hyper active in uncovering the quantitative and qualitative aspects of poverty with a view to come out with effective measures and paradigms to alleviate poverty in its multi various dimensions. While at the same time research also points to the direction of poverty becoming increasingly urban concentrated (Baker, 2008).

The incidence of urban poverty, or the share of poor as a proportion of the urban population, is the highest for South Asia and Sub-Saharan Africa. An estimated one-third of all urban residents are poor, which represents one-quarter of the world's total poor (Ravallion, Chen, and Sangraula, 2007 in Baker, 2008). Many of these are in small cities and towns where the incidence of poverty tends to be higher than in big cities. While these proportions have not changed dramatically in the last 10 years, with continued urbanization, the numbers of the urban poor are predicted to rise and poverty will increasingly be an urban phenomenon.

Coming specifically to the case of Sub-Saharan Africa, while it remains the least urbanized of the continents, it is a region where the rate of urbanization is currently the fastest. While the national population growth rates in most Sub-Saharan African countries are still well above the 2 per cent per annum level, the urban growth rates are everywhere over 5 per cent. Thus, all over Sub-Saharan Africa, the percentage of people living in urban settlements has grown to over 37 per cent by the year 2000 and is expected to get beyond the 50 per cent mark before the year 2030 (United Nations, 2009). A situation in which half the African population will live in urban centres is sure to pose a major crisis for poverty reduction, development and governance. Thus, the Millennium development goal of eradicating extreme poverty will continue to be a major challenge in Sub-Sahara Africa and huge efforts will continue to be required to halve extreme poverty by 2015.

The dominance of the poor in Sub-Saharan African cities has, thus, resulted in the extensive development of slums and unplanned shanty settlements on the outskirts of large cities or heightened concentration of population in over-crowded living spaces in already deteriorating districts closer to the centre of the cities. According to UN-Habitat (2003 in Mabogunje, 2005), nearly 72 per cent of the total urban population of Sub-Saharan Africa lives in slums. Between 1990 and 2010, the African slum population increased from 103 million to 200 million people, prompting the United Nations to claim that urbanization in Africa is 'virtually synonymous with slum growth' (UN-Habitat, 2010 in Resnick, 2011).

On the one hand, the urbanization process has played a vital role in poverty reduction by providing new opportunities for migrants. While on the other hand, they tend to face a number of deprivations which affect their day-to-day quality of life such as limited access to income and employment, inadequate and insecure living conditions, poor infrastructure and services, vulnerability to risks such as natural disasters, environmental hazards and health risks owing to living in slums and squatters and spatial issues which inhibit mobility and transport access to the poor.

Urban Poverty and Transport Interface: A Theoretical Overview

Traditionally, poverty has been pinpointed on the sole basis of economic resources available to the household. However, the emergent body of literature in the last three decades has thrown light on its multi-dimensional character (SITRASS, 2004). While poverty in its multi dimensional manifestations has been a subject of much research and debate since the 1960s, yet the studies related to exploring and analysing the complex interface between poverty and transport are few and far between; thus, highlighting a lack of inadequacy of recognition to transport as vital to poverty eradication strategies (Howe and Bryceson, 2000; GTZ, 2002; World Bank, 2002; Luthra, 2010).

As is well known that transport is a catalytic force in economic growth and development, the presence or absence of which can have major repercussions for a country's growth and progress. Cities within the context of urbanization are expanding spatially and population wise and have emerged as the accelerators of economic growth in both developed and developing countries. As such, the presence of a dynamic transportation network and infrastructure has become a priority of national and local governments aiming to attract investment and economic spillovers in the city. Consequently, the needs for mobility are ever increasing in sync with the growth of the city itself (GTZ, 2002: 1). It is assumed that for every 1000 additional inhabitants, a further 350 incidents of daily conveyance arises and every square kilometre of area expansion induces 500 new incidences of daily conveyance (p. 1).

Transport has a crucial impact on access and mobility and, therefore, directly influences the quality of life and livability. According to Howe and Bryceson (2000), the role of transport in alleviating poverty can be evaluated in terms of the context of the 'basic needs approach' generating the most fundamental of movement requirements. Therefore, the specification of the list of most basic goods and services that are essential for survival constitute the following bundle (Ghai et al., 1977 in Howe and Bryceson, 2000: 20) as shown in Figure 5.1.

Figure 5.1 *Core bundle of basic needs*

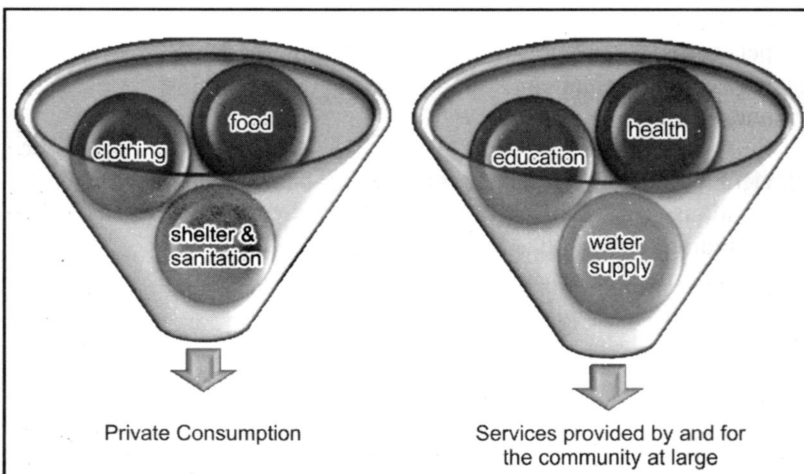

Some of these needs such as health and education services or even water supply may involve substantial transport requirement if not available locally or near the spatial locations. While, at the same time, increase in the quantity or quality of food, clothing or shelter enjoyed by a community is related to improved transport, directly in terms of the income resulting from the activities of which transport is an important component. Thereby, the need for income is manifested in the form of employment which is further connected to a workplace with a spatial location in the city. Workplace connectivity by appropriate networks, means of transport and affordability to the same plays a very important role in enhancing productivity and quality of life of the poor in a city.

Describing the state of current urban transport conditions in Africa, (Kumar and Berrett, 2008: 1) state that it is becoming increasingly difficult to get to work in Africa's sprawling commercial capitals especially when there exists a largely dysfunctional state of urban transport. The road networks are substandard with limited capacities and absence of pavements. Poor conditions reduce vehicle speeds, sapping the output and productivity of the bus fleet and resulting in increased vehicle operating costs that may be passed on to the passengers. Fares are also high in relation to the purchasing power of the poor families forcing them to either walk or resort to largely unregulated and informal paratransit services comprising mini buses and motorcycles. The weak fragmented authorities have been unable to maintain existing services appropriately and fail to meet the service demand of the urban residents, the poor in particular. Also the absence or inadequacy of land use planning and economic development is leading to the phenomenon of urban sprawl. The poor, who are usually located in the peri-urban locations due to dearth and cost of land in central areas where most jobs are located, have to deal with increased travel distances and increased cost of commuting that affects them disproportionately; thus, excluding them from work and social services. The usually insufficient public transport provision and related infrastructure in fringe locations, its poor frequency and higher fares play a major role in further excluding the poor from access and city-level facilities.

Consequently, the poor population's inability to access jobs and services acts as an element of social exclusion that underlines urban poverty (Kumar, Kulkarni and Parida, 2010: 126). With this backdrop, in terms of their mobility characteristics, the poor make fewer trips per capita than the non-poor. The composition of the trips also varies substantially wherein the poor people's trip purposes are largely restricted with journey to work and education primarily. Also, in many cities of the developing world, walking accounts for most of the urban trips owing to poor outreach or unaffordable public transport (World Bank, 2002: 7). Since walking between home and work consumes a lion's share of time and energy, the poor are highly immobilized when it comes to making other important trips from their marginalized housing locations, for example to avail vital services, green spaces and other spatial locations that every inhabitant of a city must have equal access and possibility to visit.

Public transport makes a major contribution to urban mobility for a vast majority of the population which does not have access to personalized modes such as a car and those who cannot afford costly modes of transport. Accessibility to urban public transport by the urban poor remains limited, crippled by issues of affordability and coverage. Research also indicates that the expenses for transport for the urban poor are higher in relation to their incomes (Kumar, Kulkarni and Parida, 2010; GTZ, 2002; Howe and Bryceson, 2008). In addition to matters of mobility and accessibility, a segment of the urban poor find employment in the transport sector, whether it is the paratransit operations, non-motorized transport (NMT), repair and maintenance of paratransit and NMT as also construction of road networks and related infrastructure. Thus, this additional dimension of employment is important for the urban poor to sustain themselves in the city.

Table 5.1 *Classification of the urban poor based upon mobility characteristics*

Classification of the urban poor	*Mobility characteristics*
Income poor	They are poor by income and make fewer number of trips. Most of their trips are undertaken on foot.
Accessibility poor	They have less 'direct accessibility' to public transport. They access only restricted services that are available within walking distance.
Time poor	They have relatively long journey to work. They may walk or use NMT modes which are more time consuming.
Safety poor	Poor are more vulnerable to road traffic accidents owing to their being pedestrians/NMT users.
Productivity poor	Long walking distance and waiting time periods create tiredness and also boredom that can further reduce the productivity of the urban poor leading to loss or erosion of income.

Source: Kumar, Kulkarni and Parida, 2010, p. 127.

Table 5.1 gives the classification of the urban poor in relation to their mobility characteristics. It can be visualized that these categories, although defined independently here, may severely overlap when evaluated. For instance, an income poor may also be counted as poor in relation to all other categories. The above discussion and analysis brings to fore the need to clearly identify the aspects that must be considered for evaluation as a part of research on transport and poverty interface. Making derivations from literature, the researchers construct the following framework to place their research in the context. The framework shall be applied in the case study for arriving at suitable evaluation and judgment about the topic under study.

Table 5.2 *Theoretical framework for transport-poverty evaluation*

Criterion	*Indicators*
Mobility	Network characteristics, trip distance, purposes and travel time and safety
Accessibility	Access to public transportation, coverage and frequency of transportation services
Affordability	Fare for public transport/para transit services, transportation budget of poor households
Urban Morphological Structure	Mono/poly nucleated city structure Concentration jobs viz a viz location of urban poor settlements
Employment	Employment in the transport sector

Source: Constructed by the authors.

Mobility, idefined 'as all trips made over a given unit of time, usually one day, is simply the means to carry out a number of activities that are localized in both time and space' (SITRASS, 2004: 12). Increasing the efficiency and effectiveness of transport network shall lead to enhancing the mobility. Mobility measures indicate the quality of the movement as well as the quantity in terms of trips undertaken and also the safety factors. Both quality as also quantity may depend upon the nature of the network, which therefore becomes an important variable to be analysed.

The concept of *accessibility* emerges as a complementary to the concept of mobility. The concept of accessibility measures a population's ease of travel in order to reach urban facilities or services, starting out from their place of residence (SITRASS, 2004: 13) and reaching a serviceable road to access public or other forms of transport. The concept encompasses the conditions of physical access (time or distance, possibly transport costs) to the facilities, but does not generally take into account other socio-cultural or economic dimensions that may limit or even prevent using the facilities, even if they were easily accessible from a spatial perspective. Also the road in question may not be one used by public transport vehicles and the passenger will have to continue walking to reach a transport stop. Then, the wait for transport to arrive may actually be along one (ibid.: 13).

It may be of use to mention that in the event of a citywide mobility study, the aspect of equity needs to be considered separately. Equity refers to the distribution of resources and its appropriateness (Litman, 2011 in Bogale, 2012: 9). In this case equity would refer to the distribution of transport network and services to the poor areas. However, in this study, the same would be focused in both mobility and accessibility and, hence, need not be treated as a separate aspect.

Accessibility is also measured through the costs of transport that is taken here as a separate aspect of *affordability* to highlight its role from the poverty perspective. The household monthly expenditure on transport in proportion to their total income is considered as the key indicator herein.

The study of *urban morphological structure* offer a possibility to make a conclusion about the 'spatial mismatch'[1] between the location of the impoverished neighbourhoods and jobs that leads to larger travel distances by the urban poor. In other words, the morphological structure of a city has a definite impact in increasing or reducing trip lengths and effects the trips per capita. According to SITRASS (2004: 23), the poverty of the household is perhaps not as important as the location of its residence in the city and especially the location in relation to the main radial roads when it comes to measuring the access to transport networks. Also the morphological analysis points to the form and structure of the city which inturn determines the spatial location of city centres where jobs are concentrated. The distance from the city centre to the housing location could be a highly discriminatory factor when it comes to workplace-living relationships of the urban poor.

Finally *employment* is considered as a separate aspect because of its critical importance to the urban poor in finding livelihood and the ability to survive in urban environment. The employment generated through investment in transport is of two types – direct and indirect (Howe and Bryceson, 2002: 21). Direct employment is created in both the construction and operation phases of the transport system. The operation includes both repair and maintenance and also the actual production of transport services. Indirect employment is generated by direct employment through a series of backward or forward linkages (ibid.: 21). The backward chain of linkages starts with material and service inputs used in the construction or operation of the system. Each of these inputs has to be produced, which causes additional manpower to be employed. Forward linkages in the transport system arise when additional employment is generated in consuming the transport service, such as employment created in loading and unloading, service stations and wayside amenities.

The theoretical overview has provided an insight into the complex relationship between transport and urban poverty in a generic context. Also based upon literature review, the authors have derived a framework for conducting an analysis that shall be applied in the case study of Addis Ababa as follows in the coming section.

Ethiopia: A Country Profile

The Federal Democratic Republic of Ethiopia (FDRE) is the second most populous country in Africa with a population of 84.3 million (CSA, 2010). However, with a per capita income of only USD $ 220, it is one of the countries in the world with lowest income levels, which is low even by the African standards, where the average per capita income is estimated at USD $ 450 (UN-Habitat, 2008: 7). In 2010–11, while the proportion of the population below the poverty line stood at 30.4 per cent in rural areas, it is estimated to be 25.7 per cent in urban areas (MoFED, 2012: 7).

It is estimated that 80 per cent of the urban population is living in sub-standard housing and half of these are either living in shacks or are homeless. Ethiopian cities differ from other African cities in that they do not have clearly defined slum areas. Urban settlement has been driven by a combination of archaic land tenure systems which have hindered a large part of the population to acquire land for housing legally, and the absence of colonial urban planning structures, that have prevented slums from being concentrated in certain areas. As a result, informal housing surrounds formal throughout urban areas. With 70–90 per cent of the urban population living in sub-standard housing, and growing by 4 per cent per year, the challenge is massive (ibid.: 7).

The majority of the urban population live in small settlements scattered around the country. There are only 10 cities with more than a 1,00,000 inhabitants. A quarter of the urban population lives in the capital, Addis Ababa, which is a primate city, eight times larger than the second largest city of Dire Dawa. Erratic economic activity, a burgeoning population, inadequate maintenance and haphazard upgrading has rendered Ethiopian cities unable to provide for their inhabitants.

However, in the recent times, Ethiopia has experienced a positive economic growth in the last 10 years when in 2007, the economy increased nearly 10 per cent. Agriculture is the largest single contributor to the economy, accounting for 40 per cent. The other main sector (49%) is services, which includes tourism (14%), trade, transport, public administration and defense. Industry, including food and beverage, textiles, leather, manufacturing and mining, contributes 12 per cent. Industries and manufacturing is generally confined to urban areas, in particular the capital city of Addis Ababa. As per the UN-Habitat (2008: 14), governmental spending is divided between defense (22%), education (9%), agriculture and food security (16%), roads (11%), health (5%), and water and sanitation (4%). In total, the government spends 45 per cent of its budget on poverty reducing mechanisms backed by the national level policies documented as the Growth and Transformation Plan (GTP) and the Plan for Accelerated and Sustained Development to End Poverty (PASDEP) to accelerate Ethiopia's move towards the path of growth and development and in order to meet the MDG goals of reducing its poverty by 2015.

Addis Ababa: A City Profile

Addis Ababa, the capital of Ethiopia, is one of the most prominent primate cities of Africa due to its demographic, historic, diplomatic and political significance. Covering an area of 540 sq. km and with a population of 3.04 million, amounting to 23 per cent of the national urban population, the city is experiencing a rapid pace of physical and socio-economic transformation (Woldetensae, Fanta and Haile, 2011: 8).

The city has been experiencing a high growth of urbanization with its population growing at the rate of 2.9 per cent per year and is estimated to reach 5 million by 2020. The city, located in the rough geographical centre of Ethiopia, is currently experiencing spatial spread towards southern, eastern and south western parts of the main city guided largely by its undulating terrain and development of road network. The city is also experiencing a dynamic transformation from being a predominantly administrative and service centre into an industrial and financial hub; thus, attracting high rates of mobility of both goods and people creating thereby a high transportation demand and pressure on the existing mobility networks and services. Existence and operations of a public transportation system providing the much needed services between informal settlements and crucial employment spaces is crucial but severely undermined in practice.

The household income and expenditure survey conducted by CSA (Central Statistical Agency, 2002 in SSATPP, 2002: 103) revealed that 41.5 per cent of households in Addis Ababa earned less than 4100 ETB[2]/year (less than 340 ETB/month). Recent studies estimate that about 50 per cent of the population lives below or close to poverty line while the UN-Habitat (2007 in Tolon, 2008) mentions a figure of 70–80 per cent as living at or below subsistence level. Another study (Bogale, 2012)mentions nearly 50 per cent of the population below poverty line with a monthly income less than 20 euros per household (476 ETB) and about 23 per cent households in absolute poverty with less than 13 euros per month (310 ETB). The growing manifestation of urban poverty in Addis Ababa is the overcrowding and congested living conditions and poor access to urban basic services in the city. Unemployment rates have contributed to the poverty levels reaching 34.7 per cent and the limited access to urban mobility services is highlighted by a high incidence of walking by the city residents (60%)

Figure 5.2 *Addis Ababa transport profile*

Source: Addis Ababa Road Transport Authority, 2012

can be taken as a perpetual symbol of poverty. It is fairly evident that the marginal and peripheral housing areas of the urban poor are poorly served and lack integration with appropriate public transportation systems.

Urban Mobility Profile

The road network of Addis Ababa follows a ring radial pattern encircled by the ring road to form the ring and radial roads of regional character i.e. Dessie, Debrezeit, Jima, Ambo and Gojam converging into the city to assume the arterial and sub-arterial character in addition to the other roads that traverse the city (Figure 5.2).

In terms of land use, the share of roads was just about 13.7 per cent in 2012 indicating an inadequacy when compared with the standard requirement of 25–30 per cent. Also a major part of the city is not served by asphalt roads especially the collector and local roads are unpaved. Asphalt roads account for only 39 per cent of the total road length currently and two-third of them are without any form of sidewalks. This shows that network coverage in the city is inadequate. Despite major overhauls, the current network continues to suffer from limited capacity, faulty geometrics, poor condition stretches, inadequacy of public transit, imbalanced hierarchical system and improper traffic management, all of which contribute to poor mobility patterns on one side and road traffic accident in other side in the city.

The Urban Transport Study (UTS) for Addis Ababa carried out in the year 2005 had estimated that the average per capita mobility was 1.08 trips/day and the total city population generated a total travel

Figure 5.3 *Growth and future of travel demand in Addis Ababa, an average for selected years (2005, 2011, and 2020)*

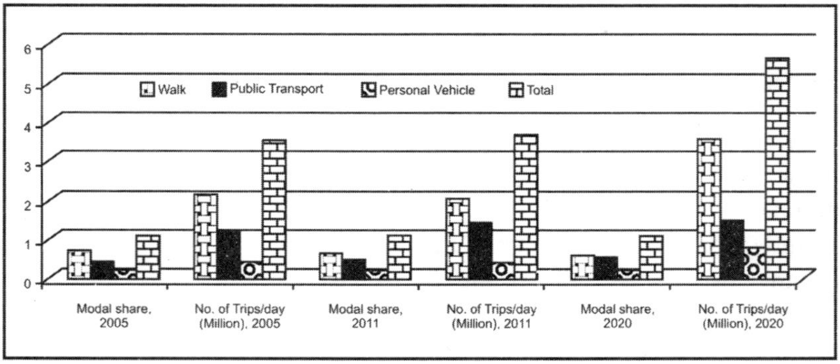

Source: Computed from UTS, 2005 and CSTAS, 2012.

demand of 3.4 million trips/day (Figure 5.3). Of this, 60 per cent were performed by walking, 31 per cent by public transport (conventional and minibus) while only 9 per cent used personal vehicles for their travel demands.

UTS (2005) has forecasted that by 2020, the per capita mobility would increase to 1.4 trips per day with a forecast population of 5 million, the city would generate at least 5.5 million trips per day (Figure 5.3). Interpolating the UTS study forecast, the per capita mobility for 2012 was 1.3 trips/day. With population of 3 million, the city is currently generating a travel demand of 3.6 million trips per day. Assuming that the modal shares changes as forecasted by the UTS study it can be inferred from Figure 5.3 that walking shall continue to be the dominant mode of urban mobility in Addis Ababa in times ahead as well. Looking at the trends of spatial expansion, the distances are likely to increase due to the rampant expansion of the city. Therefore, the urban poor located in the peripheral informal housing extensions shall have to walk greater distances if the road network and transport service coverage is not enhanced and expanded to cover peripheral locations as well. Table 5.3, based upon a random sample roadside survey result of 30 pedestrians at two spatial locations at Bole (core) and Yeka sub city (peripheral), reveals trip purposes and average distances travelled by the pedestrians.

Table 5.3 *Reasons for walking, trip purposes and average distance of pedestrians*

Reasons for walking	*%*	*Major trip purpose*	*Average trip distance (both ways in kms)*	*Average time taken*
Lack of affordability	89	Work based	10	1.5 hours
Poor transit connectivity	10	School based	8	1 hour
Preference to walk	1	Other (commercial/ personal visit)	5.5	40 minutes

Source: Survey result compiled by authors, 2013

The table indicates that a majority of the pedestrians are 'captive walkers' who lack the means to afford any form of transport to undertake work or other trips. Also, the high average walking trips to work indicate the distances that the poor must walk which is bound to have an impact on their productivity due to long hours spent commuting to work by foot. Also, as per the information provided by the Ethiopian Roads Authority (2010), the proportion of pedestrian casualties constitute 89 per cent of the total fatalities in the road traffic accidents in Addis Ababa; thus, highlighting the fact that not only the poor walk, they are also subject to perilous operational conditions on the road owing to the inadequacy of the network in terms of suitability to pedestrian mobility such as provision of adequate sidewalks.

Accessibility of the Poor to Public Transport Systems

The existing public transport system in the city comprises three types of bus services. This includes a large number of mini bus (shared paratransit) and midi buses operating alongside standard size and articulated city bus service called the Anbessa City Bus Service. Table 5.4 indicates the available fleet size and estimated average daily passengers carried by these three road-based public transport modes in the city in 2005 and 2011. At present the paratransit minibus carry 76 per cent of passengers while midi bus and Anbessa city bus services carry 8 per cent and 16 per cent, respectively. This indicates that the modal share of the paratransit services is the highest in the city. The paratransit services in Addis Ababa are characterized by their informal nature and operations that fulfil the demand of travel filling in the gaps in the absence of the formal public transport systems to meet the requirements of transit.

Table 5.4 *Average daily passenger traffic carried by various public transport modes, 2011*

Public Transport Mode	*Passenger Capacity*			*2005*			*2012*		
	Seating	*Standing*	*Total*	*Fleet Size*	*Passenger Carried (millions)*	*Share (%)*	*Fleet Size*	*Passenger Carried (millions)*	*Share (%)*
Minibus	12	0	12	12,500	1.20	65%	10,500	1.,60	76%
Midi bus	25	10	35	0	0	0	439	0.18	9%
Anbessa	30	70	100	750	0.64	35%	759	0.33	16%
Total	67	80		13,024	1.84	100	11,250	2.11	100

Source: Computed from CSTAS, 2012, p. 6–2 and Berhan, Beshah and Kitaw, 2013 p. 723

Currently, the actual number of passengers carried by the public transit system is 2.11 million per day whereas the estimated daily public transit capacity is 1.33 million per day. The ratio of these two figures works out to 1.59. This also suggests that there are about 59 per cent more passengers carried on the system than the actual capacity. This suggests that the poor are forced to walk due to inadequate supply of public transport demand. The second pertinent issue is of coverage of the services, particularly the Anbessa City Bus Service which is also subsidized by the government and preferred by the low income households. With a bus route length of 1,240 kms, a current operational fleet of only 435 out of the total of 759, the route coverage in terms of the area of the city and number of operational bus per 10,000 inhabitants is very low (Figure 5.4).

The bus route length per square km of area was 4 kms and 1

Figure 5.4 *Total fleet, passengers and distance covered by Anbessa City Bus Enterprise and relation with city population and area in Addis Ababa (2000 -2010), (Index base year 2000 = 100).*

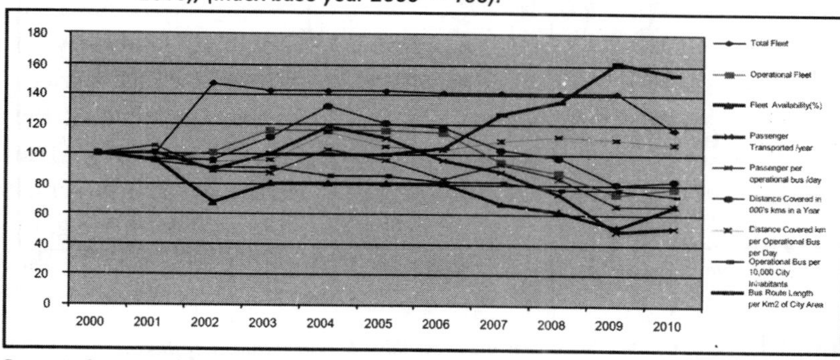

Source: Computed based on Berhanu, et al., 2010.

operational bus per 6,000 inhabitants. The proportion of buses per city inhabitants has been continuously shrinking. The city development plan has recommended one bus per two thousand inhabitants at least. Moreover, as shown in the Anbessa route network in Figure 5.5, the rapidly developing expansion areas of the east, south and southeast are poorly served by the City Bus services, thus, alienating the poor residents from access to public transport services equitably.

The road network and population coverage of existing public transit system in 2011 is assessed by CSTAS (2012) by considering the route network as shown in Figure 5.5. Road network coverage represents the proportion of city roads on which public transport services are operating and can vary from 0 per cent (no public transport routes) to 100 per cent (all roads have public transport routes). Population coverage represents the proportion of population which is within 250 metres of a public transit route. A value of 0 per cent represents non availability of public transport services while a value of 100 per cent indicates that the entire population is within 250 metres of a public transit route (Figure 5.6).

Figure 5.5 *Anbessa bus route network and bus stops*

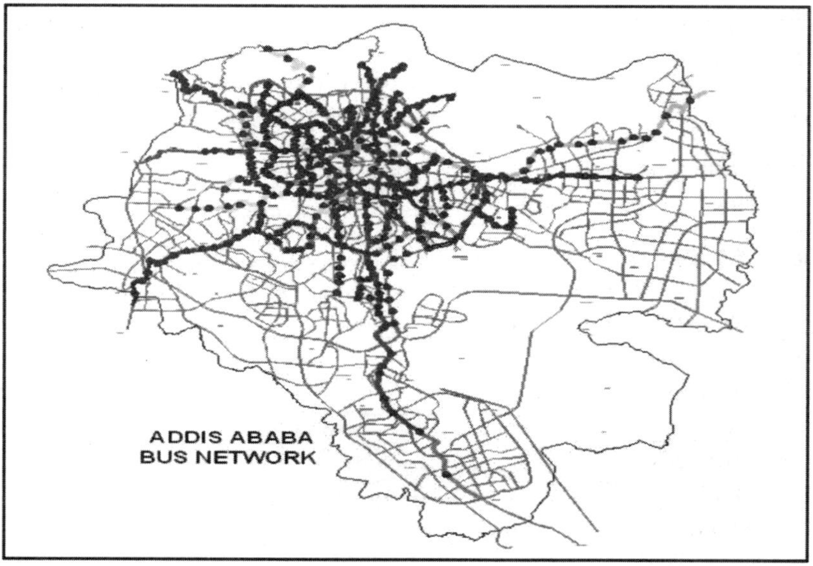

Source: Woldetensae, Haile and Fanta, 2011, p. 16.

Figure 5.6 *The existing coverage and accessibility of public transit system*

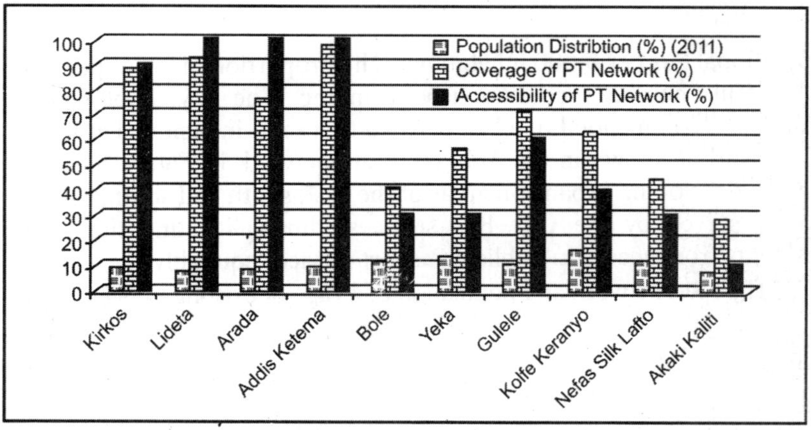

Source: Computed based on data from CSTAS, 2012.

Figure 5.6 presents the public transport network coverage of the people to the total city road network in each sub-city. The figure illustrates the proportion of sub city level population which is within 250 metres of the public transport network. As can be inferred, core areas of the city represented by the first four sub-cities have public transit service on most of their main road network. Due to small size and high residential densities in the core area sub-cities, almost the entire population is accessible to public transit network within a distance of 250 metres. On the other hand, the sub-cities located outside the core city areas have comparatively much lower public transit network coverage as well as public transport accessibility. Only about 33 per cent of the population is within 250 metres of a public transport route. About 67 per cent of city population which is residing in the peripheral sub city areas has low public transport network coverage and accessibility. Overall, about 60 per cent of the main roads have public transit routes and only about 40 per cent of the city population has access to public transport within a distance of 250 metres. A majority of the population in the outer subcities such as Yeka, Akiki Kaliti and Nefas Silk Lafto pertains to the lower segment of the society and absence of a stable public transport service provision alienates them and contributes to walking populations and long unproductive commuting distances.

Affordability of Public Transport Systems to the Urban Poor

One of the critical factors that can limit the access of the poor to urban transport services is affordability which can be precisely reflected in the usage pattern of public transport, the household budgets on public transport and the nature of fares. Coming specifically to the case of Anbessa City Bus Service, prior to its deregulation, it exercised an exclusive monopoly in the public transport services with the fares being heavily subsidized to enable a wider outreach. After deregulation, a vast segment of the public transport market has been captured by the paratransit mini bus operators. The fare is based on distance and ranges from 1 Ethiopian Birr rates (ETB) (city centre) to 7 ETB (suburb) and there is a 45-cent public subsidy per ticket. Currently, Anbessa carries 4,00,000 passengers per day. The mini bus fare levels are four times those charged by Anbessa. However, despite the subsidized fare, the Anbessa suffers from poor operational efficiency and lack of outreach in the outer peripheral parts of the city or a very low frequency of service. For instance, in the Yeka sub-city, a sample survey of 20 passengers on the Kotobe road with a varied income breakup revealed the preference of public transit users for paratransit mini bus due to its higher frequency of service that reduces waiting time even though the costs are higher. Survey revealed that even the low income group population was forced to use paratransit over the anbessa leading to a higher burden of transportation cost as the table reveals.

Table 5.5 *Income levels and average expenditure on transportation*

Income level (ETB)	*Average expenditure on transportation (%)*
Below 350	35
350–500	21
500–1000	18
1000–2000	17
Above 2000	13

Source: Sample survey findings, 2013.

It can be inferred that the people with the lowest incomes end up spending a larger amount on making urban travel trips, majority of them being work based. While there are no international benchmarks as such to arrive at a rational judgment of the more or less standard transport expenditure, it can be rationalized that appropriate provision of transport services and rational tariff setting would enable a reduction in transport cost to the poor and the money could be channelized to other important areas such as access to health care or education. The figure of 35 per cent also matches with other similar studies (World Bank, 2004; Nyarirangwe, 2008) to indicate the transport burden on the urban poor in African context. Also, the lack of affordability constrains trip-making behaviour of the low income population and makes than much less mobile than their richer counterparts.

Also as Nyarirangwe (2008) points out that the demand for public transport in Addis Ababa displays a varying levels of inelasticity owing to the inadequacy of services as well as limited alternatives to choose from between the Anbessa and the paratransit mini bus. The private cab taxis also called 'ladas' are beyond the reach of the poor with their speculator fares amounting to as high as 20 ETB per kilometre of travel. A limited number of NMTs (non-motorized transport) in the form of horse/donkey carts operate in some peripheral parts of the city on inner unpaved roads such as the CMC extension serving as a feeder to the paratransit or the Anbessa. The lack of promotion and incorporation of the NMT and its prohibition on the main roads is also a limiting factor. The road infrastructure does not cater to the provision for design space for the NMT operations, thus, discouraging its use.

Another reason that leads to the high fares is that incase of the paratransit mini buses, some trips such as from CMC to Bole road requires a minimum of three changes due to shortening of routes by operators. So, instead of a single cumulative fare, the passengers end up paying much more. The interchanges impose an additional cost which the poor can ill afford to pay.

Employment Generation in the Transport Sector

Urban transport, in particular public transport, happens to be an important generator of employment.

The Anbessa employs 2,719 people out of which 4 per cent are professionally qualified staff, 16 per cent skilled and 80 per cent semi/unskilled staff. The paratransit operations constitutes nearly 75 per cent of the total employment in the transport sector and, thus, acts as a source of employment to the poor and in fact contributes positively to tackling urban poverty (Table 5.6). Also, the development and construction works on the city roads such as Bole road reconstruction and extension, outer ring road construction of flyovers and cobblestone sidewalks paving have opened up opportunities for enlarging the labour based intensive construction methods towards poverty reduction in the city.

Table 5.6 *Employment in the transport sector*

Employment	*Number*	*Percentage share*
Anbessa city bus service	2,719	9.21
Paratransit Buses and Bajaj auto service	22,100	74.89
Non motorized transport	100*	0.33
Repair and maintenance services	1,000	3.38
City traffic police	360	1.22
City Transport Authorities staff	428	1.45
Road infrastructure development and construction	1,600*	5.42
Freight transport	1,200*	4.06
Total	29,507	100

Source: Anbessa City Bus Statistical Data, 2012; Addis Ababa Road Transport Authority, 2013.

* Refers to approximations as factual data is lacking and these figures also pertain to situations of fluctuations in casual labour.

Urban Morphological Structure

The morphological character of Addis Ababa also bears an impact on the transport burden of the urban poor. The city displays an organic spread around a multi nucleus structure. However, the multi nucleus pattern with concentration of jobs and facilities such as Bole, Bole Dili, Gurdshola, Meganenga, Merkato and Piazza is manifested in the poor having to traverse across a number of centres for employment and other services. In this context, a survey (Nyarirangwe, 2008) revealed that 80 per cent of the employees in Gurdshola and Meganegna centres are not resident there and come from distant locations.

Also, the city nucleus are not self-sufficient and generate the need for travel to fulfil specific needs of employment and access to facilities. As a result, the city morphology in reality creates the possibility for many vehicle interchanges with paratransit running over shorter routes and leading to longer trip distances between centres and, thus, higher fare rates. Consequently, this structure of the city accelerates the need for transportation, posing an additional travel demand, exacerbating transport costs and imposes a high burden on the poor to compromise their travel behaviour.

Transport Policy and Poverty Reduction Initiatives

There has been a growing recognition that development of sustainable transport both in urban and rural Ethiopia is critical to the overall socio-economic development and progress of the country and this understanding is manifested in the national level policy documents i.e. PASDEP (Plan for Accelerated and sustained development to end poverty, 2005–2010), Growth and Transformation Plan (GTP, 2010–2015) and the National Transport Master Plan (2008). The PASDEP and also the GTP emphasized on achieving the Millennium Development Goal 7, target 11, improving the quality of life of the slum dwellers as being of specific importance to poverty alleviation and socio-economic development of the country. The National Transport Master Plan is also reflective of a poverty focused intervention with one of its key objective being to reduce transport costs and improve its safety and access. In this backdrop, the Addis Ababa City Development Plan 2001–2010 identified shortage of public transport services and low affordability of mass transport as critical problems to be addressed.

As such, the Strategic Development Action Plan (SDAP) earmarked 1.4 billion ETB for strategic actions to improve transport conditions in the city. Also, the Addis Ababa City Development plan proposed the development of LRTS (Light Rail Transit System) and BRTS (Bus Rapid Transit System) mass transit services in the city.

They are currently under construction and expected to be completed by 2015. Once in operation, the LRTS being constructed at the cost of US $ 236 million is expected to reduce travel time between the major nodes with a capacity of 12,000 persons/hour/direction. However, it is important that the cost must be affordable to the majority of the population and be sensitive to the needs of the poorest sections or else this mode shall also not be within their reach.

Urban Poverty Focused Transport Interventions: The Road Ahead

The case of Addis Ababa has highlighted the complex interface between urban poverty and transport and it has been demonstrated through the analysis of five criterion, i.e. mobility, accessibility, affordability, urban morphological structure and employment. Through this research, the authors highlight the interface while also herein make a strong case for further research to establish further concrete evidence for setting the stage for targeted interventions to emerge. However, in the light of the study, the case is established for carrying forth interventions focusing upon poverty sensitive transport solutions to enhance mobility of the poor.

Saving time on urban travel is not only an important social consideration but also has a very real economic impact at national, regional and urban scales (Woldetensae, Fanta and Haile, 2011). The development of multi modal transport in Addis Ababa is a step in the right direction. However, it is important to establish appropriate modalities of inter connectivity and feeder services with a wide outreach covering the entire spatial spread of the city to ensure geographical coverage of transport services. However, even a geographical spread cannot ensure affordability and this must be done by introduction of a multi modal transport system that offers a wide elastic supply of modes and leads to competitive fare reduction. Alternatively, the poor can benefit from flat fares rather than fares based upon trip distances. However, the fare fixation demand a methodological study of sustainability and threshold which is another subject that demands research and is beyond the purview of this paper.

While the public transport system shall ensure mobility of the poor, it is envisaged that the modal shift shall also occur slowly depending upon other poverty eradication policies and programmes of the government. The *UTS* Study (2005) indicates that the number of pedestrians shall decrease from the current 60 to 45 per cent if the mass public transit system was developed as suggested by the study. That would lead to an increase of modal share of public transport to 46 per cent and the private share shall remain at 9 per cent. Looking at these estimates, it is evident that pedestrian traffic shall decrease but not drastically and largely over long distances. Therefore, it is suggested that the road networks must be designed as pedestrian-sensitive to enhance walking speed and safety. This can be done by a general provision of better pedestrian access tracks, safe pedestrian crossings, segregated walkways along all the collector, arterial and sub-arterial roads in the city. The paratransit operations must be appropriately regulated from the routing and fare aspects so that they are more accessible and affordable to the urban poor.

Despite the development of the LRTS, it is anticipated that the Anbessa city bus shall continue to play an important role in urban mobility in the city and especially of the poor due to its subsidized fare structure. However it demands improvement in terms of enhancing its fleet, geographical spread and reduce waiting times and enhance frequency by appropriate route and vehicle scheduling measures. The addition of 100 articulated buses by the city government to the existing fleet of the Anbessa is an appropriate measure to this effect.

The NMTs as horse/donkey carts provide employment and mobility options to the poor and should, therefore, be integrated effectively into the design of the feeder system on roads of lower hierarchy and level of service keeping the aspect of transport equity and employment in mind. While bicycle can be a suitable NMT option, in the case of Addis Ababa, due to its undulating terrain its use is and shall continue to be limited and, hence, unless the roads are designed to suit the bicycling grades, its use might not be completely feasible.

As has been demonstrated, transport supply and land use are mutually dependent (GTZ, 2002). Improving access for the poor can be targeted more effectively if the urban transportation planning is tied to urban expansion and development and takes account of the transport needs of the urban poor. A morphological structure of Addis Ababa can benefit from creating largely self-sufficient poly nucleated land use distributions with high order inter-linkages between the centres and the periphery to ensure fast mobility between the work places and the living areas of the urban poor while, at the same time, reduce the need to travel between and to various nodal locations.

Finally, transport by itself is a lucrative sector that can generate employment in all its components. Looking at the context of unemployment levels in the city, it is important that transport infrastructure developers be more sensitive to using labour intensive methods of construction over machine intensive such as cobblestone sidewalks paving that not only promote micro industrial enterprises (manufacture of cobblestone blocks) but also engage labour in skilled/unskilled employment.

Conclusions

In summary, it can be opined that if a city is to be socially economically vibrant and sustainable, its land use and infrastructure development characteristics must reflect equity and inclusion of all its residents and especially the poor and the disadvantaged. This calls for designing transport policies and programmes that target poverty by creating possibilities for enhancing mobility, accessibility and affordability of the urban poor to the city transport systems and also create deliberate opportunities for employment for them. Also, it is emphasized that the informal settlements housing the poor must be systematically integrated with efficient public transportation systems to provide seamless mobility to the poor and enhance their access to jobs and productivity. The same shall go a long way in addressing the needs of the urban poor in terms of reducing their travel time, enhance productivity and improving incomes and quality of life of the urban poor.

Notes

1. The concept of spatial mismatch has been used by different authors to analyse the jobs for low income groups depending upon the cost of travel to various locations (Joseph, 2011 in Bogale, 2012).
2. ETB refers to Ethiopian birr, the currency of Ethiopia and is equivalent to 23.8 euros.

References

Addis Ababa City Administration. (1997). City's Transport Service Study: A Study Project to alleviate the Cities Problem for Long Term, Addis Ababa.

Baker, J.L. (2008). 'Urban Poverty: A Global View', Washington: World Bank, D.C. siteresources.worldbank.org/INTURBANDEVELOPMENT/.../UP-5.pdfý

Bogale, Y.A. (2012). 'Evaluating Transport Network Structure: Case study of Addis Ababa, Ethiopia', Masters Dissertation, University of Twente, Netherlands. www.itc.nl/library/papers_2012/msc/gfm/bogale.pdf.

Berhanu, E., B. Beshah and D. Kitaw (2013). 'Performance Analysis on Public Bus Transport of the City of Addis Ababa', *International Journal of Computer Information Systems and Industrial Management Applications*, 5, pp. 722–728.

Central Statistical Agency of Ethiopia http://www.csa.gov.et/images/documents/pdf_files/recentsurveysreports/HCE_2010_11_Statistical%20Report.pdf

Consultancy Services for Technical Advisory Service for Addis Ababa City Traffic Management (CSTAS). (2012). Draft Interim Report, Addis Ababa: Addis Ababa City Administration.

COWI. (2008). 'National Transport Master Plan Study', Volume I Investment Plan, Addis Ababa: COWI and GOPA.

GTZ. (2002). 'Urban Transport and Poverty in Developing Countries', Eschborn. http://www.gtkp.com/assets/uploads/20091127-182046-6236-en-urban-transport-and-poverty.pdf

GTZ. (2012). 'Making Good Governance Tangible, The Cobblestone Sector in Ethiopia', GTZ, http://www.giz.de/Themen/en/dokumente/giz 2012-making-good-governance-tangible-en.pdf

Howe, J. and D. Bryceson. (2000), 'Poverty and Urban Transport in East Africa: Review of Research and Dutch Experience, International Institute for Infrastructure, Hydraulic and Environmental Engineering. citeseerx. ist.psu.edu/viewdoc/download?doi= 10.1.1.199.7184.

Kumar, A. and F. Berret (2008). 'Struck in Traffic: Urban Transport in Africa', World bank and SSATP, http://siteresources.worldbank.org/EXTAFRSUBSAHTRA/Resources/Stuck-in-Traffic.pdf

Kumar, P., S.Y. Kulkarni, and M. Parida. (2010). 'Multi Modal Public Transport for Urban Poor: Inclusive Planning Approach' in 58th National Town and Country Planner's Congress, *Inclusive Planning for Empowering Urban Poor*, Institute of Town Planners, India, pp. 126–129.

Luthra, A. (2010). 'Accessibility, 'A tool for empowering urban poor' in 58th National Town and Country Planner's Congress, *Inclusive Planning for Empowering Urban Poor*, Institute of Town Planners, India, pp. 91–96.

Mabogunje, A.L. (2005). 'Global Urban Poverty Research Agenda: The African Case', http://www.citiesalliance.org/sites/citiesalliance.org/files/mabogunjepaper%5B1%5D.pdf.

Ministry of Finance and Economic Development (MoFED). (2012). 'Growth and Transformation Plan (2010–2015) Annual Progress Report 2010–2011', Addis Ababa, *www.imf.org/external/pubs/ ft/scr/2011/cr11304.pdfý*

MoFED. (2012). Ethiopia's Progress towards Eradicating Poverty: An Interim Reporton Poverty Analysis Study (2010–2011). www.mofed.gov.et/.../Interim%20Report%20on%202010-11%20Povert.

MoWUD. (2006). 'Plan for Accelerated and Sustained Development to End Poverty', (PASDEP) 2005/06-2009/10, Volume I, Addis Ababa. http://www.afdb.org/fileadmin/uploads/afdb/Documents/Policy-Documents/Plan_for_Accelerated_and_Sustained_(PASDEP)_final_July_2007_Volume_I_3.pdf

Nyarirangwe, Maxwell. (2008). 'The impact of multi nucleated city morphology on transport Addis Ababa', in M.P. VanDijk and J. Fransen (eds) *Managing Ethiopian Cities in an Era of Rapid Urbanization*, Delft: Eburon Publishers, pp. 45–53.

Resnick, D. (2011). In the Shadow of the City: Africa's Urban Poor in Opposition Strongholds, *Journal of Modern African Studies*, Vol 49, No 1, pp. 141–166.

Saba Engineering PLc. (2005). Urban Transport Study and Preparation for Pilot Project for Addis Ababa, Volume I and II. Addis Ababa.

SITRASS. (2004). 'Poverty and Urban Mobility in Douala, Final Report' African Region', World Bank. www4.worldbank.org/afr/ssatp/Resources/PapersNotes/Douala_en.pdf

Tolon, U.W. (2008). 'Comparison of Urban Upgrading Projects on Development Cooperation in Ethiopia', upcommons.upc.edu/pfc/bitstream/2099.1/6374/7/06.pdf

UN-Habitat. (2008). 'Ethiopia Urban Profile', Nairobi. www.unhabitat.org/pmss/getElectronicVersion.aspx?nr=2719&alt=1

United Nations. (2009). 'Rethinking Poverty: Report on the World Social Situation 2010', Department of Economic and Social Affairs, New York. www.un.org/esa/socdev/rwss/docs/2010/fullreport.pdfý

United Nations. (2012). 'World Urbanization Prospects, The 2011 Revision', Department of Economic and Social Affairs.http://esa.un.org/unup/pdf/WUP2011_Highlights.pdf.

Woldetensae, B, Y, Fanta, and A Haile. (2011). 'Evaluation of the Development Plan of Addis Ababa City', Transport Sector, 2003–2010.

World Bank. (2002). 'Scoping Study-Urban Mobility in Three Cities'. www4.worldbank.org/.../TESSA4%20%20Urban%20Mobility%20in%20A.

PART II

Societal-Level Housing Provision Policies

6

Housing Questions in Hyper-Modernizing (Post-) Socialist China

Enigma of Urban Contradictions and Dualism in Economic Miracle[1]

On-Kwok Lai

Enigma of Hyper-Modernizing China's Mega-Urbanization Project

Over 9 per cent of annual GDP growth since 1980s in the People's Republic of China (PRC) is a multiple economic miracle: historical both in Chinese and global history; the hyper-modernization processes resulted in over 50 per cent of its population (2012) residing in cities (partly by migrant-workers drawn from rural areas). This is juxtaposing a socialist state-commanded yet market-driven (somewhat successful) economic development, with the result that millions of people are escaping from absolute poverty (of less than 1 US$ per day) and urban dwellers are becoming richer but having more housing problems since economic liberalization in early 1980s. To examine the underlying contradictions of the urban housing question, this paper has four parts. After a historical review on structural conditions (and limitations) of low income housing development in (post-) socialist China's rapid urbanization, Part 2 examines, through case studies, the urban contradictions of the housing question, with reference to central, regional and local government policy (inertia) initiatives to cope with hyper-urbanization and the 'compressed' modernization; highlighting the problematic urban policy derived from a neoliberal economics' bias for pro-market development. A critical discussion on current problems and future scenarios in Part 3 is followed by the ending remarks on the dilemma and normative issues on the prospect for urban development for all.

Positioning China's Rapid Urbanization in its Hyper-Modernization Project

China's economic growth has been impressively coined as miracle by neoliberal economic agencies like IMF and the World Bank: over 9 per cent for several decades since its Open Door Policy in late 1970s. More recently, it is the world's second-largest economy: despite its recent slowing economic growth, down from 9.2 per cent (in 2011) and 10.4 per cent (in 2010), China's economy still expanded impressively by 8.2 per cent in 2012, vis-à-vis the developed (like OECD) countries.

But it should be warned that Chinese development statistics are full of caveats, particularly for those measuring rapid urbanization processes – like those on land development and property market. One unique contributing factor for China for the default of problematic urban statistics is the calling for medium-range (say, the five-year plan) development goals and short-term harmony (to prevent the hard landing of a bubble economy which could exacerbate more urban chaos like social dualism)under the steering of Chinese Communist Party (CCP).

Yet, rapid urbanization in the last few decades is at an historical scale, driven by the hyper-modernization regime of growth. Since 2010, half of its population are urban dwellers and more people are now moving into cities, under an increasing dynamic momentum for further rapid urbanization processes.

In (post-) socialist China, the mode of (semi-) planned urbanization is the consequence, as well as the representation, of political struggles over socialist ideologies on pro-capitalist development: urbanization and segregations are intertwined with the state's urban governance in pre-1970s era, but more or less as structurally anchoring on the emerging market forces in the last 30 years. More specific, the development of urban governance has been shaped by two major sets of factors, namely, the influence of the CCP ideologies on national (pro-growth economic) developmentalism (to secure the legitimacy of itself) and the political struggles within the CCP, and perhaps more importantly, the national economic problems encountered and the pragmatic policy responses in different periods along the path for semi-integration with global capitalist economy (Lai, 1998, 2001, 2007). The CCP's pragmatism and expediency are evolving with their strategies as the timely *modus operandi*.

Historical Legacies of Socialist Transformation to China's Semi-Capitalism

Rapid urbanization mirrors the liberalization of the economy since 1978. The relaxation, and the subsequent demise, of the household registration (*hukou*) system was a direct result of rationalization of labour force in rural areas' modernization which produced increasing number of redundant peasants – the push factor of rural-to-urban migration, coupled with the incapability of the rural economy to provide incentive for people to stay in the rural areas. The increase of redundant rural workers is, in fact, a direct consequence of the rural reform since 1978 which aimed to improve the efficiency of agricultural sector through a new household based contractual responsibility system – the over-collectivized or communized rural sector was mostly privatized. Generally, labour was in surplus and redundant in rural areas. More specifically, the previously (1960s–1970s) collectivized rural sector had been downsized and resulted in the problem of under-employment in agricultural activities. The un(or under)-employment problem in rural areas, in the early1980s, can be seen in the central government's reactionary attempt to rejuvenate various village and township based on non-agricultural enterprises for labour absorption and out-migration containment in the rural sector. Rural-to-urban migration, manifested in terms of floating population towards, and permanent resettlement into, urban areas, has become an integral part of urban dynamics since the mid-1980s (Lai, 1998, 2001, 2007).

Consequently, the surge of housing demand from those rural-to-urban migrants became a major problem for urban municipalities and local governments which had almost no funding to cope with this sort of newly developed and differentiated demand, as most of the housing stocks were within the control of production sectors: work-units (*danwei*). Under these constraints, parallelling to the commodification (commodity housing: *shangpinfang;* commercialization) of public housing by work-units (*danwei*), it is not surprising that, having no housing stock, urban municipalities had difficulty assuming a significant role in the housing reform through the initiatives for alternative (commodity) housing. Furthermore, the urban crisis was also exacerbated by the underdevelopment of infrastructure in urban areas, or the bottleneck problem. This was coupled with the inertia against the *SOEs* reform and the monopolistic power of local authorities in (under) pricing the land and property market. Since

2004, the *hukou* system though is only serving the personal information registration purpose and no more controlling on people mobility; but the *hukou* system excludes the incoming migrants from access to public services. And most SOEs no longer consider housing provision as their basic service to their employees – all have to go for market to get residence!

Affordable housing is a key concern not just for local citizens already living in cities, but also the migrants, as well as all international investors who have to secure residence for their workers. In spite of the fact that some investors provide factory-based housing for incoming migrant workers – as employers only provide housing to meet their own profit-making purpose-minimal and subsistence housing with low quality of living in factory-compound is, therefore, the norm(Li and Duda, 2010). For the *high tech* firms, the affordable housing for employees is ranked at the lowest score for their concern and they have contributed to the most unfavourable conditions of living for emerging metropolitan areas of Pearl River Delta (Guangzhou as hub), Yangtze River Delta (the Greater Shanghai region, and Beijing-Tianjin region Lai, 2007).

The combined effects of rural-to-urban migration driven by relative poverty, breakdown of *hukou* system, and the ever-increasing population pressure with under-provision of affordable housing are the sources of social conflicts, segregation and social exclusions of various forms – all these are part of the formation of the permanence of those (over 250 million migrant, floating, population having) nomadic sub-classes of (urban) citizenship. Hence, urban problems become the China's syndrome of rapid urbanization: dualism of various forms can be witnessed in any part of China today. Perhaps, the most contrasting, if not the worst, urban phenomena are the juxtaposition of super-modern high-rise architecture with pre-modern manual (cheap) labour for service industries of domestic waste collection, and those 21st century high tech, foreign imported, luxury cars running side by side with the pre-modern, century-old, man-powered carts in Chinese world class cities like Shanghai. The CCP recently had to acknowledge this dualism with policy to address the problems – trying to demonstrate the benevolence of an affective state (Yang, 2013).

China's Property Market-driven Multiple Deprivations

Hyper-modernizing forces and rapid urbanization processes have been shaping housing question in (post-) socialist China. Slum settlements are disappearing from new urban architecture but they are remaking in different forms; mostly in the sub-markets are less concentrated or en masse in a particular location, more likely be in transient and nocturnal temporary (Mahadevia, et al., 2012). Those living in 'slum-equivalent' spaces are not just those 'laid-off workers, underpaid and underprivileged migrant labourers from the countryside', due to economic reform (Solinger, 2006: 177), but also those working as middle-lower, lower and poor sub-classes. Migrants and long-term residents alike are suffering from different forms of deprivations in China's internationalizing cities. These sub-classes have to bear with the rocket-high living cost in the market place; or the *guanxi* (functional social relationship based) 'rationing' of public housing, education and health services by the CCP cadres, who can determine who gets what with the subtle rule for the so-called '*guanxi*-privileged access to' limited urban services.

The Perpetual Nomadic Rural-to-Urban Great Migration

The influx of over millions of migrant workers from pre-modern village living to super-modern cities' temporary housing in China, since its late 1970s economic liberalization policy, has been characterized by four major dynamics. First and foremost, it is nomadic yet seasonal: not just because of most migrant workers' returning home for a few weeks during Lunar Chinese New Year (the Spring Festival). More problematically, most migrant workers do not have, and will not likely have, any formal urban resident status (no household *hukou* registration). Second, the scale of a few hundred millions – the 2011 official data from the Sixth National Population 2010 Census indicated over 261 millions – is unprecedented in Chinese and human history (NBSC, 2011). Third, there is a trend that the momentum for rural-to-urban migration due to the continual economic reform (migrant-workers at large) has been on the rise: there has been an 81 per cent increase in the population mobility with different household registration from the last place of their residence (rural) place for new working (urban) site from the year 2000 to 2010. Last but not least, the share of urban dwellers (following the official household *hukou* registration) has crossed the bench mark of 50 per cent in 2010. Rapid urbanization has been taking place in the past 30 years and will continue for the future as well.

With an ever expanding urban yet internationalizing economy, to cope with both domestic demand and external business for exports and exchanges, labourers have been drawn from the less developed rural localities *en masse*. The most obvious case is by one of the major subcontractors for information and communication technologies gadgets (iPhone, iPad, iPod, Kindle, Play Station, etc.), the Taiwanese electronic manufacturing group, Foxconn (http://www.foxconn.com/). It has employed, and provides factory-residence for, more than one million rural-to-urban migrant workers in several different major coastal Chinese cities (though some factories recently moved to inland major cities due to labour shortage and cost escalation in coastal cities).

Contrasting the export-led rapid industrialization which calls for rural-to-urban labour mobility *en masse* are, perhaps, the most significant yet invisible migrants moving into the rapidly urbanizing localities to take up the dirty, dangerous and demand jobs (which no longer attract city dwellers) in both formal and informal economies (Loyalka, 2012). Due to low status and poorly paid job conditions, the nomadic lower, sub-and-under-classes are subject to various forms of discrimination and segregation in the modernizing cities of the internationalizing market forces, and to local government neglect. Living in temporary housing or even being homeless is common for these members of the under-classes. The mega traffic, back-and-forth flows, during the one-month 'Spring Movement' before and after the Lunar Chinese New Year, when over 250 million migrant workers return to their home villages, demonstrates the deep contradictions in working, but not living, in cities.

The experience of the rural to urban migration in China context is obvious: those migrant workers not acquiring functional social networks with local residents at host locality (lineage and kinship based social relationship) were more prone to suffer from problems of adjustment, adaption and integration. They risk being trapped in permanent poverty and falling into the nomadic under-sub-classes in urban areas (Hsu, 2012; Yang, 2013; Yue, et al., 2013). There is neither much actual calling from the CCP nor any local government for actual policy initiatives for the acceptance or socio-economic integration of nomadic migrant workers in cities. Therefore, they remain nomadic!

Life chance in contemporary China is predicated on one's origin and status in the pre-modern era. This is true not just for the floating population of migrant-workers, but also those already well settled in cities. For migrant workers, among all non-productivity factors (personal characteristics, social norms and policies) contributing to the successful or failure of migrants' survival (in income distribution and inequality terms) in cities, there is consensus that the central and local state policy factors have the most profound impact on their livelihood.

The household registration system of *hukou* in particular has the strongest discrimination effect upon migrants' working life chance in Chinese transitional economy (Gravemeyer, et al., 2010; Whyte, 2010). Furthermore, local government policies, officialdom and their control of an individual's socio-economic rights in the emerging segregated markets have shaped not just the labour processes, but have also contributed to the emergence and subsequent formation of urban dualism. This dualism between rich and poor, local residents and migrants, formal and informal economic activities – along the geo-social contours of the household registration system (*hukou*) – is embedded in a highly differentiated, segregated labour market-cum-public service rationing.

Urban housing conditions in (post-) socialist China have idiosyncrasies; the most obvious ones are the institutional discrimination against migrant workers in super-modern cities, and the party cadres' power over human rights. The most salient result is the institutional bias and control of the nomadic sub-classes, exploiting them for national economic progress and political stability, and not allowing them to be settled in the urban sector. In short, the nomadic under-sub-classes in China are very different from their counterparts in other developing economies like Brazil, India and Mexico. There migrants have been settling in whatever form of temporary housing *in-site* they can find, while they launch along term battle for their urban survival. This has contributed to a differentiated class struggle in the urban arena, constituting the new metropolis (Pieters and Schoukens, 2012). But the Chinese case represents the strong control of the CCP, which through its party cadres' urban managerial control on household registration (*hukou*), rations public services, segregating and excluding the incoming migrants. Thereby making them permanent nomadic social sub-classes without socio-economic and cultural integration in cities.

The Urban Dualism in Continual Economic Reform

(Post-) Socialist China's economic reform is urban biased. Continual reform contributes to the formation of the middle class and this nascent bourgeoisie class opts for individualistic lifestyles of their own; more even so for those being brought up as the only child in the family (under *One-Child Policy* implemented at the same period with economic liberalization in the late 1970s) who yearn for foreign brand luxuries and palace-like private property-home, if affordable. This is a dramatic moving away from utopian Maoist socialism. More specifically home ownership, mostly through mortgaging one's house, becomes China's new middle class dream. But the urban dream is underlain by the risk of becoming one of those in the under-classes; disenfranchised and underprivileged in the urban core.

China is one of the fastest growing urban agglomerations in the world. It is definitely at the top of hyper-modernization and rapid urbanization thanks to its three-decade continuing reform-after-continual reform transformation. But urban transformation processes in transitional economies has a strong impact on localities and communities; more even so for those who have been settling (old residents) in cities for longer period with established social networks. A recent study on Guangzhou, the biggest city in the Pearl River Delta and the growing hub of the Southern China metropolis, highlights the common case for China's urban development. Lack of housing is still a basic problem in this (post-) socialist city. The typical neighbourhood suffered from multiple deprivations and several households had to co-live in partitioned tenements:

> the average dwelling area per capita is 9.8 m^2, which is much lower than the average standard for Guangzhou (18.19 m^2) and almost half the standard of workers' villages (17.6 m^2). Most public housing in this neighborhood cannot be sold to sitting tenants because of poor indoor facilities and the complexity of ownership (e.g. some are properties without owners and some are private property but under public trust), and only 27.8 per cent of interviewees own their housing. While the rent for public housing has been relatively stable, private rentals have increased by 2.74 times in the past 10 years, resulting in increases in living expenditure (Yuan, et al., 2011: 730).

Furthermore, many urban dwellers have experienced deprivations in urban services, and/or actual poverty since late 1980s. China's pro-market continual reform has been creating new urban poverty of various forms: not only the increasing number of those low income people who cannot catch up with the rise of housing and commodity prices, but the dis-enfranchised and underprivileged groups created by property-development's forced evictions and the ever-increasing rural-to-urban migrant enclaves. It juxtaposes the continuing destruction of neighbourhood and social fabrics under urban redevelopment strategies for new property development and nation building projects, e.g. Beijing Olympics 2008 and Shanghai Expo 2010. What is distinctive about the Chinese urban transformation process is the discriminatory-cum-discretionary role it plays in shaping and creating multiple deprivations, new and old, and poverty of all variations. And multiple deprivations are not necessarily associated just with low income (Lin, et al., 2011; Wu et al., 2012; Yuan, et al., 2011).

As a result, social inequalities in housing and urban deprivations have been causing conflict between the haves and have-nots, poor and rich, and more problematically, tearing down the social fabrics in communities, and extending the urban dwellers' cynicism, if not open criticism, of the CCP. Nobody knows whether China's aggregated urban contradictions will turn into another revolution in the quest for basic housing rights, but deprivations-driven social unrest is on the rise, challenging the governability of the CCP and its local state machineries.

Awakening from China's Urban Dream: The Middle Class' Falling Down?

The new urban dream of China has been formed with the twining of property market development and middle class' home ownership through the maximization of one's economic value in the market place with the new production of private housing and the consumption of new residential spaces (Abramson, 2011; Zhang, 2010). The urban processes shape not just the new identities of various social actors according to their social (housing) class, but also their access to economic means through a functional social network to the CCP's cadres, e.g. *guanxi*, the functional social reciprocity in socialist China. More specifically, the emergence of new social agencies for rapid urbanization, like real estate developers, property agents, homeowners – cum-investors, juxtaposing those who are excluded from new urban spaces, is historically new for (post-) socialist China. Despite their differential and heterogeneous compositions, all of them have the heightened sense of insecurity (no trust on collective commons or society as a whole), partly due to the rise and fall, gain and lost, in the property market cycles, and the problematic governance of the CCP over its economic and political project for state developmentalism (or alternatively, the party-cadre-leaders' self-interest at different level of the state machinery) (Abramson, 2011; Su and Tao, 2012).

Perhaps, the best kept twin-secret for the dark side of urban economic in China is epitomized by the permanence of the so-called 'mortgage slaves' (*fang nu*) for young (age 25 to 35) professionals who secure a better job but have to contribute a significant amount

(30–40%) of their income to housing mortgage As long as their working years continue and is further problematized by the ever-increasing numbers of the so-called 'ant tribes' (*yizu*) or recent university graduates who are entering a severely competitive labour market without much hope for securing a permanent job (*The Economist*, 28 January 2012). Accordingly, as many as three million young professionals, born in or after the mid-1980s, most recently graduated from universities, stay in slum-like conditions, e.g. underground redundant infrastructure like the sewage system or the bunkers built during Cold War era no longer in use, in overcrowded temporary housing at the peripheries, and commuting in-and-out of big cities like Beijing (*Al Jazeera,* 2012).

While the increasing number of 'mortgage slaves' is a norm for, reflecting the booming, property market, the prolonged period (say 20–30 years of mortgage for young professionals) it is not uncommon given the rocket-high property price and the stagnation of urban wage (vis-à-vis living costs and property prices). But those paying long and high mortgage payments have to forfeit their family wishlist. And as disposable income is minimally for survival, they are not happy to be property-bound and their own and family's quality of life suffers in return.

In strong contrast, those well-educated 'ant tribe' members suffer not just the bad living conditions with a downward-spiralling of their wages, social status and competitiveness, but also the urban dreams for better life and future through hard work and learning, and loyalty to the state's continual reform agenda for national development with economic liberalization, is lost. For the last decade alone, there were over 20 million Chinese graduates yearly attempting to enter the highly competitive labour market and most of them were disappointed. Surveys show young white-collar workers in cities were not happy and have no sense of security for the future:

After two decades of economic reform, per capita GDP has risen 13-fold, and average salaries in major cities are on par with those in many developed countries. The post-1980s generation, the first to come of age in this era of opportunity, has been raised on a belief that if one can do well in school, graduate from a good university and work hard on his or her career, one can enjoy a measure of success. Instead, many find themselves squeezed by skyrocketing housing costs, rising prices for basic necessities and family pressures. As a large percentage of the post-1980s generation are only children, they alone will be expected to provide for their parents and older relatives (*Al Jazeera*, 2012).

Obviously, and as happened recently, the post-1980s generation, highly differentiated in the opportunities structure of being the 'ant tribe' or the 'mortgage slaves', has commonly voiced their complaints and angers through various demonstrations, using various pretexts, say, the Sino-Japanese territorial conflicts over Daioyu/Senkaku Islands, or urban conflicts and problems arising from the officials' abuse of power. This is the most worrying problem for the CCP leadership: given the permanence of the 'ant tribe' and 'mortgage slaves', coupled with many other disenfranchised groups – these urban tribal groups become not just the source of, the incubator for, discontents and anti-government appeals, but they have the 21st century knowledge of using new media and organization strategies to challenge the CCP-party legitimacy for China's state developmentalism!

Contours of Rapid Urbanization: Unintended Social Consequences

One of the historical phenomena of China's hyper-modernization project with rapid urbanization is the nomadic population flow. The exponential growth of the urban economy has been drawing migrant workers out from villages and towns into the urban sector. The influx of migrant workers in rapidly urbanizing localities shapes the formation of new nomadic under-classes. Because they have no household registration, *hukou,* or are merely temporary residents, they have no entitlements for public services such as housing, medical care or education. According to many local governments, these migrants and temporary residents have not been considered for any urban policy development. In short, they are left to live their own life; left out of any public service development. This differentiated, if not divided or dualistic, policy reference has contributed to the formation of slum or underprivileged temporary settlements in urban China (Lai, 2009; Lin, et al., 2011; Wu, et al., 2012).

Since the economic reform in late 1970s, the commodification of land and housing development as property rights, with ever increasing pricing and speculation practices, in terms of property rights, has become the new *modus operandi* for new urban economics. Both the central government, and more importantly, local and state officials (mostly CCP cadres) can choose their ways to liberalize the local economy for both communal and private interests. In short, the sophistication of the property rights regime, coupled with its exploitation for higher prices and profits through land and housing development, is the key to local, regional and national development in China (Abramson,

2011, Chen et al., 2011; Tang et. al., 2011). These problematic rapid urbanization processes will be examined below.

Property Market Forces Changing Chinese Family Values?

Since the 1980s, the urban property market has been booming; housing prices have risen faster than wages in cities. This has prompted more people to strategize their individual and familial life course for the acquisition of the residence (home ownership) and if extra capital available, to invest and make speculation in the property market (Abramson, 2011; Lin, 2007). The newly acquired property has its multiple rights to use, to transfer or for capital gain. The result is obvious for the new property market: achieving high speed home ownership. But the (miraculous?) *modus operandi* for the free-to-buy-and-sell reciprocity has one unintended consequence: namely the transformation of family processes in urban China.

With the end of the Maoist revolutionary approach to collective ownership of housing for workers in state enterprises, the pro-market housing reform since mid-1980s has been the (post-) socialist state's policy. One of the many fundamental changes is the ending of welfare housing (*fulifang*), making (and forcing?) many urban Chinese to purchase a property for home ownership. As a result, China is one of the largest homeowner society in the world (2005 onwards) – and more importantly, the world's fastest home-ownership achiever from almost from zero to 70 per cent in less than three decades: followed by 12 per cent and 8 per cent in private and public rental housing, respectively (Davis, 2010).

By taking away the state and collective enterprises' control of housing provision to their employees, those who used to have a housing allocation had to search for their own residence in the emerging property market. Under this policy, state and collective enterprises also sell their housing stock as property. This policy has unleashed an ever-increasing demand for private property. Since the mid-1980s, people are free to choose. One of the unintended social consequences of the continual reform in housing is the change of family processes; particularly for making marital divorce easy and sometimes, compensatory. The new Marriage Law (1980) and its revision (2001) fostered a 'fair-split' (50–50) of property and wealth acquired during marriage. The seemingly timely coupling of new marriage laws and urban housing reform set off repercussions on family processes, challenging the ethos of Chinese families:

strategizing family wealth accumulation (*buying a house?*) before and during marriage, or alternatively, splitting the wealth (*whose property?*) in the contesting divorce case (Davis, 2010). All this brings back the ethos and normative aspects of the origins and fundamentals of marriage and family in Chinese society. It challenges the consensus on family values and harmony – thanks to the (separating-) couple (individual's) pricing of the (whose?) family property. It seems that the property (rights-) market in transforming the family ethos for gender equality, that there is a shift towards 'the increasing emphasis on individual contractual obligations within the institution of marriage, and in particular, they highlight greater concern with personal property within marriage' (Davis, 2010: 479–480). Given the transformative power of neoliberal economics' property market forces, families in China's (post-) socialist society are under threats!

Permanence of Urban Dualism in the CCP's State Developmentalism?

Moving beyond the consensus on neoliberalism about Chinese economic miracle, it should be stressed that there is an almost complete monopoly of property development by the state apparatus in China, particularly the local state's control over the land use (change) for rapid urbanization. Local governments (and their party cadres) can pocket the 'windfall profits' thanks to the CCP absolute power to offer any (low) compensation terms in the name of nation interests. Urban processes in many (townships to be) cities has been captured by the pro-growth alliance of the CCP leaders and their cadres and increasingly powerful businessmen (Su and Tao, 2012; Kung et al., 2013; Yang, Ed., 2012).

Hence, the active land conversion for (commercial and real estate developments in premium locations) higher land price, coupled with the speculative market forces, reinforces the state-induced urbanization process (Chen, et al., 2011; Kung, et al., 2013; Xu, 2011). The continual economic reform has completely changed the urban landscape; super-modern high-rise architecture and luxurious housing are built onto the logistic networks and hubs of highways, international airports and high-speed trains. Seemingly urbanity offers a better yet expensive quality of life. But clearly, all these have stringent monetary and social class-specific prerequisites. Urban dualism, thus, is an integral part of 21st century urban China.

One of the main problems of the Chinese differential dualism of hyper-development, which can be seen benefitting the new rich but creating the under-classes, is that it is structurally embedded in Chinese (authoritarian?) communist champion for state developmentalism. Both central and local governments are pro-economic growth, neglecting the equitable (equalization of life chances for) public services.

And the dualism between rural and urban sectors, as well as the dualistic life chance in cities, must be addressed for China's future. For instance, despite the minimal poverty alleviation impact by inter-governmental fiscal subsidies directing to specific target group like farmers, a recent detailed analysis argues that 'to reduce income disparities more effectively in the rural sector, China requires more centralized management of programme design to ensure that subsidy programmes are aimed at the poor and low income groups' (Lin and Wong, 2012: 45). There needs to be continual reform goals for equitable fiscal provisions both horizontally and vertically in the Chinese administrative system.

Obviously, this call should not be just for administrative reform, but a more fundamental change of the CCP's *modus operandi* for development at large. This also applies to any mitigating measures to address the syndrome of hyper-modernization, social dualism, with various forms of inequalities in both urban and rural sectors. More fundamentally, there should be more pro-active policies for freedom and human (economic, social and cultural) rights, enabling free access to information and enhancing public participation in decision-making for managing rapid urbanization. At the least, there should be actions to prevent the party cadres and officials from 'ripping-off' the development benefits.

The Socialist Nostalgic Rediscovery: Continual Economic Reform for Whom?

China's pro-urbanization (land asset and housing property) developmentalism is structured and aligned by the shifting of fiscal power from the central to local states, coupled with a new reciprocity exchange favouring the localities. This is demonstrated by the CCP's daunting task of using both fiscal and monetary policy instruments as counter-cyclical measures for the stimulation of real estate market development while attempting to stabilize the property (and retailing) prices (Su and Tao, 2012; Xu and Yeh, 2009, Yang Ed., 2012). Therefore, the structural linkages between central and local governments, as well as the pro-growth ideologies for a better future, are echoing each other in the powerful elitist circles; but there is not much resonance at both urban and rural grassroot levels.

Under neoliberal economic hegemony for continual urban reform, the transformation has many repercussions for every aspect of people's life and their survival. The last two decades of accumulated frustration over the broken reform promises is in strong contrast to the beginning phase of economic reform in the mid-1980s. For veteran urban dwellers, the urban experience in the early reform era was distinguishably new, from bad to good, if not euphoric, for a better future under new CCP leadership of Deng Xiaoping and his ideology of liberalizing economic development for everyone. Then, the bad experience of the past, class struggles under the 'continual' Cultural Revolution, etc. was somewhat forgettable (and forgivable). What (Ho and Ng 2008: 390) term as 'public amnesia of the socialist past', metaphorically referring to an empirical phenomenon, whereby events that occurred only decades ago seem no longer to be questioned by most people in the present.

But the daily reality check for many urban dwellers in rapid urbanization is embedded in the new social insecurity. It has been estimated that the number of employees in China's informal sectors (those not covered by any social security) has increased, vis-à-vis the formal employment. The ratio between the informal and formal sectors are from 1:4 to 1:2, for the period 1996 to 2001 (Pieters and Schoukens, 2012: 156; Cheng, 2010). More are employed with no job or social securities! Due to the new urban economy, many citizens are left out of the social security arrangements entirely; not to mention the impossibility of upward socio-economic mobility for many urban dwellers. Hence, the dualism between the formal and informal economies is also a reality for new urban China.

Arising from these frustrations and disappointments is a strong resonance from the disenfranchised groups for the nostalgic ideals about fairness and equality under Chinese Communism in those old, poor days. This is particularly the case in the mobilization for 'Singing Red Songs', which originated from the largest inland city of Chongqing (one of the four special designated cities like Beijing, Tianjin and Shanghai) by its party chief Bo Xilai 2008–2012 (CMP, 2013; Huang, 2011). Though the movement has faded out due to CCP suppression, with the political purge and subsequent downfall of Bo Xilai in early 2012, it has been well received by the underdogs of the continual economic reform in the urban sector. What the red songs praise are the Maoist revolutionary ideals of the goodness, justice and fairness of Chinese communism under CCP leadership. These and other social virtues have been burnt in the fire of continual pro-market reform. As the 'Red-Song' episode is one of the many legacies of communism in China, they will be haunting the CCP as long as social dualism continues. These recent rejuvenated supports for communist ideals have put the CCP in a very embarrassing position, including threats to its legitimacy.

Beyond China's Urban Future: Instability with Unsustainability?

Many scholars argue that the uniqueness of China's ascendency, the three-decade long economic miracle with over 9 per cent GDP growth annually, and its geopolitical success in the global capitalist system, has created both internal and external tensions and conflicts. These reinforce the rise and fall of economic cycle-driven labour unrest, coupled with the exacerbating political un-governability of the CCP's project for communist-state capitalism (Hung, 2009; So, 2010; Yang, 2012; Yang, 2013). China's ongoing continual economic reform, plus its ascendency in global system, is controversial and contradictory if compared with the CCP goals for socio-economic development. China embraced neoliberal economic strategies up to the early 2000s but then shifted to state developmentalism (for perpetual economic supremacy to serve the CCP's legitimacy to govern 1 billion 300 million population), while at the same time benefitting those self-chosen communist agencies and power elites. The CCP claims for providing basic services, housing and health care alike, for free, are merely propaganda, as experienced by urban dwellers. The actuality is the permanence of the exploited under-classes and underprivileged in cities. For these alone, there will be challenging issues for China's urban future. We provide some ending remarks here for China's project for urban sustainability and urban development for all.

The 'Exploitative' Urban Project for State Developmentalism

Perplexity is always the case for post-socialist, or transitional, economy; more even so for the so-called economic miracle since the 1980s. Comparatively, little public attention has been given to the withering away of social fabrics in rapid urbanization, against the backdrops of hyper-modernization. The terms 'slum' or 'poor settlement', within the wider glossary of social dualism and inequalities of various kinds, has been rarely used in China's policy documents and scholarly work. This is further misled or complicated by the problematic status of statistics and their possible use for political purposes.

Far from the claim for reducing urban poverty, its formation and permanence, for both formal and informal economies, is due to the fact that benefits of economic reform have not been fairly distributed, or tickled down to the lower social sub-classes as claimed. Those in urban poverty have been left alone to face the cruelties of the crude (as the 19th century capitalist) market economy. And the longer they are trapped in hyper-modernizing state development for global cities or transnational urbanization, the more they are living in slum-equivalent temporary housing and marginalization, tending towards homelessness in the long run (Cheng, 2010; Lin, et al., 2011).

Hyper-modernization and rapid urbanization in China are driven not just by speculative forces of the market, but also by the officials who have to achieve both public (the planned growth indicators) and private individual gains within a wider context of bribes and corruption *guanxi* networking. In spite of its 'guided' economic policy framework for pro-growth development, the central state has to mitigate the market forces of speculation by both fiscal and monetary means; this is particularly the case for urban land development for exploiting economic growth. But there is cyclic movement of property prices, like any property market (speculation). To prevent the market from inflating into a full-fledged bubble, Chinese government policies on property and land development have been restrictive since 2010 (*Financial Times*, 19 February 2013). Still, the property market is the most important motor for Chinese economic growth for decades (Chen, et al., 2011; Lin, 2007).

The continual urban syndrome in (post-) socialist China is the result of the contradictory experimental (never confirmed or definite) reform policy. Coupled with the experimental adoption of 'neoliberal' policies, the CCP-controlled political regime has given extraordinary privileges to powerful party cadres and agencies like People Liberation Army, to build up, control, exploit and to monopolize real estate activities which are for their own interests – although some have been clawed back to local governments (Kung, et al., 2013; Su and Tao, 2012; Yang, 2012). In other words, the full property development cycle is controlled by, and profits, those new rich interest groups consisting of officials and party cadres and officials-turned businessmen. These abusive, malpractices have enabled the CCP to plan and develop China as if in a planned economy; with phenomenal hyper-modernization and rapid urbanization within a short 30-year historical span. This has provided revenues to local government and its government leaders, a super-modern urban landscape, and making the middle class' dream of a luxury home skyrocket in price.

Moving beyond the consensus idea that China's latest developmental pattern is unique and historical beyond any economic history, this chapter argues that the uniqueness is embedded in urban contradictions of the (post-) socialist, transitional economy, within a wider dys-functional network of CCP agencies and party cadres' greed. But the repercussions of the permanent urban dualism are critical indeed: billions of Chinese have to pay the price and social cost for hyper-modernization. At the least there is the possibility to lose, if not totally lost, one's own home.

Worsening East Asia's Quality of Life – Unsustainable Urbanity Beyond China?

China's urban syndrome is more than slum – equivalent dualism: the under-classes and underprivileged groups comprising not just nomadic migrant workers, but also the disenfranchising under-class of low paid white collar workers, the ant-tribe and mortgage slaves and others who are suffering not just from socio-economic exploitations but ecological disasters in China's new urbanity.

The worst thing is the rapid urbanization and industrialization-driven environmental pollution and disasters which have resulted (He, et al., 2012). In February 2013, China's environment ministry confirmed the problem of the so-called 'cancer villages' which have exceptionally high incidences of cancers and high exposure to environmental pollutants near or at major industrializing and rapid urbanizing centres like Beijing, Shanghai and Guangzhou (*BBC News*, 23 February 2013).

People are losing patience with urban promises and become intolerant of the *status quo*. The sentiment against dualistic urban processes in Chinese cities is also among the elites. For instance, Jack Ma, Chairman of the Alibaba.com, the largest business-to-business online market and trading platform in China, cynically commented on the smog pollution in Beijing 'as the elitist class has privileged water and food supplies, but this time, they have no [specially supplied clean] air for them' (*Phoenix Finance*, 22 February 2013). Furthermore, he stressed that in urban China, people have no clean water or food, and environmental pollution generating cancers have increased urban mortality in the last 30 years. More people will die due to worsening environmental quality. Obviously, China's problematic economic liberalization for state developmentalism is a short-cut to its unsustainable future, and might be for the whole world as well.

In the mid-2010s, there was the impression that China's management on urban pollution was a success, say, through strong state intervention the battle on air pollution during 2008 Beijing Summer Olympics and Shanghai EXPO 2010. But the recent environmental disaster of urban air pollution of PM2.5 (the smaller than 2.5 micrometre) particulates can penetrate into human lungs. And due to its smallness, not much can be done to prevent it when air quality is so bad. It demonstrates the losing war against environmental pollution in many cities. In January 2013, Beijing was blanketed in smog; beyond the World Health Organization's PM2.5 standards and hazardous to human health. The problem is no longer just for urban China. The pollution goes from bad to worse as the PM2.5 drifted to different countries in Northeast Asia. The cross-border PM2.5 has been recorded in Japan recently (*NHK News*, 23 February 2013).

In addition to its urban dualism, China's hyper-modernization and rapid urbanization growth model bears more than a passing resemblance to the environmental degradations during and after both the 19th century Industrialization and the post-Second War economic miracle, because its environmental impact is global. The above-mentioned PM2.5 air pollution is just tip of the iceberg if measured against green house gas emissions and other environmental pollutions made in, and exported from, China's rapid urbanization.

To recapitulate, people living in urban China and their neighbours in Northeast Asia are suffering from China's economic miracle – driven environmental pollution disasters. Therefore, an international mitigating strategy is called for. All these prompt us to reconsider the normative and ethical issues of China's problematic continual economic reform – *whose benefits?...development for whom?* For the future, the public's awareness and intolerance of urban dualism and environmental problems will continue to increase and, thanks to new media of mobile communication, there will be greater willingness and ability of the people to take action. The question is: *how could (post-) socialist state of China respond?*

Note

1. Acknowledgement: This chapter is from an ongoing project on *Sustainable Society in Comparative Perspectives*, with generous supports from KwanseiGakuin University, Honorary Professorship, Department of Social Work and Social Administration at The University of Hong Kong,

and Visiting Professorship at United Nations University – Institute of Advanced Studies. Many colleagues and informants provide views during the study. The normal disclaimer applies. Comments are welcome:
O-K.Lai; E-mail:oklai@kwansei.ac.jp

References

Abramson, D. (2011). 'Transitional Property Rights and Local Developmental History in China', *Urban Studies,* 48(3), pp. 553–568.

Al Jazeera, (2012). 101 East: China: Broken Dreams, 24 August 2012: http://www.aljazeera.com/programmes/101east/2012/08/20128229 4320474807.html British Broadcasting Corporation (BBC). *BBC News,* various dates

Chen, J., F. Guo, and A. Zhu. (2011). 'The Housing-led Growth Hypothesis Revisited: Evidence from the Chinese Provincial Panel Data', *Urban Studies,* 48(10), pp. 2049–2067.

Cheng, Zhiming. (2010). 'Poverty in China's Urban Communities: Profile and Correlates', *China Report,* 46(2), pp. 143–173.

China Media Project. (CMP, 2013), A Brief History of the 'Red Songs', Journalism and Media Studies.

Centre of The Hong Kong University: http://cmp.hku.hk/2011/06/10/13105/

David Kennedy and Joseph E. Stiglitz (eds.), (2013) *Institutional Design for China's Evolving Market Economy,* Oxford: Oxford University Press.

Davis, Deborah. (2010). 'Who Gets the House? Renegotiating Property Rights in Post-Socialist Urban China', *Modern China,* 36(5), pp. 463–492.

Gravemeyer, Stefan, Thomas Gries, and JinjunXue. (2010). 'Income Determination and Income Discrimination in Shenzhen', *Urban Studies,* 48(7), pp. 1457–1475.

He, C., F. Pan, and Y. Yan. (2012). 'Is Economic Transition Harmful to China's Urban Environment? Evidence from Industrial Air Pollution in Chinese Cities', *Urban Studies,* 49(8), pp. 1767–1790.

Ho, W.C. and P. Ng. (2008). 'Public Amnesia and Multiple Modernities in Shanghai: Narrating the Postsocialist Future in a Former Socialist "Model Community"', *Journal of Contemporary Ethnography,* 37(4), pp. 383–416.

Hsu, Jennifer. (2012). 'Layers of the Urban State: Migrant Organisations and the Chinese State', *Urban Studies,* 49(16), pp. 3513–3530.

Huang, Philip C.C. (2011). 'Chongqing: Equitable Development Driven by a "Third Hand"'?, *Modern China,* 37 (6), pp. 569–622.

Hung, Ho-Fung. (ed.). (2009). *China and the Transformation of Global Capitalism,* Baltimore, MD: Johns Hopkins University Press.

Kung, James K.S., C. Xu and F. Zhou. (2013). 'From Industrialization to Urbanization: The Social Consequences of Changing Fiscal Incentives on Local Governments' Behavior', http://ihome.ust.hk/~sojk/Kung_files/KXZ_Industralization_3–31–09.pdf, in

Lai, On-Kwok. (1998). 'The State's Governance and Housing Question in a Transitional Economy: The Political Economy of Housing Policy in China Reconsidered', *Habitat International*, 22(3), pp. 231–243.

Lai, On-Kwok. (2001). 'Rise and Fall of the Production Based/Bias Housing Regime in China, 1949–1999: A Political Economy Perspective, R.S. Sandhu, S.S. Minhas and Jasmeet Sandhu (eds). (2001). *Sustainable Human Settlements: The Asian Experience*, New Delhi: Rawat Publication, pp. 124–152.

Lai, On-Kwok. (2007). 'Urbanization and Social Segregation in Chinese Cities under Globalizing Forces: China's Rapid Urban Transformation in Question', R.S. Sandhu and Jasmeet Sandhu (eds) *Globalizing Cities: Inequality and Segregation in Developing Countries,* New Delhi: Rawat Publications, pp. 231–270.

Lai, On-Kwok. (2009). 'The (Il) Logics of Urban Poverty in a Globalizing World: The Nomadic (sub) Citizenship in Chinese Societies in Comparative Perspective', in R.S. Sandhu, J. Sandhu and B. Arora (eds), *Urban Poverty in Developing Countries: Issues and Strategies for Sustainable Cities*, New Delhi: Bookwell, pp. 29–56.

Li, B. and M. Duda (2010). 'Employers as Landlords for Rural-to-Urban Migrants in Chinese Cities', *Environment and Urbanization, 22(1),* pp. 13–31.

Lin, G.C.S. (2007). 'Reproducing Spaces of Chinese Urbanisation: New City-based and Land-centred Urban Transformation', *Urban Studies*, 44(9), pp. 1827–1855.

Lin, W. and C. Wong. (2012). 'Are Beijing's Equalization Policies Reaching the Poor? An Analysis of Direct Subsidies under the 'Three Rurals', *China Journal*, 67 (January), pp. 23–45.

Lin, Y., B. de Meulder, and S. Wang. (2011). 'Understanding the 'Village in the City' in Guangzhou: Economic Integration and Development Issue and their Implications for the Urban Migrant', *Urban Studies*, 48(16), pp. 3583–3598.

Loyalka, M.D. (2012). *Eating Bitterness: Stories from the Front Lines of China's Great Urban Migration*, Berkeley: University of California Press.

Mahadevia, D., Z. Liu, and X. Yuan (2012). 'Housing of Urban Migrants in India and China', *Environment and Urbanization ASIA*, 3(1), pp. 143–163.

National Bureau of Statistics of China (NBSC) (2011). Communique on Major Figures of the Sixth National Population Census in 2010, No. 1 (in Chinese). http://www.chinanews.com/gn/2011/04-28/3004638.shtml

Nippon Hoso Kyoka (NHK). *NHK News*, various dates.

Phoenix Finance (2013) Report on Jack Ma 22 February Speech on Beijing Air Pollution: http://big5.ifeng.com/gate/big5/finance. ifeng.com/news/special/ybl2013/20130222/7691973.shtml

Pieters, D. and P. Schoukens. (2012). 'Social Security in the BRIC Countries: Brazil, Russia, India and China', *Compensation and Benefits Review,* 44: 154–164.

So, Alvin Y. (2010). 'Globalization and China: From Neo-Liberal Capitalism to State Developmentalism', BerchBerberoglu (ed.), *Globalization in the Twenty-First Century: Labor, Capital, and the State on a World Scale*, New York: Palgrave Macmillan.

Solinger, Dorothy J. (2006). 'The Creation of a New Underclass in China and its Implications', *Environment and Urbanization,* 18(1), pp. 177–193.

Su, Fubing and R. Tao. (2012). 'Visible Hand or Crippled Hand: Stimulation and Stabilization in China's Real Estate Market', in Dali L. Yang (ed.) *The Global Recession and China's Political Economy*, New York: Palgrave Macmillan.

Tang, Bo-Sin, S.W. Wong, and S.C. Liu. (2011). 'Institutions, Property Taxation and Local Government Finance in China', *Urban Studies,* 48(5), pp. 847–875.

The Economist. (2012). 'Ant Tribes and Mortgage Slaves: The Subdivisions of Urban China', 12. January, http://www.economist. com/node/ 21543590

Xu, Chenggang. (2011). 'The Fundamental Institutions of China's Reforms and Development', *Journal of Economic Literature,* 49:4, pp. 1076–1151.

Xu, Jiang and Anthony Yeh. (2009). 'Decoding Urban Land Governance: State Reconstruction in Contemporary Chinese Cities', *Urban Studies,* 2009 46(3), pp. 559–581.

Whyte, Martin K. (ed.) (2010). *One Country, Two Societies: Rural-Urban Inequality in Contemporary China.* Cambridge, MA: Harvard University Press.

Wu, F., F. Zhang, and C. Webster. (2012). 'Informality and the Development and Demolition of Urban Villages in the Chinese Peri-urban Area', *Urban Studies*, Online First Version: 26 November 2012: DOI: 10.1177/0042098012466600.

Yang, Dali L. (ed.). (2012). *The Global Recession and China's Political Economy*. New York: Palgrave Macmillan.

Yang, Jie. (2013). '*Song wennuan*, 'Sending Warmth': Unemployment, New Urban Poverty, and the Affective State in China', *Ethnography,* 14(1), pp. 104–125.

Yuan, Y., F. Wu, and X. Xu. (2011). 'Multiple Deprivations in Transitional Chinese Cities: A Case Study of Guangzhou', *Urban Affairs Review.* 47(5), pp. 721–736.

Yue, Zhongshan, Shuzhuo Li, Xiaoyi Jin, and M.W. Feldman. (2013). 'The Role of Social Networks in Integration of Chinese Rural – Urban Migrants: A Migrant – Resident Tie Perspective', *Urban Studies*, pp. 1–20. DOI: 10.1177/0042098012470394.

Zhang, Li. (2010). *In Search of Paradise: Middle-Class Living in a Chinese Metropolis*. Ithaca, NY: Cornell University Press.

7

The Crucible of Housing the Bottom of the Pyramid in Egypt

Ahmed M. Soliman

Egypt is approaching the figure of 92 million, and it will reach around 151 million by 2050 where 62.4 per cent will be urbanized. Most Egyptian cities are surrounded with belts of informal housing built on agricultural land. The result is a growing divergence in Egyptian cities: between the old and the new part of the urban agglomeration, a 'Great Divide' between 'establishing', 'struggling' and 'emerging' urban spaces. As of 2007, there were an estimated 8.5 million informal housing units with at least 21.2 million and 12.8 million Egyptians in urban and rural areas, respectively. The chapter highlights the state's various housing policies that have been applied during the last six decades for housing the urban poor, and it shows the effects of the new regime on housing policies and practice. It also sketches the growth of the Egyptian cities during the last six in relation to land reform act and how it led into informal development processes and activities that have provided suitable and affordable land mechanisms for gaining access to urban land for the urban poor who have created 'cultural struggle' to housing problems. In absolute terms, the progress made on housing the urban poor target has certainly not been sufficient to offset the growth of urban informality in Egypt. It concludes that housing policy should be viewed from three perspectives; an institutional, a social, and an implemental perspectives based on a common ground among the stakeholders to lock in the pattern of urban informality at national and local levels, otherwise urban informality will sustain its perpetuation to meet the increasing demand of housing the urban poor.

In Egypt, informal housing development is as old as modern urbanization and urban development, which have existed in the country for more than nine decades. Scattered evidences indicated that the appearance of informal housing in Cairo dates back to the 1900s where squatters' areas (*Ezbet El Saiiaada*, and *Tall El Hosen*) were found in *El Matarya* area at North West of the city of Cairo (GOPP, 2012). These squatters' areas accommodated the workers who came from Upper Egypt for the construction work of *Heliopolis* Oasis which was built between 1906 and 1929 by a Belgian, Baron Edouard Empain (Ilbert, 1984). In Alexandria, scattered squatters areas were located on the banks of *El Farkha* canal in the mid-1930s. The urban agglomeration of informal areas in both cities began to appear in the 1960s and stretched in the 1970s where there was little interest in what was at first a very marginal and not very visible phenomenon, neither from government nor academics.

Urbanization, rapid population growth, and increasing housing demand for the urban poor were among the causes that led into the appearance of informal areas, in which it renovated, or enlarged throughout the cities without recourse to zoning and construction regulations. The work of many literatures established on Egypt's informal areas is well illustrated elsewhere (Bayat and Denis, 2000; Soliman, 2004; 2007; 2010; Dorman, 2009; Kipper and Fischer, 2009; Singerman, 2009; Sims, 2010), while this paper traces the state policies on housing, and maps cities' growth in relation to land reform. The various state policies on housing have affected by one way or another the urban landscape of the Egyptian cities, directly or indirectly or both, and have facilitated the spreading of urban informality on the periphery of the urban centres. Most Egyptian cities are surrounded with belts of housing informality on agricultural land, which it constitutes about 88 per cent of housing production in Egypt. The result is a growing divergence in Egyptian cities: between the *old* and the *new* part of the urban agglomeration, a 'Great Divide' between 'establishing', 'struggling' and 'emerging' urban spaces. The former space is the new gated communities of the elites of the society, the middle, is the formal city and symbolizes the community that follows the prevailing laws, while the latter is the *peri-urban informal* settlements and mirrors the marginal groups. Cairo and the other Cairos within the city, the formal city, informal city and desert city are found in 'The Egyptian landscape' (Silver, 2010; Sims 2010; AlSayyad, 2009).

Between 1982 and 2004, an estimated 1.2 million *faddan* (one *faddan* is equal to 0.42 hectare) of agricultural land has been decimated through housing informality which has come to account for 35–40 per cent of the total housing production during the same period (GOPP, 2006). Agricultural land is being lost at an estimated annual, daily, and hourly rate of 54,545, 149.4, and 6.22 *faddan*, respectively. In the 1980s and 1990s, attempts were made to legislate away the informal phenomenon, culminating in 1996 with the promulgation of two presidential decrees which stipulated that any new construction on agricultural land and any urban construction without a valid building permit would be severely punished through military courts.

As of 2007, there were an estimated 8.5 million informal housing units with at least 21.2 million Egyptians in urban areas. Of which, 4.7 million units were on agricultural land within or outside municipal boundaries; 0.6 million on government-owned desert land within municipal boundaries; and 3.2 million units (12.8 million Egyptians) outside administrative village boundaries (Egypt Human Development Report, 2010), worth of around US$ 241.4 billion as estimated in the year 2000 (De Soto, 2000). During the inter-census period (1996–2006), the annual urban housing production was conservatively thought to have grown to reach 2,63,838 units. Of these, 55.6 per cent were formal and 45.4 per cent informal. In Cairo, 81 per cent of informal units sited on privately owned agricultural land, with 10 per cent on government owned desert land and the remainder on state-owned agricultural land (Cities Alliance, 2008; UN-Habitat, 2012). In 2008, the government has established the Informal Settlements Development Facility (ISDF), as an important step towards institutionalizing and upgrading the informal areas, but little progress has been made.

These statistics reinforce the argument that the crucible of urban housing in Egypt is a problem not of scarcity but of distortions to both urban development and the housing market caused by an accumulation of ill-conceived and inadequate policies that led over time to a mismatch between supply and demand and to severely curtailed private sector investment in housing construction. The government policy's failure to provide affordable, viable housing for the urban poor has led many to build homes – semi-legally or illegally – on privately-owned agricultural lands. Approximately, 40 per cent of the urban inhabitants of Egyptian cities now live on these so-called *ashwaiyyat* or housing informality.

In the early 2013, the total population of Egypt is approaching the figure of 92 million, the largest population in North Africa (CAPMAS, 2013; UN-Habitat, 2012) in which 83 million live inside the country and the remainder is living abroad. About half of the urban population is concentrated in two major urban centres: Cairo and Alexandria, while the remaining is scattered in 226 small and intermediate urban cities along the Nile river valley and delta. Most of the General Strategic Plans for 226 cities, 4600 villages, and more than 27,000 hamlets indicate expansion on adjacent agricultural areas, accordingly, it is expected that Egypt will lose formally around 66,300, 1,38,000, and 6,750 *faddan* of the best fertile areas surrounding Egyptian cities, villages, and hamlets, respectively to the year 2027, given a total lose of 2,11,050 *faddan* or 14,070 *faddan* per year (Soliman, 2012a). Despite the political context in Egypt has radically changed after the 25 January revolt of 2011, but till now nothing has been done on the ground, while during one and a half year after the Revolt, Egypt has lost between 1,00,000 and 1,20,000 *faddan* of agricultural land to housing informality. The total population of Egypt will reach around 151 million by 2050 (CAPMAS, 2012) where 62.4 per cent will be urbanized (UN-Habitat, 2008). With this trend of future urbanization, it is expected that agricultural land conversion to housing informality will be perpetuated, unless an appropriate policy is achieved. This current urban pattern of the Egyptian cities was accumulated over time due to the arbitrary urban and housing development policies.

This chapter is organized as follows: the following section traces government policies on housing during the last six decades and show how the various policies have created a '*crucible*' for housing the urban poor, and then, mapping cities' growth and land reform draws section two. A concluding section offers directions for further research.

Government Policy on Housing

During the era from 1952 to 2013, the Egyptian government introduced housing policy for the urban poor, in five principal ways: (1) demobilization mode, (2) the participatory mode, (3) the manipulative mode, (4) the cost-recovery mode, and (5) the 'transitional socio-economic and political mode' (Soliman, 2012b). Of course, these are idealized type of responses that do not fit every situation and sometimes exist in combinations or variations.

Demobilization Mode

During the Nasserism era, from 1954 to 1971, which reflected socialist ideology and trend, in attracting the lowest strata of the society towards the new political transformation, and against the external international powers. It was characterized by 'demobilization mode', the government actively sought to promote community mobilization, from rural to urban areas, and its contribution as a mechanism for sustaining the political system, and the low-income groups were used by politicians for strengthening their own political power and continuance (Hopkins, 1969). It was aimed at satisfying the urgent needs for goods and services, for the bottom strata of the societies, in order that they would be a buffer against the external 'imperialism'. It was to be the basis to establish a 'Socialist society' and to mobilize the working classes from rural to urban areas in order to accelerate the development processes. In the mid-1950s, the Egyptian government introduced three policies to tackle housing shortage; the development of social housing programmes; rent control act, and land delivery system for housing to accommodate middle and low-income groups. In 1954, the construction of workers' housing, sometimes called dormitory towns, was the first public housing programme and was mainly for workers and employees who were attached to major industrial centres established at that time. Subsequent huge public housing projects were constructed in Cairo and Alexandria. The second policy targeted the private sector, where the private real estate market was thrown into a state of disarray by the promulgation of stiff rent control laws, starting in 1954. Private development for the rental market virtually stopped (The Aga Khan programme, 1984). The third policy was the allocation of land for housing development on the periphery of the major urban areas. In 1960, President Nasser was assigned the roles of securing land to set up housing projects, provide utilities, and sell and distribute plots. The socialist movement was in full swing as government endeavoured to become solely responsible for providing housing for middle and low-income groups, while the involvement of the private sector was reduced (Hopkins, 1969). In the early1960s, housing policy shifted into condominiums in new large-scale land subdivisions such as *Madinet Al Awqaf, Naser city, Maadi,* and *Heliopolis* districts near Cairo, taking advantage of the liberal credit terms available under the government-subsidized cooperative housing programmes. The role of the private sector in housing supply was eliminated, causing a sharp decline in the housing market.

However, the 1967 war with Israel, the subsequent war of attrition, and the run up to the 1973 war froze formal housing programmes in Egypt, as public funds were reserved for the war effort. Large urban centres had to accommodate a significant number of internal migrants in Egypt. Shifting demobilization – from one urban to another urban area – had taken place, with the landscape of the Suez Canal cities in confrontation with Israel changing radically, resettlement of many residents from war front cities, and a huge increase in housing production in other cities, but much of it was informal, such as in Cairo, and Alexandria. The informal housing development accounted for between 25 and 35 per cent of the total housing production.

Participatory Mode

The 'participatory mode' was characterized by an elastic housing programme through encouraging involvement of the private sector in decision-making and in housing production for accelerating the development process. During the Sadatism era from 1973 to 1981, Egypt witnessed a period of active but ad hoc intervention in housing production. After the 1973 war, President Sadat introduced the Open Door Policy, or *infitah* in 1974, and the government intervened more positively in the housing market. Rebuilding Suez Canal cities of Suez, Ismailia and Port Said was a first step towards providing housing for immigrants. The housing approaches developed in the Canal Towns' demonstration projects depended on the government's objectives in making housing affordable to low-income groups. One of the main projects implemented according to these objectives was *El Heker* project in Ismailia City. In this project, housing policy changed from one of direct provision of subsidized housing by the government using central funds, to one of basic infrastructure only, with user control of the building process (Davidson, 1981; 1984; Davidson and Payne, 1983).

The government recognized private developers as the principal means of tackling the shortage of housing. This era witnessed various experiences in public housing, sites and services, core housing, and upgrading schemes in the new and old towns of Egypt (Davidson, 1981; Stewart, 1981; Welbank and Edwards, 1981). The urban poor and those on fixed incomes were hit the hardest by *infitah* policy. In addition, this era, often referred to as the 'boom years', was based on the large contingent of emigrants who worked in the oil-rich states of the region, many of whom sent back substantial remittances, and this accelerated the boom in housing productions.

Consequently, the government of Egypt intervened more positively in the housing market and recognized that the private sectors offered an important means to tackle the housing shortage. Housing policies involved the private developers and embraced three sets of actors, the formal and informal private sectors, and the public sector, where the private housing developers were considered an important actor in the housing development in new and old towns. Thus, the private sector had gained the privilege of becoming the main supplier for housing production. At the same time, for low-income groups, the states adopted self-help that was advocated by the first congress of UN-Habitat in 1976. This was achieved by facilitating the flow of subsidized building materials, forming cooperative housing societies, and allowing a free market within the formal private housing sector. In the late 1970s, the role played by the informal sector as an indispensable part of housing production was recognized in Egypt with at least 75 per cent of housing construction being undertaken by the uncontrolled private sector (Soliman, 2004).

Adequate shelter for all was the declared objective to be achieved through private and public sectors. The idea was a shift of focus from providing completely subsidized housing to providing other means of housing in terms of goods, services, or both. As a consequence, site and services and upgrading programmes, core housing, and wet core units were developed to house this bottom stratum of the society. Learning from the experience gained from the rebuilding of the Suez Canal cities, the Egyptian government implemented sites and services and core housing policies in the first generation of new towns (*Tenth of Ramadan*, *Sadat*, and *Bourg El Arab*). Many projects were also implemented in Egyptian cities – Alexandria, Ismailia, Helwan, Aswan, and Cairo (Davidson, 1984). This was based upon two main principles: first, land policy introduced to allocate large land plots in various locations within the cities to cover various social classes of the required population (The Joint Land Policy team, 1977), and second, applying self-help housing technique by leaving housing production in the hands of private developers who catered only to a small minority of the privileged who could afford to build their own homes. The self-help techniques faced many challenges (Soliman, 2012c). Initially, sites and tenure allocation in the new towns were poorly designed. Criteria for landownership and utilization of land for shelter were unclear. Management failed to provide housing plots to most of the industrial employees. Three alternatives were available to the cities' civil servants:

owner-occupier, or to the industrial employees, or housing plots allocated to people who live, work, or were born within the city's jurisdiction. In all cases, certain restrictions were imposed on land allocations: 25 per cent of the total price of the land plot was to be paid in advance with the remainder to be paid over 10 years at subsidized interest rates with monthly payments amounting to 25 per cent of the employee's salary.

Manipulative Mode

The 'manipulative mode' constituted a vaguely formulated or poorly implemented policy whereby at the beginning of Mubarak era of the 1980s, the state played an arbitrary role within the housing market and had begun to impose new restrictions on private developers in terms of building procedures and regulations. Yet by 1986, the new-found orientation of international agencies induced new economic reforms, and the state once again recognized the private sector as the principal housing sector to develop housing construction for middle and low-income groups (Soliman, 2004). This era witnessed a great fluctuation in housing policies and the real estate market, where new private developers in the form of money-lending companies became a major supply of housing units, not for the poor, but for the middle and the upper-middle classes.

In 1989, former Prime Minister *Attaf Sadekey* interpreted '*informal housing areas to be like cancers, belonging neither to the city nor the village*'. To address this problem, in 1991, the Egyptian government established a wide range of Economic Reform Structure Programmes, according to which the private sector was engaged in a policy of market-based remedies. With the beginning of the 1990s, the terrorist movement occurred in Egypt which has encouraged politicians to address the problem of informal housing areas where much of the unrest is concentrated. After the terrorism of *Imbabah* at the beginning of 1993, in May 1993, President Mubarak announced a national programme to upgrade the informal housing areas in Egypt, which also meant an increased official presence in such areas, in which 550 million Egyptian pounds were allocated up to the year 2002. According to this programme, around 707 informal areas in Egypt, which accommodated more than eight million people and represented 38.6 per cent of the total of the cities' urban population (Soliman, 2004), were assumed to be upgraded. Thus, the state has a double role, widening its control over society and providing some improvements to the informal settlements. Such improvements are seen as a way of gaining political support from the large number of people who live in these settlements.

Between the years 1995 and 2000, the government also initiated a new economic policy through its privatization programme. This programme took three forms. First was outright privatization, where the government sold certain assets, franchised other operations, and contracted for other services. Second was the introduction of certain free-market mechanisms, including a new rent law that allowed the private sector to put housing units on the market without restriction and according to supply and demand. Third was a programme of pragmatic privatization, according to which initial agreements with private management agents might eventually lead to more extensive commitments. The urban poor continued to rely on informal methods to shelter themselves. Due to the arbitrary housing policies in this era, many laws were passed and later on amended and replaced by new ones where many informal areas had been created on the periphery of the major urban centres in Egypt. Therefore, the state had accepted a status quo for the arbitrary urban growth in seeking to recover from the financial burden that it had inherited from the 1973 war, housing shortages in the 1970s, and the increasing price of oil, and began to speed up the process of implementing new economic policies, making the best use they could of the substantial remittances from people who worked abroad.

Cost-recovery Mode

The 'cost-recovery mode' was an attempt to involve community participation programmes and the private sector on a cost-recovery basis for increasing the level of housing production and for the state's own ends. Lack of resources, in cash, in kind, or both, forced the state to follow the cost-recovery mode in order to increase housing production for the urban poor. One of the main issues to be tackled was taking account of the invisible resources of middle and low-income groups and guiding their efforts to participate in housing construction. As De Soto (2000) identified, 'the potential value of an asset, to effectively "unlock" $241.4 million, the value of informal housing property in Egypt, of what he calls "dead capital", and so allows us to control it'. Therefore, with the beginning of the New Millennium, and after 11 September, the role of government was recast to strengthen its essential functions of facilitating real estate markets and correcting market failures, promoting socio-economic stability, and ensuring distributional equity. The Egyptian government initiated a new economic policy through privatization programmes that paid attention to the urban poor. This process included efforts to expand opportunities for citizen participation; to increase innovation, openness, and cost-effectiveness; and to promote public-private partnership. All these efforts were challenges for local government for ensuring an environment conducive to good business, a strong civic society, and for alleviating the heavy financial burden to be paid on housing projects. Egypt was committed to poverty alleviation and had acquired clear momentum through the explicit adoption of the goal of reducing poverty to 15 per cent by 2015 (UN-Habitat, 2012). The Egyptian government explicitly articulated a package of actions and programmes designed to empower the poor on cost-recovery basis. Applying these guidelines in Egypt, slum areas have not only increased (from 1174 to 1210 between 2004 and 2006) but also the share of urban population living in slums has increased by 3.5 per cent from 2004 to 2006. If this trend persists, it will limit Egypt's ability to contribute to the MDGs (Ministry of State for Economic Development, 2008).

The cost-recovery programmes, policies, and strategies were rapidly developed with the participation and consensus of all stakeholders under different national and international housing projects. However, the important point was the stability of the implementation of the housing policies and its contribution to the development process within Egypt. In the meantime, after 10 years of relative deprivation in real estate market investment (between the years 1994 and 2004), a boom in the private housing development occurred in Egypt, and other Middle Eastern countries. International, regional, and national real estate companies entered the Egyptian market; prices rapidly rose, forcing the urban poor to acquire their goods and services in their own way.

Urban informality was perceived as potentially dangerous, and the state introduced new approaches to attack the poverty belts on the periphery of urban areas, and to prevent the growing of illegal housing development (Soliman, 2007). In 2005, the Mubarak administration launched the National Housing Project (NHP) to provide 5,00,000 housing units within six years at an estimated cost of USD 6.23 billion (GOPP, 2010). Half of these units were located in old cities and half were to be built in new cities. The NHP was based on the seven principles shown in Table 7.1 and heavily relied on self-help technique or *'Ibni Beitak'* scheme. It is estimated that 2,09,373 total housing units were built in 2008–2009, distributed as follows: 92,378 units were built by the private sector, comprising 44.12 per cent of the total units; 105,578 units were built according to the low-cost housing projects in governorates and new cities, comprising 50.43 per cent of the total units; 11,408 units (rural and urban) were implemented by the government, comprising 5.45 per cent of the total units. The deficit of the NHP constitutes around 58.13 per cent of the total target units.

In 2008, the government took an important step towards institutionalization by upgrading informal settlements through the creation of the Informal Settlements Development Facility (ISDF). However, little progress was made, and ISDF provided only technical advice to various governments. The programme does not include self-help as an approach for upgrading the unplanned areas; rather, it relies on a cost recovery approach in which housing is treated as an asset.

In sum up, the urban informality expanded rapidly on agriculture and desert land. Government efforts in urban planning, land management, provision of housing and social services are ineffective in providing integrated urban development especially in support of the urban poor.

Transitional Socio-economic and Political Mode

The 'transitional socio-economic and political mode' was an attempt to cope with the transitional state of affairs that occurred after the peaceful revolution of January 2011 in Egypt in responding to the increasing demand for housing units to absorb the massive anger of the societies. The Egyptian uprising in 2011 caught the Islamists by surprise. After Mubarak was forced to step down, the Brotherhood formed a new political party to run for office. After decades of repression, the Brotherhood has gone from being an embattled opposition to the most powerful bloc – holding 216 of 498 seats in a parliament charged with writing Egypt's new constitution. The Brotherhood is now poised to play critical roles as Egypt attempts to make the transition to democracy.

The role of the state shrunk, while the housing mechanisms controlled by the private sector in informal housing development being flourishing. The immediate response of the interim governments is to modify the current housing delivery system for low-income groups and to meet the rapid demand for housing units. These transitional governments intervened in several ways.

Table 7.1 *The National Housing Project (NHP) under Mubarak Election Programme (2005–2011)*

Pivot	*Aims*	*Type of housing*	*Number of units*		*Rate of implementation %*	*% of Targets units*
			Targeted	*Actual*		
Providing ownership of residential units with an area of 63 square metres in Governorates and new cities.	Aiming to implement a number of housing units with an area of 63 square metres in new cities, 1,05,000 units thereof have already been delivered to applicants, and the remainder are currently under delivery according to the plan.	Public	2,68,756	1,05,587	39.3	53.75
Providing plots of lands with small areas in new cities to the project of 'Build your House' or 'Ibni Beitak' scheme.	88,800 plots of land of an area 150 square metres per plot were allocated for those who meet the conditions of the National Housing Project/Build Your House, with the aim to build a residential building consisting of ground floor and two floors (three units) with an average area of 63 square metres for each unit, priced at LE 70 per square metre, and in the event of complete building of three residential units, the citizen is fully exempted from the price of the land.	Private	88,889	76,852	86.5	17.78
Building housing units by investors.	Providing lands in new cities to investors to build housing units (63m2) and facilitating ownerships to the beneficiaries. 6675 *faddan* in 14 new cities were allocated to 141 companies with the purpose of implementing 35,400 thousand residential unit within the framework of the National Housing Project.	Private	35,469	14,642	41.3	7.09
Building the 'Family House' in 6th of October City and providing ownerships for families.	3000 residential units were implemented in 6 October and delivered to applicants, and utilities such as schools and markets are currently under implementation.	Private	3020	884	29.3	0.60

Cont'd…

...Cont'd

Renting small housing units with area 30–40 m2 for the most-privileged brackets.	The Project aims to facilitate housing units, with an area of 42 square metres per unit, for the citizen of more needs who cannot afford down payments. A number of 13,000 units is currently being implemented in 6 October and 1,500 units were preliminary delivered.	Public	74,958	3,449	4.6	14.99
Syndicates and Housing Co-Ops. Renting 63 m2 housing units in Governorate and new cities.	Aims to provide 20,216 thousand residential units with an area of 63 square metres per unit for members of housing co-ops and syndicates	Public	20,216	3,831	19.0	4.04
Building and providing ownerships of the 'Rural House' in the Governorate and Back Desert.	Aiming to implement a number of housing units with an area of 63 square metres in the Governorate and Back Desert.	Public	8,692	4,128	47.5	1.74
Total			5,00,000	2,09,373	41.9	100.0

Source: Ministry of Housing, Utilities and Urban Development (MHUUD), 2008/2009, adopted by Soliman, A. (forthcoming) Pathways towards innovations for self-help housing in Egypt, in Jan Bredenoord, Paul van Lindert, Peer Smets (eds) 'Housing and the Urban Poor – Stakeholders, Planning, Sustainability', Earthscan Book.

First, two months after the revolt, more than one million people had applied to the Ministry of Housing and Urban Development (MHUD) for housing. The multiple transitional governments responded to this huge demand for housing by introducing a National Social Housing Programme (NSHP) to build one million housing units within five years to meet the immediate demand for housing; turning a blind eye to illegal construction on existing residential buildings; and continuing the laissez-faire attitudes towards illegal residential development on agricultural land to absorb the people's anger.

The NSHP depends on two principles: allocating family's land plots in the new towns with a size of 300–400 m2 for developers who are able to finish the construction process within two to three years; and continuing the *'Ibni Beitak'* scheme in new towns. This plan recalls the previous scheme, NHP, in its size and ambition. Analysis of NHP found that the government achieved barely 42 per cent of the total target units. Comparing the NSHP to what has already been implemented on the ground, the picture is unclear. Assuming that each 400 m2 plot will contain 16 housing units, with an average height of four floors and four units per floor, a residential area of 25 square kilometres will be required to hold one million housing unit. In addition, 50 per cent of the needed area will be allocated for roads, services and open spaces, bringing the total area needed to meet the requirements of the NSHP 37.5 square kilometres. This area constitutes 60 and 40 per cent of the total size of *Sadat* and *Tenth of Ramadan* new cities, respectively. It also represents 11 and nearly 50 per cent of the total serviced built-up area (349.166 square kilometres) and the total housing production (5,71,770 housing units) of 17 new towns, respectively, in the year 1990. The total cost of land and of the installation of infrastructures for the NSHP will be around USD 5 billion. The total cost of housing construction for the NSHP will be around USD 16.66 billion, given a total cost of the NSHP around USD 21 billion. However, an annual estimated cost of USD 4.2 billion will be needed to implement the NSHP. This constitutes around three and a half times the total subsidy for the housing of the NHP, which was dispersed over six years and not even completed. And it also constitutes the amount of the loan that the Egyptian government is currently negotiating for it with the International Monetary Fund.

Secondly, the closed and vacant housing units in the Egyptian cities, should be exploited as rental units in the real estate market. It is estimated that the total closed and vacant housing units in Egypt are about 4.58 million housing units of which 1.18 million were closed and 3.40 million were vacant. Some privilege should be allocated to the property owners of vacant units by exempting them from paying properties tax, and providing financial support to the property owners ranges between 25,000–30,000 Egyptian Pounds (LE is equal 0.143 $) with zero interest rate. This financial support is to be paid off in monthly installments of 120 LE for the state out of the actual rental value of a free contract between property owners and tenants. The differences between the actual rent agreed upon with the owner of the property and the imbursement of loan to be covered by the tenant over a period between 10–15 years.

Thirdly, the government tries to temporarily control the unregulated construction on agricultural land and existing buildings, where some individuals have taken advantage of the transitional circumstances that the country has been passing through for personal interest, building on agricultural land and the exploitation of what can be exploited in the absence of a security presence in Egypt. Since Mubarak's resignation in 2011, nothing has been done on the ground for the urban poor. On the contrary, urban sprawl on agricultural land at the periphery of urban areas has flourished. It is estimated that during the 18 months following the 2011 uprising, Egypt has lost between 1,00,000 and 1,20,000 *faddan* of agricultural land to informal housing. Therefore, agricultural land is being lost at an estimated monthly, daily, and hourly rate of 6.11, 0.203, and 0.008 *faddan*, respectively. This is unlike the many roles of the establishment in violation of the conditions to build on the existing buildings in cities of Egypt, estimated at around 150–2,00,000 residential units in the same period. The interim government is reluctant to implement laws for fear of the negative perception at street level to the responsible authorities in the country.

It could be said that during this critical transitional period, the housing mechanisms are fully controlled by the masses of the people without adhering to the laws governing the construction process, and the shrinking role of government in controlling the real estate market. In other words, the role of the state shifted from *an enabler* to *an observer*, in which it lost control over the built environment. It is expected that Egypt will face many urban problems because of the indiscriminate construction and the rapid erosion of agricultural lands in over time.

Figure 7.1 *Various layers of urban growth for selected small cites in Egypt, middle, urban development of Alexandria city, right middle, housing informality in Alexandria city, below, urban development of Cairo city in various phases, blow-right, housing informality in Cairo city*

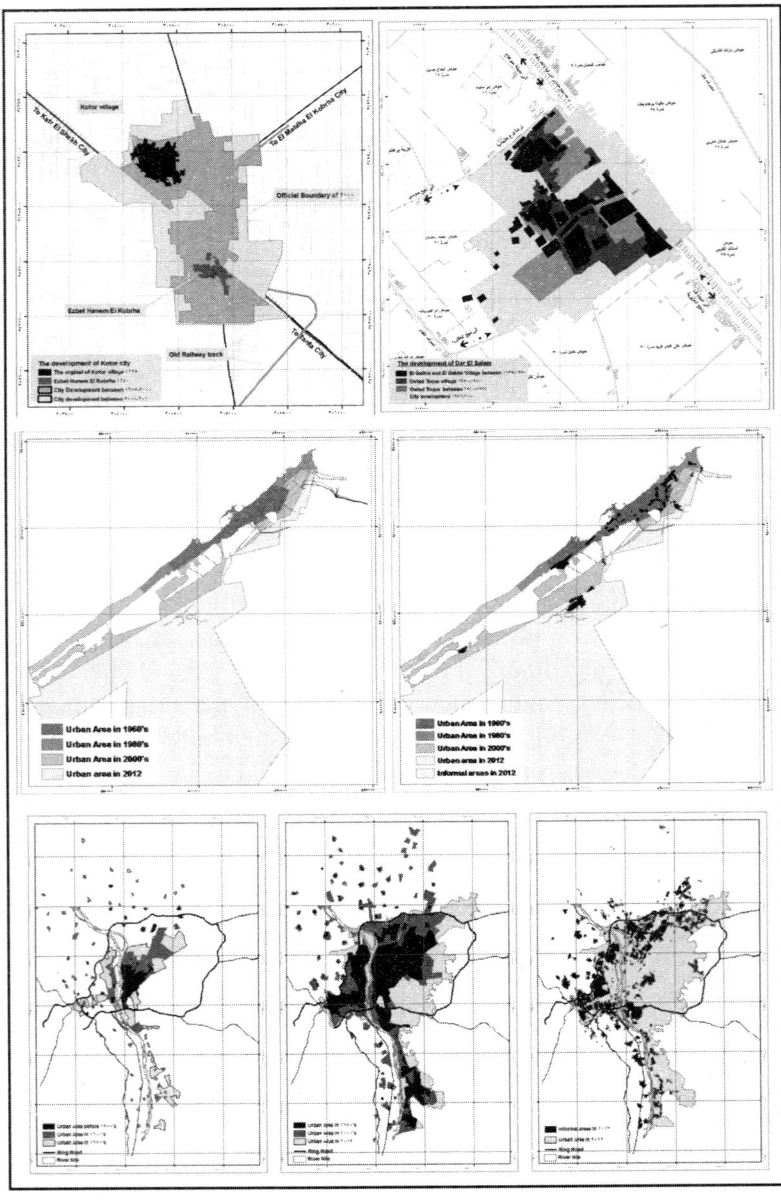

Source: GOPP, 2012

Mapping Cities' Growth and Land Reform

The land question is central to economic analysis. Its use in an urban context is crucial in shaping how effectively cities function and who gets the principal benefits from urban economic growth (Stilwell and Jordan, 2004). Land acquisition and housing production with a people's process of urban informality within the urban setting is linked with informal markets, informal institution mechanisms, and the actors who are rolling these processes. The following part traces urban development in relation of land reform act in the Egyptian cities and links it with the housing policies that Egypt has adopted.

Historically, most Egyptian agglomerations were not predominantly urban areas and it has never been classified as distinct by the state. The historic city (*medina*), such as Cairo and Alexandria, typically consists of a dense agglomeration of dwellings, with commercial uses on the ground floor. As illustrated in Figure 7.1, the urban form of the Egyptian cities consists of a series of historic layers, epitomized by relatively homogeneous land markets, each with their own rules. Small and intermediate Egyptian cities are originally characterized by a compact rural agglomeration, which formulated the first layer of the urban fabric, and by the time, more district layers were added on. Over time, many properties have deteriorated for lack of maintenance by absentee owners, or of the conflict of the fragmented ownership patterns.

On the eve of the 1952 Revolution, ownership of agricultural land was heavily concentrated in a few hands. About 0.1 per cent of owners possessed one-fifth of the land and 0.4 per cent controlled one-third, in contrast to the 95 per cent of small owners with only 35 per cent of the land, and 44 per cent of all rural inhabitants were landless (Osman, 2010). The land reform law no. 178 of 1952, and the subsequent laws, no. 127 and no. 15 of 1961, and 1963, respectively limited individual ownerships to 50 *faddan* per individual and a total landholder for a family of 100 *faddan*. It targeted the property of the upper class of landowners, dubbed 'feudalists' by the government, for distribution to the poorest villagers and landless. According to these laws, the agricultural landownership is right kind original on the land and gives its owner the power to use, abuse, and dispose of the fact that the land is for an agricultural use that leads to a definition of property of this description. During this era, urban growth on adjacent agricultural land was prohibited, and planning control was in force.

At the beginning of the 1960s significant improvements in public spaces, streets, markets, historic buildings, and new districts had been established in the majority of the Egyptian cities, which formulated the second layer as planned cities. The *awqaf* and Agrarian Land Reform foundations owned significant proportions of new added district properties. Planned and arbitrary extensions on agricultural land were added on with distinct neighbourhoods reflecting the socio-economic mix of the population, such as *El Mohandseen* and *Bulq El Daqrur* districts in Cairo (see Figure 7.2) and *Smouha* area in Alexandria, through a combination of public improvements and private investment. By June 1966, the pyramid of landownership truncated at the top part and widened at the base part while large holdings were not entirely eliminated. The 95 per cent of owners came to control 52 per cent of the land instead of the 35 per cent they had owned before the reforms (Hopkins, 1969), and the former landless became landlords of agricultural areas adjacent the urban areas.

The third layer is the *scattered-urban informal urbanization* that started in the mid-1970s and has accommodated most of Egypt's sustained annual urban demographic growth rates of 2 to 3 per cent since the 1980s. Most of this expansion occurred on privately owned

Figure 7.2 *Left part Bulaq El Daqrurwith arbitrary extension, right part El Mohandseen area with planned extensions on agricultural land, both areas in Cairo city*

Source: Google earth, 2012

agricultural land that was distributed according to Agrarian land reform (see Figure 7.2). From 1975 to 1985, urban land values doubled every three to four years while prices on agricultural fringes rose up but by less than the prices of urban land. The number of small owners, those with fewer than five *faddan*, increased to nearly 3.29 million in 1984 from 2.92 million in 1961, while the area they owned dropped from 3.17 million *faddan* to 2.9 million *faddan* (Osman, 2010). Because of low revenue of agricultural production, many of small landowners sold their properties for private developers who converted these areas into informal residential development. This suggested that land fragmentation worsened, because of the continual division of land among heirs in accordance with Islamic inheritance laws.

Between the 1970 and 1980, the Open-Door Policy of Sadat and the privatization policy of Mubarak was diminished as the government relaxed its controls over agricultural land. However, land reforms resulted only in the redistribution of about 15 per cent of Egypt's land under cultivation, and by the early 1980s, the effects of land reforms in Egypt drew to a halt as the population of Egypt moved away from agriculture. The issuance of law 96 in 1992 revoked the former Agrarian Land Reform of 1952 that had given tenants security of tenure and legalized the right to inherit tenancy agreements. The new law fully enacted in October 1997 after a five-year transition period, but the rent after 1992 was increased from 7 to at least 22 times the fees of the land tax. After the enactment of the new law, all landowners could take back their land and charge tenants market-based rent, which in some cases increased to 300–400 per cent. Despite contract renewal, the tenants remain vulnerable and insecure because of threats of eviction from proprietors. Due to the endorsement of the new law, the fourth layer appeared by which the *peri-urban informal urbanization* was dominating the new fabric of urban areas. This trend was facilitated by traditional tenure systems where the privately owned land was subdivided into three types. Privately registered owned land is an area guaranteed full land registration and has a permanent security of tenure. Privately no registered owned land, with *Hiyazah* (land holding), is an area with *de Jure* tenure recognition but does not have full security of tenure. Privately in doubt, ownership is an area with *de facto* recognition but does not have tenure title. With this type of urban informalization, land parcels are, therefore encumbered, with three instances of non-compliance: (a) illegal agricultural land subdivision; (b) change in use; and (c) unauthorized construction.

The fifth layer, which occurred in parallel to the fourth layer, is the planned urban extensions that existed in new towns, gated communities, and development corridors, but it is located only in Cairo and Alexandria, and other scattered cities that have Back Desert areas (Singerman, 2009).

The sixth layer occurred before and after the January revolt. With the introduction of a strategic urban plans for 230 cities, but despite good intentions, strategic urban plans prepared for cities are not being implemented. These plans have opened the door for further arbitrary expansion on agricultural land. Due to the political instability across the country, arbitrary informal development are spreading vertically and horizontally, where many floors are informally clinging to existing buildings (around 150–200 thousand housing units), and more agricultural land (100–120 thousand *faddan*) is converted into informal settlements. It could be said that '*the biggest destruction of the urban environment is currently taking place on the Egyptian landscape*'.

Several factors have historically been associated with urban informalization on agricultural land in Egypt. First, the government, either directly or indirectly, had played a major role in all cases, by which the land reform measures of the early 1960s, and changes in economic policies have taken economic power away from the traditional landholders and spread ownership across a wider section of the society. The original owners of the allocated land, who received land parcels according to law no. 178, after so many years died and left his/her land to his/her heirs, who were always in a conflict and were forced to put on sale their land parcels to other people. However, this often results in parcels being abandoned when multiple progeny cannot agree over subdivision or sale. Alternatively, if a proprietor dies without children, his property is transferred to Nasser Bank (*Bait-Elmaal*). Most of these lands have converted to housing informality, and fragmentation of ownership became inevitable. Secondly, the enactment of land policy in the early 1990s has stimulated greater inequality in land holdings, and it has been seen as a far safer investment in uncertain times than industrial production. Finally, further instability was created by the Agrarian Land Reform, which resulted in the change of large ownership areas from a private freehold to a public title, then to a private ownership, and vice-versa. This had a major impact on the agricultural land patterns, and led to the insecurity of land tenure

A Possible Pathway

In the last six decades, various housing policies have been applied in order to accelerate the efficiency of the housing delivery system and, at the same time, to improve the physical environment of the urban centres for the purpose of competing with the continuous development process for the welfare of the society. The development of housing policy of Egypt has passed through various stages and has had various policy makers.

The changing of housing policies was related to the changing of presidency and the fluctuation of the socio-economic and political situation of society, which led to a failure of a continuous housing policy within the country. This failure is related to the absence of correlation between different stages of housing development, misunderstanding of the environment of the urban poor on which arbitrary decisions have been taken towards the housing delivery system, lack of a clear urban development policy, the changing mode of intervention in housing sector, the absence of a future urban development vision, and a lack of land delivery system. Also, the unwillingness of politicians to understand the housing issue with regard to the treatment of housing as consumption, as a product, a commodity, or as an activity has led to setting up unrealistic housing programmes, not only for the urban poor but also for the wider range of society.

Also, the various land reform laws, socio-economic and political transformations associated with the absence of a proper land delivery system for the urban poor have contributed directly or indirectly in changing agricultural land pattern surrounding the cities. In addition, most of the cities' growth was expanded arbitrarily on the adjacent agricultural land which opened the door for land speculators and developers to conquer agricultural land and change its use into illegal residential areas.

This failure of housing policy has led to a housing puzzle in Egypt. The consequences are an increase in the demand for housing over supply, a shortage of housing supply for the bottom of the pyramid of the society, the spreading of housing informality on the periphery of the Egyptian cities, and a surplus of housing needs (around 4.8 million housing units are empty). This housing puzzle should be resolved and adjusted to meet the housing demand for the various strata of the society.

Housing policy is considered an integral part of the urban development, and the informal mechanisms for gaining access to agricultural land became 'cultural struggle' for the urban poor to house themselves. As well as, the absence of planning control, lack of local government finance, improper urban law, ineffective land reform act, weak urban governance, and improper land management over the built environment within Egyptian cities has led into the spreading of urban informality. Given the acute institutional, social, and economic constraints, in the short or medium term, it is not likely that the state or the market will effectively reach the urban poor in terms of formal access to land for housing. The dynamics of change of land delivery system, land use and land prices across different income segments of the market have to be studied.

Housing informality markets and land conversion procedures need to be formulated in line with socio-economic reforms and poverty alleviation strategies with the context of socio-economic needs of the bottom of the pyramid of the society, as well as, with the top of the pyramid. The government has to adopt an approach that supports what people do, and to regulate to the benefit of the collective resources by which enabling affordable housing standards, rather than standards so unfeasible that leave most of the housing stock unregulated.

In contrast, it has been argued that when the state and the market are as weak as in Egypt, both historically and actually, underlying social structures are more obviously, and crucially, engaged in economic activity, not only social and cultural activities. New approaches to housing policy and to urban development in general, thus need to be based on the very social mechanisms and structures whereby the majority of the populations manage their survival. Housing policy obviously needs a comprehensive set of policies, or a complete package of policies rather than a piecemeal approach in which one issue is tackled while others are ignored.

Housing policy should be viewed from three perspectives: an institutional perspective, a social perspective, and an implemental perspective. From an institutional point of view, it is appeared that housing policy can take different formal, legal shapes, but have in common that they are (to different degrees) hybrid institutions that deal with legal/illegal competing drivers stemming from public, market and community forces and values. These drivers occur in varying combinations, sometimes reflecting the origins of these organizations and affecting the motivations of the key stakeholders involved. From a social perspective, housing policy has in common that the users (again to different extents) adopt entrepreneurial strategies to fulfil their objectives (versus traditional 'bureaucratic' or 'management-oriented' behaviour); by which conflicts between principles are played out in organizational strategies and day-to-day decisions. From an implementation perspective, housing policy do not operate in isolation, rather it depends on the domination of capital, labour, collective resources, decision-makers, and a cooperation among the stakeholders, by which the governmental institutions are included and excluded at the same time. Any housing policy should recognize people as a potential to invest money, to manage and maintain the physical environment, to control the local resources, and to participate in national economy.

This then is the starting point for a society-driven urban development policy, as opposed to a state or market-driven policy. In this perspective, the organizations of civil society need to be enabled to adapt and strengthened to guide their own development, engaging with the state and the market where possible and desirable. They would appear to be the most productive means to assist the urban poor, as the state and the market are increasingly unable and unwilling to do. However, throughout the various potentialities, constraints, and the facts that Egypt has been magnified by the political goal of saving and rescuing agricultural land, therefore, from the perspective of an over all control desired by the local powers, the passage from 'a market-driven policy or a policy of containment' to 'a society-driven urban development policy or a policy of integration' has become vital and it represents an inescapable reversal. Thus, suggestions that working on the basis of these concepts can permit a more nuanced and appropriate analytical basis for understanding the perception of Egyptian urban dwellers, as well as mechanisms for consolidating urban development.

References

AlSayyad, N. (2009). 'Whose City?', in D. Singerman, and P. Amar, (eds) *Cairo Cosmopolitan: Politics, Culture, and Urban Space* in the New Globalized Middle East. Cairo: The American University in Cairo Press, pp. 539–542.

Bayat, A. and Denis, E. (2000). 'Who is Afraid of *Ashwaiyyat*? Urban Change and politics in Egypt', *Environment and Urbanization*, 12(2), pp. 185–199.

CAPMAS. (2006). General Statistics for Population and Housing: Population Census, Cairo: Central Agency for Public Mobilization and Statistics. Egypt.

CAPMAS. (2012). General Statistics for Population and Housing: Population Census, Cairo: Central Agency for Public Mobilization and Statistics.

CAPMAS. (2013). General Statistics for Population and Housing: Population Census, Cairo: Central Agency for Public Mobilization and Statistics

City Alliance. (2008). *Slum Upgrading Up Close: Experiences of Six Cities*, Washington: City Alliance.

Davidson, F. (1981). 'Ismailia: From Master Plan to Implementation', *Third World Planning Review*, 3(2), pp. 161–178.

Davidson, F. (1984). 'Ismalia: Combined Upgrading and Sites and Services Projects in Egypt'. In G. Payne. (ed.) *Low-income Housing in the Development World: The Role of Site and Services and Settlement Upgrading*, Chichester: John Wiley, pp. 125–148.

Davidson, F. and G. Payne. (1983). *Urban Projects Manual: A Guide to Preparing Upgrading and New Development Projects Accessible to Low-income Groups*, Liverpool, UK: Liverpool University Press.

De Soto, H. (2000). *The Mystery of Capital: Why Capitalism Triumphs in the West and Fails Everywhere Else*, London: Black Swan Books.

Dorman, W. (2009). 'Informal Cairo: Between Islamist Insurgency and the Neglectful State?', *Security Dialogue*, 40(4–5): pp. 419–441.

Egypt Human Development Report. (2010). United Nations Development Programme, and the Institute of National Planning, Egypt.

GOPP. (2012). The Detailed Plan of *El Matarya* Area in Cairo City, Cairo: The General Organisation for Physical Planning.

GOPP. (2010). *Ibni Beitak* Scheme, Cairo: General Organization for Physical Planning.

GOPP. (2006). Terms of Reference for Strategic Urban Plan for Egyptian Cities, Cairo: The General Organisation for Physical Planning.

Hopkins, H. (1969). *Egypt, The Crucible: The Unfinished Revolution of the Arab World*, London: Seker & Warburg.

Kipper, R. and M. Fischer, (2009). (eds), 'Cairo's Informal Areas: Between Urban Challenges and Hidden Potentials', SA: Portugal: No print.

Ilbert, R. (1984). 'Heliopolis: Colonial Enterprise and Town Planning Success?', *The Expanding Metropolis Coping with the Urban Growth of Cairo*, proceeding of seminar nine in the series architecture transformations in the Islamic World, Cairo, Egypt, November 11–15, pp. 36–42.

Ministry of State for Economic Development. (2008). Egypt: Achieving the Millennium Development Goals, Cairo.

Osman, T. (2010). *Egypt on the Brink: From Nasser to Mubarak*, New Haven and London: Yale University Press.

Silver, H. (2010). 'Divided Cities in the Middle East', *Community and Development*, 9, pp. 345–357.

Sims, D. (2010). *Understanding Cairo: The Logic of City Out of Control*. Cairo: The American University in Cairo Press.

Singerman, D. (ed.). (2009). *Cairo Contested: Governance, Urban Space and Global Modernity*, Cairo: The American University in Cairo Press.

Soliman, A. (2004). *A Possible Way Out: Formalizing Housing Informality in Egyptian Cities*. Lanham, USA: University Press of America.

Soliman, A. (2007). 'Urban Informality in Egyptian Cities: Coping with Diversity', Paper presented at the 2007 World Bank Fourth Urban Research Symposium, Washington DC.

Soliman, A. (2010). 'Rethinking Urban Informality and the Planning Process in Egypt', *International Development Planning Review*, 32(2), pp. 119–143.

Soliman, A., (2012a). 'Tilting at Pyramids: informality of land conversion in Cairo, paper presented in *Sixth Urban Research and Knowledge Symposium 2012*, Rethinking Cities: Framing the Future, organized by the World Bank, Barcelona, Spain.

Soliman, A. (2012b). 'Housing and the State in the Middle East.' In J. Susan Smith, Marja Elsinga, Lorna Fox O'Mahony, Ong Seow Eng, Susan Wachter, Peter M. Ward, (eds). *International Encyclopedia of Housing and Home*, 3. Oxford: Elsevier; pp. 346–354.

Soliman, A. (2012c). 'The Egyptian Episode of Self-Build Housing', *Habitat International Journal*, 36(2), pp. 226–236.

Stewart, Roy. (1981). 'The Development of the City of Suez', *Third World Planning Review*, 3(2), pp. 179–200.

Stilwell, F. and K. Jordan. (2004). 'The Political Economy of Land: Putting Henry George in his Place', *The Journal of Australian Political Economy*, 54 (December).

The Aga Khan Programme. (1984). 'Cairo: 1800–2000: Planning for the capital city in the context of Egypt's history and development', The Aga Khan programme for Islamic Architecture, Harvard University – Massachusetts Institute of Technology, in Proceeding of Seminar Nine in the Series Architectural Transformations in the Islamic World entitled *The Expanding Metropolis Coping with the Urban Growth of Cairo,* Held in Cairo, Egypt, November 11–15, pp. 91–120.

The Joint Land Policy Team. (1977). Urban land Use in Egypt: Report of The Joint Land Policy Team, Ministry of Housing and Reconstruction and Ministry of Planning, Arab Republic of Egypt with Office of Housing Agency for International Development, USA.

Welbank, M. and A. Edwards. (1981). 'Port Said: Planning for Reconstruction and Development', *Third World Planning Review*, 3(2), pp. 143–160.

World Bank. (2011). 'Was Growth in Egypt between 2005 and 2008 Pro-Poor: From Static to Dynamic Poverty Profile', *Policy Research Working Paper 5589*, Washington DC: World Bank.

UN-Habitat. (2012), *The State of Arab Cities 2012: The Challenges of Urban Transition,* Nairobi: Kenya.

UN-Habitat. (2008). *The State of African Cities 2008: A Framework for Addressing Urban Challenges in Africa*, Nairobi: Kenya.

8

Intervention Policies and Practices Regarding Favelas and Other Precarious Dwellings

Brazil and the City of Sao Paulo

Suzana Pasternak and Camila D'Ottaviano

Urbanization and globalization impact cities and societies differently at different times. Changes in industrialization, political regimes, economic development along with the consequences of a particular history, each has its own effect as well. Brazil, as a society, has had its share of changes, each one of which has in turn, had consequences for the housing of the urban poor. The effect of these changes, and the attendant interventions at both the societal and the metropolitan level, Sao Paul, on favelas and other precarious dwellings is described in the chapter which follows. Questions about public policy for housing the urban poor are raised by the complexity of the problem.

Cardoso (2007) summarizes current interventions in precarious settlements by using three basic models: urbanization, re-urbanization and removal. Urbanization involves interventions that do not change the structure of the settlement, providing only infrastructure and paving. This type of intervention has been the most prevalent, despite the fact that favelas and precarious dwellings usually feature urban patterns that do not meet regulations. Re-urbanization consists of interventions that completely redesign the settlement's structure, resettling the families in the same area. This was the case of the model urbanization of the Brás de Pina favela in Rio de Janeiro. Removal implies total displacement of residents and relocating them to a different area. In practice, many interventions rely on the three alternatives to some degree, re-parceling parts of the settlement, working on infrastructure wherever possible, and even removing part of the population in very crowded areas, when additional space for roads and infrastructure is required. Such removals usually entail the payment of indemnities. Interventions can also be more specific – targeting a part of the settlement or the whole thing. Specific interventions have resulted due to political motives or emergency needs, such as the reconstruction of areas hit by fire and/or floods.

Total interventions, or re-urbanization, were seen for example, in programmes like Favela-Bairro in Rio de Janeiro, and *Santo André MaisIgual*, a programme in a municipality of the Greater Sao Paulo area. The focus of both programmes was the integral improvement of a group of smaller favelas, and the projects took two years to complete. Huge amounts of resources are required for programmes of this nature, making them unfeasible for most local administrations, as funding is very restricted. Both Rio de Janeiro and Santo André relied on foreign resources (European Community and the IDB).

As for management models, interventions can be classified as participatory, as in the Plan for Regulating Special Interest Zones in Recife (PREZEIS, *Plano de Regularização das ZonasEspeciais de Interesse Social, de Recife*), or authoritarian e.g. Cingapura in Sao Paulo, or Favela-Bairro in Rio de Janeiro. Costs vary greatly depending on the different standards of the favela interventions used. Simulations by the Sao Paulo Technology Research Institute (IPT) for urbanization projects for the favelas located on the banks of the Guarapiranga dam estimated costs ranging from U$ 1,000.00 to U$ 13,000.00 per family, depending on the intervention model adopted. When analysing different projects carried out in the same Guarapiranga region, local Sao Paulo officials came up with costs ranging from U$ 2,000.00 to U$ 5,000.00.

The Favela-Barrio project did not adhere to the minimum density or dwelling condition standards, and the criteria for accessibility were quite flexible as well. In some cases, such as in Ladeira dos Funcionários, demographic density reached 1,000 inhabitants per hectare. The decrease in density was kept at the bare minimum required to open roads and supply equipment. Improvements to individual households was left to the residents themselves, and driven by the urbanization of the area. Accessibility to all residences was not ensured: a roadway was built within reasonable distance, but alleys and unfit housing units were not removed.

The arguments in favour of Favela-Bairro stress the high density of the Rio de Janeiro favelas, their level of consolidation, their size, and the difficult geographic and geological conditions of Rio's settlements in the hills. With the high density levels present, a substantial portion of the population would have to be removed to adopt the highest standards. This argument, however, touches on a serious issue for public authorities: on the one hand, there is the respect for the population's right to remain in their place of residence; on the other hand, of settlements that do not meet the city's urban standards should not be legalized. This creates two regulating principles for the conditions of urban life: one for the formal city, and a more flexible one, for the favelas. A tragic dilemma ensues: are we to accept just about anything in the name of keeping people in their places of residence? Are any settlement standards to be accepted? Aren't we sanctioning two levels of citizenship?

Land regularization is another challenge. Special Social Interest Zones have proven to be an efficient way to promote land tenure and prevent removals. For the resident population, this has generally proven to be sufficient. De Soto's argument, that real estate and land regularization, along with the granting of deeds to favela residents that would bring them into the market, would be beneficial by allowing such properties to be used in the mortgage market, has not been confirmed. In Lima, titles were granted, and favelas have only proliferated. And no bank accepts such deeds for a mortgage guarantee. In Sao Paulo, many favela residents don't want deeds because that would entail the payment of property taxes.

The urbanization of housing for the urban poor raises many challenges. Scholars sometimes refer to these efforts as 'trying to dry ice with a towel.' Wouldn't the urbanization of favelas encourage [new] invasions? The small supply of new subsidized housing units has turned favela-upgrading programmes into the only alternative. However, the growth rate of favela populations has been historically higher than that of the population as a whole. Thus, housing conditions have been deteriorating. Besides, even in the improved favelas, the density increases again, thus deteriorating the living conditions in those that have already been upgraded. The topic of the city having double standards is also pressing. Precarious dwellings, even if upgraded, will never become neighbourhoods. The integration of favelas is an illusion that conceals the profound inequalities in Brazilian society.

Table 8.1 *Brazil total households and favela households per region. 1980, 1991, 2000, 2010.*

Region	Total Households				Favela Households			
	1980	1991	2000	2010	1980	1991	2000	2010
North	12,19,496	23,76,607	33,53,764	39,88,832	12,721	97,760	1,78,326	4,63,444
Northeast	80,36,803	1,09,20,830	1,39,11,413	1,49,57,608	69,974	2,86,130	3,06,395	9,26,370
Southeast	1,37,61,346	1,88,39,621	2,46,99,909	2,52,27,877	3,57,330	6,75,846	10,38,608	16,07,375
South	48,26,030	65,98,962	85,09,284	89,04,120	30,077	73,325	1,10,411	1,70,054
Midwest	18,12,176	26,57,621	37,91,248	43,49,562	10,493	11,257	16,808	57,286
Brazil	2,96,55,851	4,13,93,641	5,42,67,618	5,74,27,999	4,80,595	11,44,318	16,50,548	32,24,529

Source: Censuses 1991, 2000 and 2010.

Housing Policy and Interventions in Housing in the Metropolitan and Municipal Regions of Sao Paulo

Favela dwellings and populations have been growing since 1980, and increasing at higher rates than the total population. From 1980 to 1991, the number of total households grew by 3.08 per cent per year, while the number of favela households grew by 8.81 per cent per year. During the following period – 1991 to 2000 – the number of total households grew by 0.88 per cent per year, while favela households had an annual increase rate of 4.18 per cent. From 2000 to 2010, the annual growth rate of Brazilian households was 0.57 per cent, while favela households increased each year by 6.93 per cent. In 1980, the favela population was 2.25 million people, by 1991 it had hit more than 5 million, and in 2000, in the 32,24,529 households in subnormal agglomerates, there were 14 million residents. While the population in favelas accounted for 1.62 per cent of the total population in 1980, it climbed to 2.76 per cent in 1991, to 3.04 per cent in 2000 and by 2010 had reached 5.61 per cent.

Until 1984, the policies on social housing in Brazil, and especially those regarding favelas and tenement houses, were highly centralized at the federal level. There have always been interventions at the local level, but prior to the closing of the National Housing Bank (BHN) in November of 1986, these interventions were not as relevant as they later became in 1990. One detailed analysis of the policies at the federal level can be seen in Pasternak Taschner, 1997.

The first favela urbanization programmes in Brazil took place at the end of the 1960s, and were largely inspired by the ideas of John Turner. However, it was only after the 1980s that this type of intervention was consolidated under the responsibility of local and/or state governments.

The interventions that occurred over the last 30 years can be broken down into eight chronological periods (Figure 8.1) For each period, we discuss the type of analysis conducted as well as the reactions caused by these interventions, using an analysis scheme previously been used by Pasternak (Pasternak Taschner, 1997), and enhanced by Patton (1988).

By analysis, we mean here the prevalent ideas, concepts and hegemonic theories of each time period. Solutions are the actions actually carried out in efforts to solve the problems, as based on the theories. Reactions mean the new problems detected, which subsequently redefine new theories and actions.

Figure 8.1 *Policies for Favela Clearance in Sao Paulo*

From the 1940s to the 1960s	Emergence of favelas in Sao Paulo, removal policies
1970s	Proliferation of favelas
	Additional removal policies, temporary shelters were constructed
1980s	Increased proliferation of favelas
	Urbanization efforts by local governments
Mid 1980s to 1988	Removal policies resumed
	Low-income housing built in partnership with public and private administration through interconnected operations
Beginning of 1990s	Urbanization of favelas by local administrations, through self-managed programmes, with a special focus on social participation
Mid 1990s	Vertical units constructed by contractors in occupied areas,
	without resident participation, with funding from
	IDB (Cingapura project)
Beginning of 2000s	Continuation of favela urbanization policies, efforts to promote
	social inclusion;
	Urban centres upgraded with social housing
	Issues of land legalization on private spaces
Mid 2000s	Attempt to recover urban centres by promoting economic
	activities, reducing emphasis on social housing
	and adopting a different approach: efforts to maintain
	existing structure and population as much as possible

The Decade of the 1960s

The first interventions for the eradication of favelas (*desfavelamento* in Portuguese) took place in the city of Sao Paulo (capital of the state and metropolitan centre) in the 1960s. Favelas were not yet a major issue in other municipalities outside the metropolitan area.

The first favela intervention in Sao Paulo involved removing inhabitants and resettling them in other different sites. The underlying idea behind this type of intervention was based on the concept of favelas being a den of disease, crime, social disorder and delinquency. This pathology would no longer exist when settlements were eradicated and its inhabitants transferred to adequate housing units. It should be highlighted here that the favela population in Sao Paulo at the time was relatively small, around 100 thousand people, making removal feasible. In Sao Paulo, removal never reached the truculent levels of Rio de

Janeiro during the era of Carlos Lacerda (1960 – 1965). The results of this policy, both in Rio and in Sao Paulo, were not encouraging. The state-subsidized housing where favela residents were sent was often in peripheral areas that were difficult to access. The result was that families had to pay more for transportation, which was a heavy burden on their budgets. Additionally, the distance between their new homes and their places of work prevented many women from working and subsequently contributing to the family income. Purchasing power dropped, it became more difficult for residents to pay mortgages or rent, and people went back to the favelas.

The Decade of 1970s

During the 1970s, it became clear that removal was justified only in emergency situations or for settlements located in at-risk areas. As a modal form of intervention in favelas, a more efficient, less traumatic policy was needed. Thus, instead of taking favela residents to a housing unit where they would eventually live, they were sent to Temporary Housing Villages (VHPs, or *Vilas de HabitaçãoProvisória*) which had existed in Rio de Janeiro since the mid-1940s, under the name proletarian parks (*parques proletários*) (Pasternak, 1997). VHPs were temporary shelters, built in the same areas as the favelas and where intense social services were provided. The core objective was professional education, literacy and the provision of legal documents to the population, so that these people would be better able to integrate into city life and participate in the real estate market. The lodging project itself showed the temporary character of the programme, as non-permanent construction materials were used. VHPs were made out of wood, not brick and mortar, and the bathrooms were communal. The expectation was that after a year, families would be ready to integrate into housing and job markets.

The theoretical rationale for this sort of intervention was based on the social integration principles of the functionalist sociology school of thought. They highlighted the fact that favelas were the first housing alternative for rural migrants, a 'springboard' to the city, and a necessary phase prior to integration in urban life. In VHPs, the basic idea was to shorten the 'necessary time' migrants had to stay in the favela, by providing some basic infrastructure, professional guidance and formal education.

VHPs were met with significant criticism. In addition to the presumption of social integration – which proved to be untrue – empirical data from the Favelas Census, the systematic collection that began in the mid-1970s, showed that favela residents were not recent migrants at all. Nor were the favelas the first place they had come to live. The reason favelas were growing had more to do with impoverishment than with direct migration. Favela residents had not settled in the shacks where they lived at first. They had actually moved around urban spaces in a 'downward filtering trajectory', corresponding to the process of land appreciation and working class impoverishment, moving from the central areas to the periphery, from brick and mortar houses to shacks in the favelas (Pasternak, 1997: 54).

The insight gained by the end of the 1970s, showing that favelas were here to stay and that favela residents were workers, mostly employed in the Sao Paulo industrial sector, spoke in favour of seeking new solutions. Temporary housing eventually became permanent. In a society like Brazil's, the assumption of social integration faced serious limits: Sao Paulo's economic capacity for integrating additional labour into the dynamic centres of the economy has always been limited. Additionally, professional skills and education were also significant limiting factors.

Period Between 1980–1985

In this era, we see increased awareness that favelas are not dysfunctions of the system but rather the physical expression of its contradictions. This leads to an operational impasse: how can the issue of intervention be handled? How does one create a methodology for action that is not a total break from the system itself?

Some technical sectors believed that large-scale construction, prefabrication, industrialization and rationalization of constructions could bring home costs down, making housing affordable to all. Thus, housing developments such as the one in Itaquera were built, where some lower cost systems were introduced (lighter prefab systems with 'outinord' metal surfaces, brick and mortar structural construction, etc.), in line with the effort by Sao Paulo's housing company COHAB-SP (acronym for *Companhia Metropolitana de Habitação de São Paulo*) to build 80,000 housing units between 1980 and 1985.

On the other side, cooperation, self-help and mutual help were advocated as tools for overcoming problems in favelas. The middle classes in Brazil tried to convey to favela residents a certain idea of society so that they would come to believe that their daily lives could be improved by their own efforts and from help from their community. Urbanization of the favelas was then conceived as a basic policy.

In the city of Sao Paulo in 1979, a programme called Pró-Água was launched, which was aimed at supplying drinking water to favelas and ultimately to the individual residences, whenever possible. Pró-Luz, a similar programme for supplying electric power to the favelas, also started in 1979. By 1987, almost all favela houses already had electric energy. These programmes were part of what were known as compensatory policies, and the amount charged to the users was always the minimum rate. In 1981, a more ambitious programme named 'Profavela' was launched, which looked not only to provide favelas with infrastructure, but also with education and health services, as well as highly subsidized financing for the improvement and/or construction of housing units. The programme was very costly and abandoned in 1984. Another federal programme, 'Promorar', also sought to eradicate favelas by replacing the shacks with 'embryo' units in the same area, with land tenure regularization.

Critics of favela urbanization programmes argue that the certainty of permanent settlements encourages new occupancy and overcrowding of the existing favelas, bringing the occupied areas a simulation of the real estate market. At any rate, even for a conservative administration such as that of Reinaldo de Barros (1979–1982), solutions based on the removal of favela residents was not feasible, as the population amounted to 4,00,000 people in 1979, around 5 per cent of the city's population.

Period Between 1986 and 1988

In January of 1986, the first local government since 1964 directly elected by the people took office in the city of Sao Paulo. 'Supported by conservative forces and large sectors of the middle class who were frightened by the ever-growing urban violence and attributed this violence in part to the 'concessions' made to lower income classes, the administration went back to entertaining the idea of removing favelas, especially those around wealthy neighbourhoods' (Pasternak, 1997: 61).

Prevailing logic at that time viewed favela residents as the poor to be segregated, and favelas situated on prime locations inside the urban network as pieces of land to be reclaimed and recovered for middle-class housing. In 1986, as a result of the Cruzado Plan (which froze prices), a real estate boom occurred.

The housing plan of the Jânio Quadros administration (1986–1988) resulted in more talk than action. Two favelas were removed from upscale areas. The period's most interesting contribution was a partnership with private companies to promote favela removal. Urban advantages were offered in exchange for the construction of houses for favela residents. Interconnected transactions provided developers with larger construction areas than those permitted by zoning laws in exchange for the donation of residential units for favela residents.

1989 to 1992 Period

In 1989, the city of Sao Paulo elected a representative from the Workers' Party (PT, *Partido dos Trabalhadores*), a party committed to social movements and union struggles. The diagnostics made and the plans of action prepared during the Luiza Erundina administration are evidence of this commitment. A portrait of the city prepared by technical analysts under her administration showed an enormous illegal city that was sheltering the lower income classes. According to these estimates, 3,50,000 households in Sao Paulo, most of which were smaller than 125 square metres, did not adhere to zoning laws and construction codes. Adding to these figures the favela households, tenement houses and irregular land divisions, approximately 65 per cent of the city was irregular.

Urban segregation was seen as something to avoid. The right to the city belongs to everybody. This stance led to attempts to maintain tenement house populations in inner city areas. Favela upgrading projects were resumed, this time with the participation of the people. Social movements demanded the removal of middlemen, with increased end user participation in the decision-making processes for planning and building homes. Projects that included private home construction and self-management were encouraged. To the 'old-left's' criticism of collective housing unit construction as an exploitation of the workforce, the 'new left' answered that self-managed, community-built housing initiatives helped reduce costs by fostering political awareness and citizenship, as 'organizing to build homes eventually becomes a school of self-management and collective organization' (Bonduki, 1992: 164).

In regards to Sao Paulo favela re-urbanization, as from 1990, '26,000 families in 50 favelas were provided with infrastructure improvements: road paving, land re-parceling, water, sewage and drainage systems, and the opening of access points. At the same time, 3,500 families in 70 favelas benefitted from smaller improvements, also as a collective effort' (Sao Paulo, 1992: 12). The concept of environmental risk was introduced in favela urbanization initiatives in order to set priorities in interventions. This assessment involved geomorphologic risks for residents: collapse, flooding or washouts. Regarding the supply of housing units outside the favelas, construction was continued on approximately 33,000 units, a share of which had been initiated in the previous administration. The guidelines set forth by the Luiza Erundina administration (1989–1992) regarding low-cost housing can be summarized as:

1. Elimination of bureaucratic red tape and simplification of construction regulations;
2. Organization of the people, wherein social movements were privileged parties in dialogues;
3. Home construction by self-managed collective housing initiatives (local administration and residents);
4. Urbanization of favelas, with priority given to sites at environmental risk;
5. Intervention in tenement houses;
6. Maintenance of partnerships with the private sector (interconnected transactions);

Criticism of the policies in force abounded, especially regarding the sluggishness of the community-built process, the transformation of social movements into political machines, generating a new form of cronyism, the continued emergence of new favelas and overcrowding of existing ones, as well as increased speculation in urbanized favelas.

1993 to 2000 Period

In 1993, the newly elected administration (Paulo Maluf/Celso Pitta) had a totally different political stance vis-à-vis the previous government. That same year, research coordinated by the Economic Research Institute Foundation (FIPE) showed an increase in the number of brick and mortar units in favelas – an increase of approximately 75 per cent. The profile of favela residents was changing, in terms of both constructive and economic features. This study also indicated a relative increase in household income in favelas.

Unlike during the Erundina administration, the new local government administration did not have any commitments to social movements. However, the idea that favela residents were poor workers who had a right to the city and to be integrated into the urban fabric had already consolidated itself. The local government's housing policy focused on the Project of Favela Urbanization through Verticalization

PROVER (*Projeto de Urbanização de Favelas com Verticalização*). This project later came to be known as the Cingapura Project.

The Cingapura Project was based on the principle that favela residents were to stay on the same favela land, but in vertical units built by developers. The project differs from the favela urbanization initiative adopted by the previous administration in that it does not make use of the urban fabric already built by the favela residents, instead providing non-expandable finished housing units. In the Paulo Maluf administration (1993–96), approximately 9,000 units were delivered. The administration that took over after Maluf continued with the same favela policy.

The Cingapura Project's buildings have five to eleven floors. The apartments are small – 42 square metres – and cannot be expanded. They are expensive, each costing approximately US$ 18,000. The architectural design is standardized, and the project is exclusively residential – no commercial units are intended. The fact that there is no input from the population is considered a sort of trade-off for how quickly the project was carried out. The project was also criticized by the media for the sites where the buildings are located: highly visible sites were given preferential treatment, as the criteria for choosing the favelas was based more on propaganda than technical reasons.

Another undertaking worth mentioning is the Guarapiranga Project, which urbanized favelas located in regions around the basins in Sao Paulo, Cotia, Embu and Taboão da Serra.

2001–2004 Period

At the turn of the century, a different political party – once again the Workers' Party (PT), took over the Sao Paulo administration. The housing situation continued to deteriorate, with an increase in the number of favelas and homelessness. The revitalization of the centre was the main proposal prior to the beginning of the second semester of 2001, and it emphasized the city centre as a housing space for the lower class. People were encouraged to participate as a way of building citizenship.

The discourse on revitalizing the centre, highlighting its primary role as a housing space for the poor, did not lead to concrete actions. Despite the work of the Integrated Recovery Programme (PRI), which defined areas for urban intervention in some of the region's more deteriorated areas, and the Municipal Master Plan, which included the demarcation of what were called Special Social Interest Zones (ZEIS) in the inner city, very little was actually done in this region. Some of the interventions were carried out by the state government through a Tenement Houses Services Programme (PAC), led by a state government agency, and others were effected by the federal government through a Home Financing Plan (PAR).

The municipal administration at the time used the Bairro Legal Programme as a tool for implementing its housing policy. This programme can be defined as a set of integrated actions in continuous and delineated territories, occupied predominantly by lower income populations. It includes the urbanization and regularization of favelas and irregular land developments, as well as housing project classification. The intervention projects must consider land regularization, access to public services and facilities, and access to green and recreational areas (in addition to trying to include favela residents in the municipality's regular social and job/income generation programmes, rather than starting a special plan of action in the settlement).

The objective was to implement the programme in the 10 areas with the most significant social exclusion in the city. The difference from previous administrations' programmes was the requirement for integrated action between different municipal agencies; therefore, it also sought the involvement of other public spheres, non-governmental organizations, and civil society.

In the project description, one item describes the city's history and housing conditions. According to the 2005 National Sampling by Household Plan (PNAD) data, at that time the number of vacant properties in the total metropolitan area was estimated at 6,66,257, or 11.5 per cent of the total number of households counted. The information provided by the 2005 PNAD also showed that of these 6,66,000 households, only slightly more than 7,000 were totally deteriorated; 5,84,000 were fit for living, and 74,620 were under construction.

In addition to living in favelas, the poor met their housing needs by building, on their own, on irregular lots. In April of 2002, a survey estimated that there were approximately 2,866 such developments. According to an agency in the local administration of the Municipality of Sao Paulo, the Department for the Regularization of Land Parceling (RESOLO, *Departamento de Regularização de Parcelamento do Solo*), illegal and irregular land developments and condominiums took up one-fifth of the surface of Sao Paulo: a total of 338.8 million square metres. This map of irregularities does not include favelas and tenement houses. In the municipality's peripheral neighbourhoods, self-built housing units have been estimated at 35 per cent of the total houses.

According to official documents, despite the different concepts applied over the previous decade, interventions in favelas were not able to significantly change the urban scenario. The urbanization efforts geared toward basic sanitation and resettlement into new units have proven not to be adequately sustainable. The former was due to difficulties incorporating settlements that had vastly different urban standards into the formal city. The latter was due to the fact that only partial interventions were attempted, and implemented without the participation of the people, disrupting consolidated relationships and ignoring the residents' investments, thus creating new debt.

Thus, a paradigm shift was proposed: the policy on new housing unit production and the policy on sanitation were to be replaced with holistic actions, which would take into account, in an integrated manner, urban qualification, land regularization, access to public services, facilities and green areas, as well as social programmes.

The priority for action was decided using different criteria regarding social exclusion (defined as a situation of collective deprivation, including poverty, discrimination, subordination, inequity, non-accessibility, lack of public representation). During the first phase, a programme called *Bairro Legal* was implemented in Capão Redondo, Brasilândia, Lajeado, JardimÂngela and Grajaú, areas where 15 per cent or more of the population were in favelas. During the second phase, the programme reached the districts of Campo Limpo, Guaianazes, Iguatemi and Anhanguera.

The Marta Suplicy administration's housing programme was divided into three parts:

1. Stimulus to produce housing units
2. Funding plans
3. Legalization and upgrading of lots and favelas

In previous administrations, the flagship of the low-cost housing policy had been the construction of new units (for favelas, vertical units in building projects – with or without elevators – in the very same site where the favela had been, construction done by contractors). In the Suplicy administration, priority was given to favela urbanization, lot upgrades and to the regularization of occupied areas.

According to the Housing Secretary, the rationale for these actions is based on these actions' better cost-benefit ratio, thus allowing services to be extended to a larger portion of the population in need. Additionally, some of these favelas and land developments were already quite consolidated, and the idea of removing them would be absurd. Therefore, they would be converted into neighbourhoods.

The main focus of that municipality administration was a programme to rehabilitate the Center Rehabilitation Programme (*Programa de Reabilitação do Centro*). Resources were invested in low-cost housing and in rehabilitating vacant commercial lots in order to re-populate the region, which was densely occupied during the day but empty at night.

Period Between 2005–2012

While under the administration of Marta Suplicy, the intention was to re-populate the central area by means of the Center Rehabilitation Programme, the Serra/Kassab administrations (PSDB, Brazilian Social Democracy Party) felt that the programme should not focus on low-income populations. What are seen are moves to restrict the programmes designed to help poorer populations settle in the central areas, although 59 vacant buildings in the central area should have been retrofitted to accommodate low-income families.

The programmes to regularize and grant deeds for irregular properties have continued, as have the re-urbanization actions in some favelas such as Heliópolis (population of 41,118 living in 12,090 units, according to the 2010 census), Paraisópolis (42,826 inhabitants living in 13,064 units) and other large favelas. The Guarapiranga Project, which focuses on sanitation and regulation of settlements surrounding natural basins, was continued. This was probably the first large-scale favela urbanization programme in the city of Sao Paulo. With an end result of more than 100 favelas urbanized, this became an example to model. Many lessons were learned during this period.

As a result of the 7 first interventions, planners realized the importance of implementing public spaces that would ease integration with the surrounding areas.

Favela interventions showed the possibility of restructuring physical spaces while preserving the investments residents had previously made in their housing units, and doing so in a sustainable way while ensuring integration with the neighbouring areas (Sao Paulo, 2008).

The core concept behind this type of intervention is providing permanence for the majority of residents and ensuring the continuity of the investments made in building housing units. Projects are developed specifically for each site, tailoring them to the area's features and topography. Proposals must be discussed with residents, since the communities' cultural diversity is deemed a relevant factor in determining the architectural concepts to use. As of the year 2000, 22,808 families had been served by urbanization projects in favelas, 11,226 of these in the Guarapiranga programme/basin areas; between 2001 and 2008, another 24,855 families benefitted, 7,412 in the Basin area programme (Castilho, 2013: 34). As of 2012, 82,581 families had been served by the favela urbanization programme in the city of Sao Paulo, and 74,621 by the Basin area programme (Sao Paulo, 2012, vol. 1), i.e. 26 per cent of the nearly 5,97,000 favela residences in 2010.

After a settlement has been urbanized, the programme provides regularization in both public and private areas, using the following instruments:

1. ZEIS (Special Social Interest Zones). In ZEIS 1, the parametres for land parceling, especially for plots, paths and setbacks, were more flexible in order to favour the regulation of settlements as they appear.
2. Concession of Special Use for Housing Purposes – (CUEM) – An instrument used widely in the areas under the scope of the Municipal Programme for Public Land Regularization. Article 183 of the Federal Constitution indicates that these concessions are tools of urban policy that ensure the right to residence for individuals inhabiting urban areas up to 250 m^2, living there for five uninterrupted years, as long as they do not own other real estate property. Concession of use does not constitute any transfer of ownership, i.e. the Public Authorities maintain ownership of the urban property as a way to ensure the area was used for its proper social purpose. Concession of use is granted on an individual basis or by undivided interest, and may be registered as with the notary public of the Register of Deeds, being transferable by acts either *inter vivos* or *causa mortis.*
3. Granting of Real Right of Use – In Sao Paulo, this instrument is used under the scope of the Municipal Programme for Public Land Regularization as an alternative for residents who do not meet some of the requirements set by the CUEM. Its intent is to provide legal support for ownership, having the same effect as the Concession of Special Use for Housing Purposes.
4. Authorization of Use – An instrument used under the scope of the Municipal Programme for Public Land Regularization that

authorizes commercial, institutional and service uses of real estate property in programme areas that are already being used for one of the said purposes and whose activities are of interest to the local community.

The regulation of private areas is supported by the following instruments:

1. Urban Demarcation – administrative procedure whereby the public authorities, acting within the bounds of social interest land title regularization, demarcate public or private lands, defining the boundaries, area, location and neighbouring occupants in order to identify the land's occupants and qualify the nature and terms of ownership, without having to file claims for registration modification. Urban demarcation was created by the enactment of law 11.977/09 (My House, My Life programme), and aimed specifically at dealing with the predicament that formed over decades regarding the precarious settlements that could not be regularized by normal methods of regularizing irregular developments, nor by the methods used for regularizing settlements in public areas.
2. Enforcing Ownership – governmental act designed to confer a title recognizing the ownership of real estate property that is the object of the urban demarcation, with due identification of the occupant and time and nature of ownership. Five years after having been granted the title, the beneficiary may register the property with a notary public where the demarcation was registered and convert it into a property right.
3. Special Urban Adverse Possession (*Usucapião especial urbano*) – original form of acquiring property by individuals who have held uninterrupted and undisputed possession of an urban area up to 250m^2 for a minimum five-year term, when the property is used for the purpose of housing for the individual or his/her family; the individual acquires the property rights to the real estate as long as he/she does not own any other rural or urban property.

References

Abreu, M. (1994). 'Reconstruindoumahistóriaesquecida; Origem e Expansão Inicial das Favelas do Rio', *Espaço e Debates,* Sao Paulo, 14(37), pp. 34–46.

Baltrusis, N. (2000). A dinâmica no Mercado Imobiliário Informal naRegião Metropolitana de São Paulo: Umestudo de Caso nas Favelas de Paraisópolis e Nova Conquista. Master's Degree, PUC Campinas.

Banco Nacional Da Habitação. (1966). Relatório de Gestão, Brasília.

Bonduki, N. (1992). Habitação e Auto Gestão. Construindoterritórios de utopia. Rio de Janeiro, FASE.

Cardoso, A.L. (2007). Urbanização de Favelas no Brasil: Revendo a Experiência e Pensando Desafios – Paperpresented at the XII National Conference of the *Associação Nacional de Pósgraduação e Pesquisa emPlanejamento Urbano e Regional*. Belém, Pará, May, CD Rom.

Castilho, J.V. de. (2013). A Favelização do Espaço Urbano em São Paulo. Estudo de Caso: Heliópolis e Paraisópolis, Master's degree dissertation presented to the School of Architecture and Urban Design – *Faculdade de Arquitetura e Urbanismo*, Habitat concentration area.

Guimarães, B. (2000). As vilas Favelas em Belo Horizonte. O desafio dos Números. In Queriroz Ribeiro, *LC (org) O Futuro das Metrópoles: Desigualdade e Governabilidade*, Rio de Janeiro: Revan/FASE, pp. 351–374.

Ibge. (2011, 2010). Census Enhanced the Identification of Subnormal Agglomerates. IBGE, Comunicação Social. Available at http://www.ibge.gov.br

Leeds, A Leeds, E. (1978). A Sociologia do Brasil Urbano, Rio de Janeiro, Zahar.

Pasternak Taschner, S. (1997). Favelas e Cortiços no Brasil: 20 Anos de Pesquisa e Política. Cadernos de Pesquisado, LAP 18, Sao Paulo, FAU-USP.

Pasternak Taschner, S. (1995). 'Squatter Settlements and Slums in Brazil: twenty years of research and policies; In B.C. Aldrich and R.S. Sandhu, *Housing the Urban Poor: Policy and Practice in Developing Countries*, London, Zed Books, pp. 185–223.

Pasternak, S. (2006). São Paulo e suas Favelas. *RevistaPós,* FAUUSP.

Pasternak, S. (2004). 'Desenhando os Espaços da Pobreza', *Cadernos* LAP 39, Sao Paulo: FAUUSP.

Patton, C. and Palmer, E.K. (1988). *Spontaneous Shelter*. Philadelphia, Temple University Press.

São Paulo, Município. (2012). Plano Municipal da habitaçãonaCidade de São Paulo, Sao Paulo: Prefeitura Municipal de São Paulo.

São Paulo, Município. (2008). Urbanização de Favelas, A Experiência de São Paulo. Sao Paulo, BoldariniArquitetura e Urbanismo.

São Paulo, Município. (1992). Secretaria da Habitação e do Desenvolvimento Urbano – Urbanização de Favelas em São Paulo: Umaexperiência de Recuperação Ambiental. Sao Paulo, Prefeitura Municipal de São Paulo.

Soto, H. de. (1990). *The Other Path*, New York: Perennial Library.

Valença, MárcioMoraes and Bonates, Mariana Fialho (2010). The Trajectory of Social Housing Policy in Brazil: From the National Housing Bank to the Ministry of the Cities', *Habitat International34* pp. 165–173.

Zaluar, A.E. and M. Alvito, (org, 1998). *Umséculo de Favela. Rio de Janeiro*, editora da FGV.

9

Review of State Role in Provision of Housing for Low Income Community in the City of Colombo

R.G. Ariyawansa and M.A.N. Rasanjalee Perera

Finding effective and sustainable solutions for the unmet housing needs has been a crucial issue in the world (Joan, 2011; Sandhu, 2008). The situation in developing countries in this regard is much more critical. Urban areas in such countries are facing the problem, particularly in connection with the 'urban poor' in a higher degree owing to the rapid urbanization (Adesoji, 2011; Ariyawansa, 2009; Berner, 2000). Hence, countries have made several attempts to supply housing in different scales through different policies and programmes such as direct construction, slum and shanty upgrading programmes as well as self-help housing programmes, etc. for the raising demand of poor communities in urban areas (Barnabas, 2006; Ganepola www.hdm.lth.se/alumni/al accessed on 10. 03.2010; Wakely, 2008).

However, many countries have not yet solved the problem of homelessness; instead the problem has been continuing. This is clear according to the literature in the last 10–15 years. For instance, as per the literature in early 2000, the annual demand for houses from new families and replacements was said about 35 million in urban areas in developing countries during the next two decades (Erguden, 2001). Further, the previous estimates shows that more than 600 million people in world cities were homeless or lived in life or health threatening conditions (Berner, 2000). About 7 million of people were living in slums and shanties only in the city of Delhi (Sivam, 2003). In Sri Lanka, more than 50 per cent of total population was living in under-serviced settlements in the city of Colombo (UDA, 1998). And as a whole, 40–50 per cent of population in many large cities in developing countries lived in informal settlements in 1987 (UNCHS, 1987).[1]

After a decade of the above status, new literature and data sources also reveal that the housing problem of the world cities is the same or worsening in regard to some aspects of the problem (Adesoji, 2011; Claudio and Christopher, 2011). Accordingly, 'fifty-five million new slum dwellers have been added to the global population since 2000. Sub-Saharan Africa has a slum population of 199.5 million, South Asia 190.7 million, East Asia 189.6 million, Latin America and the Caribbean 110.7 million, Southeast Asia 88.9 million, West Asia 35 million and North Africa 11.8 million. It is unacceptable today that about 1 billion people live in slums and other sub-standard housing, with precarious security of tenure and inadequate water and sanitation' (Claudio and Christopher, 2011).

In this way, it seems that finding a suitable solution to provide necessary housing for urban poor is a huge challenge to city authorities. As far as the Sri Lankan situation is concerned, the country's urban housing problem also has been continuing similar to the world situation. It is evident in the literature in the beginning of 2000s and up to the present that there is a continuing housing problem in connection with the urban poor. For instant, the Sri Lanka Central Bank annual report in 2003 estimated the then housing shortage in the country as 4,00,000 units.[2] The report also indicated that the shortage was expected to increase to 600,000 units by year 2010. This implies that the annual demand for new housing could not be met by implemented housing delivery projects and the market system in the country including the housing for the urban poor. According to the housing index, total approval of housing in the city of Colombo has been increased by 19.6 per cent during the period. However, according to the total building approvals index, demand for all buildings has increased by 13.1 per cent (Central Bank of Sri Lanka in www.centralbank.ac.lk accessed on 07.03.2010). Hence, it is clear that housing demand in the city is more than the other buildings during the period. While, the continuation of the housing problem in the city of Colombo is the same as the country in general, some aspects of the problem are growing rapidly in Colombo such as affordability, slum and shanty dwellings and lack of adequate infrastructure, etc. (Ariyawansa, 2010; Rajapaksa, 2010; Wakely, 2008).

In addition, the above shortfall was supposed to be increased due to the December 2004 tsunami devastation. Many urban areas of the country such as Hambanthota, Galle, Matara and many urbanized coastal areas in Southern Sri Lanka were highly affected by the tsunami and, thereby, the urban housing problem in the country was aggravated. Housing problem of the city of Colombo also was heavily affected by the war situation during the last 30 years (Sepani, Zainudeen, and Weddikkara, 2006). Moreover, analysis of the quality of housing reveals that significant need of upgrading in existing housing will determine the real need of urban housing (UDA, 1998). Further, the official website of the National Housing Development Authority (NHDA) of Sri Lanka describes the continuing housing problem of the country in general, including the urban housing problem as stated below.

> Since independence in 1948, the successive governments have taken many efforts to fulfil the housing needs in Sri Lanka. But it was impossible to secure expected result on these efforts. Whatever talking in political arena, the problem for housing in Sri Lanka seriously worsened rapidly. It is experienced that the problem for housing was not talked about a major problem in Sri Lanka. However after the unexpected Tsunami catastrophe in Sri Lanka in 2004, it was created a new atmosphere to focus the immediate attention on the housing problem of this country. (www.nhda.gov.lk, accessed on 22.02.2013)

Recent literature and the census provide clear evidence for the continuing nature of the problem of urban low income housing in countries. For instant, at the inaugural session of World Habitat Day 2007 conference, UN-Habitat Executive Director, Mrs Anna Tibaijuka said that '... the UN-Habitat research showed that across the planet the rate of slum formation was today almost the same as the rate of urban growth. This implies that most of the people who are migrating to cities, and who are born in cities, are joining with the urban poor and slum dwellers'. This is the same situation in the city of Colombo. It is identified that during the last six decades after independence, Sri Lanka was unable to reduce the percentage of slum and shanty dwellers in the city of Colombo, even though it is the wealthiest region in the country (Rajapaksa, 2010).

Therefore, to meet the rising demand for housing by the urban poor, new approaches and strategies are very essential. 'What is the best or a better housing delivery mechanism?' is still a problem to all countries. In Sri Lanka, as provider based housing delivery systems are heavily expensive, many community participatory based policies have been tested. Currently the market mechanism has also been widely trusted to supply housing. Theoretically, market based solutions expect a situation of a higher degree of (may be 100%) community responsibility in provision of their housing. This means that through the market mechanism, it is expected that families should build or purchase built houses. For this, accessibility for all major ingredients of housing such as land, materials, and finance is the key determinant. Can this be expected directly for lower and even lower-middle class families? It is, in fact, a difficult target. Therefore, what is needed is to find a mechanism(s) of a combination of public, community and the market participations, which is a general argument in global housing policy debates. In fact, it is needed to determine the different roles of the public sector, markets, and the families, etc. Considering all these circumstances, this paper aims to discuss how Sri Lanka has been struggling with the low income housing problem with special reference to the city of Colombo.

Housing Policy of Sri Lanka and Urban Housing Problem

Current Situation

According to Ashraff[3] (2007), it is the experience that planning and management of housing, particularly for urban low income communities, is a very complex and complicated process. Therefore, she emphasized that the country's housing policy framework should be a more understanding and flexible, one that simultaneously makes an adequate response for changing demands in well-planned human settlements taking into consideration the population density, effective land use planning and environmental sustainability. Similarly, she argued that the solution to the housing situation should not be ended by keeping poor people in high-rise apartments for the sake of so-called city development. Hence, as it is described, provision of low-income urban housing is a complex matter and the existing housing policy is being challenged.

When it is considered the housing in Sri Lanka, the housing issue in rural areas and estate sector in the country is somewhat different from that of urban areas. Most of rural families living in owner-occupied houses, of which some are marginally fulfilling the requirements needed for a decent family. In general, rural households suffer from land tenure issues and, thereby, access to housing finance. These are the same issues in the urban sector while higher land prices and cost of construction are some additional barriers for poor. Hence, countrywide housing sector is suffering from issues of quantity as well as quality of housing of poor. Therefore, according to the traditional definition, nearly 13,00,000 housing units require improvements to make them habitable islandwide (www.nhda.ac.lk accessed on 07.03.2010). Particularly, in Sri Lanka, urban housing problem is severe than other areas of the country.

As a nation, Sri Lanka has been making considerable efforts to mitigate the housing issue. Earlier, the state agencies undertook the total responsibility alone according to the adopted economic policy in the country and the world at that time. However, responsibility was transferred to the community and the market in different scales time to time. For instance, in the period before 1977 when the country adopted a closed economic policy, the state attempted to provide houses for homeless families. This was changed along with the 1.5 Million Housing Programme, which was implemented according to the participatory approach which altered the housing policy. Thereafter, most of housing programmes adopted this feature in Sri Lanka. In fact, the community participation is a highly accepted and known concept in the housing sector in the country; particularly in the areas of urban low and lower-middle class communities. In this connection, slum and shanty upgrading projects were a popular effort in Colombo.

Currently, several steps have been taken to strengthen the market system and the construction industry particularly targeting the urban poor. For that purpose, it has introduced cost-effective construction technology and energy saving, eco-friendly designs to suit different climatic conditions to the beneficiaries, providing land tenure and services and micro financing for urban poor. Many advantages of such measures are expected. For instance, the enabled beneficiaries involved in the construction of their own house have a house according to their affordability and aspirations. Furthermore, it is expected to have a house which is worth over five times of that made by the direct investment in construction (in www.nhda.ac.lk accessed on 07.03.2010).

The former Minister of Housing and Construction of Sri Lanka, Mrs Ferial Ashraff (2006) said that 'the people who are in need of houses should provide their fullest cooperation to the government as it is difficult to provide housing facilities by the government itself', while addressing 2006 World Habitat Day National Conference held at Bandaranaike Memorial International Conference Hall (BMICH) on 2 October 2006 (as available in www.nhda.ac.lk accessed on 07.03.2010). This speech very clearly indicates the state capacity and the interest of changing the housing delivery policy. This statement implies two things: the government is unable to bear the full cost of housing even for the needy families and there is a need for effective community and market participation in housing. Therefore, as the cost of urban sector (cost of land and materials etc.) is more than rural sector, urban low income housing problem in the country has become a huge challenge.

Further, the vision and the Mission of the Ministry of Construction, Engineering Services, Housing and Common Amenities of Government of Sri Lanka show the current housing policy directions. The vision is stated as '*development of sustainable settlements and a re-awakening of the construction industry*'. And the mission is stated as '*creation of a planned, environmentally friendly and high quality construction industry by strengthening Sri Lankan entrepreneurs, professionals and labour force with skills and resources and contributing to economic development by generating settlements with basic facilities through community participation*' (http://houseconmin.gov.lk/, accessed on 21.02.2013). The vision and the mission of the ministry clearly indicate two phenomena 'sustainable settlement' and 'community participation', as the direction of the current housing policy of the country. However, these directions have not directly addressed the problem of urban low income housing. Instead of that, one can argue that the vision and mission of the ministry may aggravate the problem of urban low income housing. Lack of suitable land (Jayaratna, 2002) for housing and cost of material and labour, approvals and financing issues (Rajapaksa, 2010), etc. which are severe hindrance in achieving housing for the urban poor have not been directly addressed by these policy directions.

Evolution of the Policy: The History in Brief

As the housing problem has been continued, housing policy should also be a continually formulated or adjusted in finding better solutions for the problem. In urban contexts, there is an urgent need of unconventional policy as the housing problem is becoming more and more complex than other areas of countries. This is a matter of huge debate among the housing-stakeholders in the world. Also, in many countries, including

Sri Lanka, housing policy has become an integrated part of the housing problem. Countries are still struggling to formulate suitable housing policies particularly for urban low income communities.

The mode of the solution for housing is determined according to the socio-economic and political context of a country and its overall policies. Therefore, urban areas were not highly emphasized as it is today. For instance, prior to 1977, Sri Lanka practiced a state-sector oriented (closed) economic and political policy. The social context of the country was also confined mostly to the local norms and practices. Also rural development and agriculture were more emphasized. Therefore, the urban housing problem was not heavily recognized. Also, the housing provision of the country was taken as a total responsibility of the state and in turn the provider-based approaches were practiced even for the housing requirement of the urban poor. However, along with the overall political and economic policy changes of the country by 1977 and thereafter, a community-based approach and the market-based approach, were adopted in both rural and urban housing sectors. It was also needed to formulate new policies along with the rapid urbanization under the market oriented economic policy. High-rise apartments through land liberation became a strategy for urban low income housing problem in Colombo. These policies are continued up to now. However, there is a mix of approaches for housing provision in the country. Generally in area of urban low income housing, public sector intervention has been essential requirement and it is playing a crucial role from direct construction to various facilitator roles.

It seems that there were no specific attempts taken as policy on housing during the colonial era of the country. However, along with the huge investments in plantations, there were many physical developments including residential and non-residential buildings (Bandarage, 1983). The legacy of such initiatives has provided positive as well as negative lessons for the present policy framework, including the urban housing sector of the country. After independence in 1948, the first purposely designed comprehensive housing policy was prepared in 1954. This was officially introduced with the establishment of the National Housing Act No. 37 of 1954, Department of National Housing, and the National Housing Fund (Mirihagalle, in http://www.lth.se/fileadmin/ hdmalumni/papers accessed on 10. 02.2010). However, at that time, the 'urban low income housing' was not a severe issue as it appears today in the country.

In the communist political era of the country during the early 1970s, the government policy was based on social equity and, therefore, the state sector took housing as an obligation, revising the previous policies built based on colonial lessons. Accordingly, the government strengthened the legal system of the country by introducing several housing related laws such as the Ceiling on Housing Property Law, Rent Control Act, Protection of Tenants Act, Apartment Ownership Law, Common Amenities Board Law, and Land Reform Act, etc. Also the country accepted provider-based expensive housing as a policy until the late 1970s in the country. Accordingly, in urban areas, public housing schemes with apartments were established for poor communities.

A drastic change in the socio-economic and political arena of the country took place in late 1970s (after 1977), leading to the promotion of many housing initiatives through innovative policies. Some of influential steps connected with the urban low income housing can be summarized as follows:

- State role was changed from provider of housing to facilitator of housing provision.
- Community participatory policy was adopted enabling the empowering of families and the whole society to build houses by families.
- Innovative housing finance through micro-finance schemes was established.
- Institutional framework was enhanced.
- Nationwide housing programmes by state patronage created a culture of housing throughout the country.
- During 1989–1993, the concept of community participation in housing and community development programmes in slums and shanties' was the main strategy in Sri Lanka. The state involvement in the above programme gave small housing loans as incentives.
- Security of tenure of lands was given by the state to encourage families to invest their own resources in housing (Dolapihilla, in http://www.lth.se/fileadmin/hdmalumni/papers accessed on 10. 02. 2010).

In the meantime, along with the political change, further major transformations in the housing policy were put in place in 1990s with regard to the urban low income housing. Particularly, the housing policy makers attempted to integrate the market system with the participatory approach. This policy initiative was supported by the proposal made by the Presidential Task Force on Housing and Urban Development in 1998. This was planned with a view to provide decent houses for all poor communities in the city of Colombo while assuring the supply of required land for the overall city development. Through this strategic policy, it was planned to liberalize land from dwellers who established their housing horizontally by means of providing new houses in vertically developed high-rise apartments for all under-serviced settlers in the city. This programme was implemented in 1999 under the 'Sustainable Township Programme', which targeted the total low-income community in the city of Colombo with some innovative strategies with public, private and community participation. This was a dual purpose project to provide houses for poor in high-rise and to increase land supply for the commercial and the environment activities in the city.

Accordingly, it seems that all successive governments of Sri Lanka had implemented various approaches in order to increase the availability of housing for the urban poor in the city of Colombo; however, it has not been able to come up with a long-lasting solution. Even at present, the city is under the pressure of adverse effects of low-income housing problem.

Throughout the housing policy evolution, Sri Lanka has some landmark developments, some of which highly relate with the urban low income housing problem can be indicated below:

- Establishing the first Ministry of Housing in 1952.
- National Housing Department which was established in 1952.
- Ceiling on Housing Property Law of 1973.
- National Housing Development Authority was established in 1977.
- Urban Development Authority was established in 1977.
- Hundred Thousand Houses Programme (1984–1988).
- 1.5 million Houses Programme (1993).
- Presidential Task Force on Housing and Urban Development (1998).
- Sustainable Township Programme with emphasis on the city of Colombo (1999).
- Pura Naguma with emphasis on the city of Colombo (at present).
- Jana Sevana: One-million housing project including the city of Colombo.

Actors of Provision of Housing for the Urban Poor

The most significant actor in the housing sector should be the households. In fact, the households represent the 'demand side' of the market, playing different roles such as 'key beneficiaries' in the housing delivery system, and the 'most important participants' in community participatory approaches. Apart from the households, there are several actors representing the institutional framework of the housing sector in the country including the state sector, private and non-government sector institutions. The following table includes the key actors and their role in brief.

Table 9.1 *Key actors and their role in the urban low income housing sector in Sri Lanka (relevant to the last two-three decades, 1980–2010)*

Actor	*Role*
Ministry of Construction, Engineering Services, Housing and Common Amenities	Formulating policies, encouraging stakeholders at national level, keep up with international links, planning and implementing national level housing projects especially for needy people.
National Housing Development Authority (NHDA) provider of housing on behalf of the state	Carry out on-site upgrading and management of urban housing projects. Carry out housing projects for lower, middle, and upper middle class people. Role of the NHDA in providing housing for low income community in Colombo city is significant through public housing schemes and other projects.
Urban Development Authority (UDA)	Preparation of zonal plans, building regulations and provide building approvals and approval for special projects for urban low income communities. Conducting some special housing projects for urban low income communities. Under the Colombo regeneration, many housing projects are undertaken.
Land registry, Local Authorities and Provincial Secretarial Offices	Registration of deeds mainly by the land registry. Approval of site plans and building plans by the local authorities.
Electricity, Water and Telecommunication companies and state agencies	Provision of services and maintenance.
Sustainable Townships Programme (STP)/Real Estate Exchange Pvt. Ltd. (REEL) (this was active from 1998 up to recent past)	Carry out housing projects for urban under-serviced settlements in the city of Colombo, through land sharing and redevelopment process.
Urban Settlements Improvement Programme	Provision of water and sanitary facilities in urban settlements.

Cont'd...

...Cont'd

NGOs and CBOs	Community-based housing development, provision of infrastructure facilities and awareness programmes for low income communities.
Private Developers	Constructing houses for medium and high rise as well as detached houses for middle and upper income community, and improving and selling land, etc. This may provide several benefits for low income communities like career opportunities.
Professional bodies and professionals	Surveyors, Valuers, Architects, Engineers, Quantity Surveyors, lawyers, etc. providing their professional services.
Individuals and organized informal sector	Brokerage, finance, information, etc.
Material manufacturers and vendors	Providing materials, transportation, credit facilities, etc.
Contractors and labour suppliers	Providing labours and supervisory services.
Housing Development and Financing Corporation, State Mortgage Investment Bank, other banks and Financial institutes	Provision of housing finance. Formal sector role in financing for urban low income housing is mainly through public projects.

However, the state role in urban low-income housing is more crucial as a facilitator. The following table briefly indicates the key activities played by the state sector according to the Sri Lanka experience.

Table 9.2 *State role and responsibilities*

Role	*Details*
Top-level policy maker	Having taken into consideration the nature of the economic situation of the country, political aspects, and resources etc.; in a macro level, different governments have formulated different policies and implemented from time to time regarding land and property development, proving houses for urban poor, etc.
Regulating agency	Zoning, planning and building regulations, environment and density control, creating policies and laws for land and property ownerships etc. Providing land title/certificate for urban poor, formulating special regulation for urban poor, etc.
Property administrator	In doing this, state encourages private sector investors in real estate production by offering different concessions such as tax, duty, and land at concessionary terms, etc. In the meantime, urban low income communities are protected by ensuring their land rights.
Developer	Direct housing construction for lower income and lower middle income communities and some other property for public uses of poor communities.

Cont'd...

...Cont'd

Financer	Providing finance through state banks, special schemes and employer's loans, etc.
Infrastructure developer	Water supply, electricity, drainage, sewerage system, roads, and sanitations, etc. are provided through local authorities, Water Supply Board, and Electricity Board, etc.
Social infrastructure	Provision of facilities for education, public transportation, health, security, law and order, environmental safety, etc.
Operation and maintenance manager	This function is mainly for the state rental housing, slum gardens and public places. State body called Common Amenities Board was established particularly for this. Further, all local authorities are responsible for the maintenance of essential services.
Landlord/land supplier	Still the state sector acts as the major landowner, buyer, seller, acquirer, giver, etc. Providing land title/certificate for already occupied land and providing land for landless families, etc.

Sources: Author compiled the table using data and information from Dolapihilla (2000), Siriwardana (1999), Central Bank of Sri Lanka (1998)

Instead of providing built houses for the poor of the poorest, the state role was changed to facilitator from the provider of housing for urban low income communities. In this process beneficiaries have become more active players. The state role is, however, to stimulate the community for the higher level of active participation. The following are some of actions taken by the Sri Lankan government to empower the urban low income households in construction of their houses during the recent past.

(a) Stimulating low cost housing methods and technologies.
(b) Rehabilitation and development of traditional skills in the construction industry.
(c) Make available raw material and services to support small and large projects and programmes.
(d) Training of youth in masonry, carpentry, electrical wiring and bar bending and so on in line with the new technology.
(e) Encouraging micro-finance on housing.
(f) Scientific studies and experiments on building materials, techniques, etc.
(g) Promoting the stakeholders through mass media.
(h) Keeping the housing as the first level matter in political debates and manifestoes.
(i) Strengthening the market system as a whole.

Major Programmes Undertaken by the NHDA

The NHDA has taken measures to implement several programmes in rural areas where the majority of the people are living, and urban areas as well as for estate workers in plantation areas. The following table briefs the present and past projects and programmes implemented mainly by the National Housing Development Authority (NHDA).

Table 9.3 *Current and previous housing projects implemented by the NHDA for urban poor*

Programme	*Details*
'Jana Sevana' Housing Programme	This programme is mainly implemented to provide housing facilities to the poor community who cannot construct a house by obtaining a loan including the urban low income communities. Also this attends on special housing projects such as disable soldiers and public servants housing, etc.
Urbanization and The Provider Approach	This programme aims to fulfil the urbanization needs that is taking place at a rapid speed by putting up high rise buildings as to release land as far as possible in urban areas for other non-residential purposes.
Urban Renewal and Construction of Flats/Relocation	This programme aims to develop substantial number of low density, dilapidated settlements or flats located within the inner city areas in a planned development effort. This expects to release lands to be used for appropriate development maximizing the utility value of valuable lands.
Construction of Flats/Housing For Sale	This programme aims to cater the demand for 'ready to occupy' houses where a huge demand exists in the city of Colombo. This does not target poor families. Even the lower-middle class may not be the target group. By this programme, houses are constructed to sell in the open market. The quality of housing may be questionable compared to the private sector houses. This indirectly benefits the urban poor.
Public Servants Housing	This programme aims to provide housing facilities within close proximity to Colombo for the large number of public servants who travel daily to office spending a larger proportion of their time on travelling. These houses are supposed to offer concessionary terms and cost of land may be taken at subsidized rates in determining the price of houses. This programme directly increases the housing supply. Question of quality level exists in case of even these houses.
Site and Service Blocks with Housing Assistance	Through this programme, NHDA mainly aims to cater the low and lower-middle income groups living in urban settlements which will not be covered under the earlier mentioned programmes. The programme includes regularization of tenure, offering the tenure, provision of basic amenities, etc.

Cont'd...

...Cont'd

Low Income Community Development Programme	Under this programme, agencies like JICA, USIP, and UNICEF extend financial support as well as human support through volunteers for educating and improving the living standards of densely populated low income settlements in and around the city of Colombo. Through this, housing condition of the city is improved.
The 'Million Houses Programme'	This programme was implemented during 1984–1988 covering the entire country. This was undertaken mainly as a provider-based approach. Through this project, low income communities in Colombo were provided with constructed housed.
The 'Million-and-a-Half Houses Programme'	This was implemented during 1989–1993, as very innovative programmes changing the role of state from a provider to a facilitator of a people based housing process. This was the first mass scale housing programme implemented in the country empowering the benefited families including low income families in the city of Colombo.
'Sustainable Cities Programme' (in collaboration with other state agencies like CMC, UDA)	This was expected to implement late 1990s enabling Colombo for a rapid development. This was the largest housing programme proposed for the Colombo city to provide houses for all families living in under-serviced settlements while increase the supply of land for the city development through liberalizing some lands used for residential purpose. This was an innovative approach combining of the state, community and the markets.
'Pura-Naguma'	This newly launched programme may contribute immensely to upgrade the housing quality of all under-services settlements in the city of Colombo.

Source: Authors compiled the table using the data available in www.nhda.ac.lk accessed on 07.03.2010; and in http://www.lth.se/fileadmin/hdm/alumni/ papers accessed on 07.03.2010

Current Housing Needs in the City of Colombo

The urban population in Sri Lanka was 31,49,852 as of 2010; which was 15 per cent of the then total population (http://www.indexmundi.com/facts/sri-lanka/urban, accessed on 09.03.2013), which comprised Municipal Council areas, Urban Council areas and built-up areas in Pradeshiya Sabhas (Name of the local authorities rural areas). However, the actual percentage is considered to be more than this figure in the whole country of which about 70 per cent is concentrated in the Western Region, including Colombo, Gampaha, and Kalutara districts. The growth rate of total population in the country is less than one per cent according to the 2012 census, i.e. 0.7 per cent, while the urban areas recorded above the national growth as 1.1 per cent in 2010 (http://www.indexmundi.

com/sri_lanka/demographics_ profile.html, accessed on 09.03.2013). The following table presents the growth rates of population in the country and the districts of the Western province.

Table 9.4 *Population growth in Sri Lanka and districts of Western province*

Region	*Population*			*Average growth Rate (%)*		
	1981 Census	*2001 Census*	*2011 Census*	*1981–2001*	*2001–2011*	*2001–2011*
Sri Lanka	1,48,46,274	1,87,97,257	2,02,77,597	1.16	1.00	0.71
Colombo	16,75,847	22,39,696	23,23,826	1.43	1.05	0.35
Gampaha	13,67,813	20,60,470	22,98,588	2.01	1.67	1.02
Kalutara	8,23,964	10,65,635	12,14,880	1.26	1.25	1.23

Source: Authors compiled the table using the data of the Department of Census and Statistics Sri Lanka, 2012.

In fact, it shows that the Sri Lanka's population grew only by 0.7 per cent annually over the last 10 years. According to the population census of 2012, the Western Province (Colombo, Kalutara and Gampaha districts) of the country accounts for the majority of concentrated population. It is about 28.8 per cent of the total population in the country. This population data implies that the housing needs of the Western Province are higher than the rest of the country. Instead of the total amount, the higher growth rate of the Western Province further indicates the raising demand for the housing in the area. According to the 2012 census, population growth rates of the Colombo district is 0.35 per cent, Kalutara district is 1.23 per cent and Gampaha district is 1.02 per cent. Except Colombo, other districts record higher growth rates more than the country's growth rate.

Further, it is evident that Colombo has recorded continuous population growth at an increasing rate according to the previous census. However, this picture has changed during the last decade. This may be due to the fact of immigrants to Western Province opting to settle down in Gampaha and Kalutara districts. Migration from other districts to the Free Trade Zones in Katunayake and Biyagama has contributed to the population growth visible in Gampaha district (Department of Census and Statistics Sri Lanka, 2012; http://www.colombopage.com/archive_12A/Jun27_1340813142CH.php, accessed on 07.02.2013). However, according to the following table, it seems that the population growth rate of Colombo has been continuously increasing.

Table 9.5 *Population density and growth rate of city of Colombo (1871 – 2010)*

Census Year	Extent (Ha)	Population	Density (P/Ha)	Growth Rate
1871	2,448.6	98,847	40	–
1881	2,448.6	1,10,509	45	1.18
1891	2,448.6	1,26,825	52	1.48
1901	2,720.6	1,54,691	56	2.20
1911	3,091.1	2,11,274	68	3.66
1921	3,350.3	2,24,163	73	0.61
1931	3,368.4	2,84,155	84	2.67
1946	3,438.4	3,62,074	105	1.83
1953	3,593.9	4,25,081	118	2.48
1963	3,710.4	5,11,639	138	2.04
1971	3,711.0	5,62,430	152	1.24
1981	3,711.0	5,87,647	158	0.45
1994	3,729.0	7,21,443	193	1.75
2010	3,729.0	10,00,000	268	2.42

Source: http://www.buildsrilanka.com/CDP/8_City%20of%20Colombo.htm accessed 11 February 2013.

Even though the total population is the primary determinant of residential property requirements, population growth rate is also an important variable in determining the housing needs in a city. Accordingly, it seems that the Colombo district growth rate is reducing while the Colombo city population growth rate is increasing. Referring to this, Wakely (2008) describes that there are some irregular characteristics in urban population in Sri Lanka. Net migration and natural population growth are factors to increase the population. The pattern of migration, which is highly dynamic in a city like Colombo as an immerging cosmopolitan city, is also a complex matter in determining the real requirement of housing quantity and the quality (Parnwell, 1993).

Higher population growth has created specific housing and housing-related issues in Colombo and suburbs. Generally, increased population is a positive factor for industries, commerce and businesses as populated cities provide a large pool of labour and a large domestic customer base for markets. Yet, the worse case is the challenge of providing decent accommodation to permanent dwellers and regular visitors. In connection with the city of Colombo, the housing problem is severe due to its multiple facets as indicated in some analysis. For instance:

- The magnitude of the housing problem in the city is very high as around 50 per cent of the city population is living in underserved settlements (UDA, 1998). In these underserved settlements, many severe housing issues have been identified. However, it is recorded that there are considerable numbers of such settlements, which have not yet been assisted by any housing development projects satisfactorily until the recent past (Rajapaksa, 2010).
- More of such settlements are in environmentally sensitive areas and reservations along the railway, and canal banks, etc.
- They are heavily suffering from lack of basic infrastructure services and health as well as many basic necessities required even for an ordinary family.
- Further, the land price/value of city centres have gone up rapidly due to the severe scarcity of land in the city.
- Therefore, compensation to dwellers in slum and shanties is a big problem. Other problem is, with scarcity and high price, providing alternative land is also difficult. Therefore, only available alternative is relocating families in high-rise apartments. This solution is financially expensive, technically riskier, and socially less attractive and more complicated.
- City development has been obstructed by settlements. There are low density dilapidated underserved settlements (urban slums and public servant/labour quarters) in prime urban locations, which are potential for urban development in Colombo (UDA, 1998).
- Lack of Infrastructure facilities: The underserved settlements that have already been regularized and allocated for construction of houses for the poor communities in urban areas are adversely affected due to the lack of individual infrastructure services and other shelter related assistance (www.nhda.ac.lk accessed on 07.03.2010).
- Maintenance of Public Housing Schemes: Several low-cost housing schemes delivered by the government on rental basis in urban areas have been suffered from maintenance and other related issues (www.nhda.ac.lk accessed on 07.03.2010). This is a critical issue as most of schemes are old and poorly managed. As the maintenance of the public housing schemes has become a severe issue, the NHDA that has the management authority of schemes began to transfer the ownership of houses so far constructed islandwide to recipients of the houses (in www.nhda.ac.lk accessed on 07.03.2010). This mechanism

generates some benefits as well as shortcomings. Transferring of the ownership may increase market activities in forms of formal transactions. However, the said issue i.e. maintenance problems, may become more serious if newly built maintenance bodies will not be effective and efficient.

- Households' Satisfaction: Satisfaction of households in public housing schemes is questionable. It has been examined empirically considering a few important aspects such as 'privacy', 'facilities', 'security', 'housing unit conditions', 'neighbourhood', and 'location'. This was evaluated using four scales as 'highly', 'somewhat', 'less', and 'no'. Table 9.6 shows the summary of the results.

It is very clear that 'higher' satisfaction for all aspects in each and every scheme is 50 per cent and for many it is even as low as 25 per cent. Many have refused to answer. The majority are in 'somewhat' and 'less' satisfaction levels.

Housing Requirements of the Urban Low Income Community

Generally, in Sri Lanka, irrespective of the sector either urban or rural, human settlement issues are more prominent among low income groups. However, in urban areas of Sri Lanka, demand for housing is acute due to internal migration in addition to the prevailing higher population growth. In Colombo district and other main urban centres with higher economic activities, there is an immediate need for more than 75,000 housing units for the low income communities alone by the year 2007 (Ashraff, 2007). This figure is presumably higher in the present context.

The national ratio of home ownership in Sri Lanka is about 80 per cent. However, in urban areas it stands at about 60 per cent. The reason for the lower percentage in urban areas is said to be the higher price of land, usage of large stock of rental housing and other categories of shelter in urban areas compared to rural areas. It seems that particularly in the Western province and even in regional urban areas, demand for houses and urban infrastructure is expanding rapidly with the population growth and urbanization. For instance, the population is growing at 0.7 per cent annually in the country whereas the urban population is growing at a higher rate as indicated by more than 1–2 per cent in many urbanized districts like Gampaha, Kalutara, Galle, Kandy, etc. Estimates indicate that more than a half of the population of the country will be living in urban areas by 2016. This will raise more demand of urban infrastructure including suitable housing and necessary facilities.

Table 9.6 *Satisfaction of households in public housing schemes in Colombo city*

Aspects		*Satisfaction levels in Housing Schemes*				
		Scheme 01	*Scheme 02*	*Scheme 03*	*Scheme 04*	*Scheme 05*
Privacy	Higher	9.3%	16.3%	14.0%	20.9%	39.5%
	Somewhat	29.1%	23.6%	23.6%	9.1%	14.5%
	Less	Not replied	Not replied	50.0%	Not replied	50.0%
Facilities	Higher	12.9%	22.6%	19.4%	35.5%	9.7%
	Somewhat	21.3%	19.7%	18.0%	4.9%	36.1%
	Less	37.5%	12.5%	37.5%	Not replied	12.5%
Neighbourhood quality	Higher	9.1%	22.7%	9.1%	22.7%	36.4%
	Somewhat	24.6%	14.5%	21.7%	13.0%	26.1%
	Less	14.3%	57.1%	28.6%	Not replied	Not replied
	No	Not replied	50.0%	50.0%	Not replied	Not replied
Security	Higher	5.3%	26.3%	15.8%	23.7%	28.9%
	Somewhat	32.7%	12.2%	22.4%	10.2%	22.4%
	Less	15.4%	30.8%	23.1%	Not replied	30.8%
About the Housing Unit	Highly	Not replied	27.8%	16.7%	38.9%	16.7%
	Somewhat	25.0%	19.1%	19.1%	10.3%	26.5%
	Less	18.2%	18.2%	27.3%	Not replied	36.4%
	No	33.3%	Not replied	33.3%	Not replied	33.3%
Location of the Scheme	Highly	Not replied	31.3%	12.5%	37.5%	18.8%
	Somewhat	19.7%	19.7%	21.1%	11.3%	28.2%
	Less	40.0%	10.0%	30.0%	Not replied	20.0%
	No	66.7%	Not replied	Not replied	Not replied	33.3%

Source: Ariyawansa, 2010

The average annual new demand for houses in Sri Lanka was estimated to be around 1,00,000. In addition, the estimated housing shortage was 3,50,000 in recent years. Further, about 30 per cent (about 1.3 million) of the existing houses are semi-permanent or improvised or unclassified needing substantial improvements as well (Samaranayake, in http://www.lth.se/fileadmin/hdm/alumni/papers accessed on accessed on 12.02.2009).

The increase of housing units in the country during a decade period according to the last census is indicated in the following table. During the inter-census period of 1991–2001, in the 18 districts, where the enumeration was done, the number of occupied housing units has increased from 24,90,114 to 39,69,211 by 59.4 per cent. The salient feature in this statistic is the higher rate of increase in Western province which is the most urbanized region in the country in the period. As per the census 2012, increase of houses in these three districts are 17.5 per cent, 24.4 per cent, and 17.7 per cent, respectively. These figures are very low compared to the previous census period. The reason may be that the country experienced a drastic change in socio-economic context as a result of the liberalization of economic policy during 1980s.

Table 9.7 *Housing units and inter-census increase 1991, 2001 and 2012*

District	*Occupied housing units*			*Inter-census increase*	
	Census 1981	*Census 2001*	*Census 2012*	*Number and % 1981–2001*	*Number and % 2001–2012*
Colombo	272,489	473,045	5,55,926	2,00,556 (73.6%)	82,881 (17.5%)
Gampaha	2,65,954	4,75,847	5,92,064	2,09,893 (78.9%)	1,16,217 (24.4 %)
Kalutara	1,60,423	2,45,784	2,99,321	85,361 (53.2%)	43,537 (17.7 %)
Sri Lanka	24,90,114	39,69,027	51,65,331	14,78,913 (59.4)	n/a*

* Note: Country growth rate was not calculated as 1981, 2001 census were done only for 18 districts.

Source: Authors compiled the table using the data of the Department of Census and Statistics Sri Lanka, 2012

Quality of Housing in the Country and the Western Province (Colombo, Kalutara, and Gampaha Districts)

It is also important to analyse the key areas of housing to understand the depth and width of the problem in terms of quantity and quality. There were 40,54,385 households in 39,69,211 occupied housing units in 18 districts[4] according to the 2001 census. It has been identified that more than 98 per cent of the occupied housing units in all the three sectors have one family and a very small number of housing units have two or more families. The average size of household in the 18 districts is 4.2 persons and the average occupant per room is 1.1. Comparison with 1991 census figures reveals that the average size of household has reduced by 0.7 from 4.9 and average number of occupants per room has also reduced by 1.0 from 2.1.[5]

According to the latest census in 2012 which has covered all the country, the average occupancy rate in a house of the country is 3.9. It is in Colombo 3.01, Gampaha 2.31, and Kalutara 2.75. Hence, within the province, Colombo seems to have lesser availability of houses for the population.

As far as the quality of housing is concerned, it seems that districts in Western province are comparatively in a better situation. However, there are some areas to be seriously taken into account. Table 9.8 shows the general picture of the type of houses in the country and the Western province by year 2012.

Table 9.8 *Type of houses in the country and districts in the Western province*

Region	*Total Houses*	*% of Types of houses*			
		Single house	*Flats/condo*	*Twin houses*	*Raw/slum*
Sri Lanka	51,65,331	93.3	0.7	0.7	5.3
Colombo	5,55,926	90.3	5.0	0.5	4.2
Gampaha	5,92,064	95.2	0.2	0.4	4.2
Kalutara	2,99,321	97	0.2	0.6	2.2

Source: Authors compiled the table using the data of the Department of Census and Statistics, Sri Lanka, 2012.

It is very clear that the majority of residential condominiums are centred to Colombo. Underlined fact is that more than 90 per cent of houses are single units even in the highly urbanized districts i.e. in the Western province of the country. This is a critical factor with regard to the highest and the best use of urban land in these areas. Particularly, land supply for commercial, recreation, green space, services, etc. in these urban area are heavily affected by this type of land uses for housing. For instance, very recently (during July/August 2013), a densely populated area in the Gampaha Urban Council was identified as an area where the ground water is highly polluted due to the chemical waste of a factory located in the area. After several community protests and many pathetic incidences, government decided to provide drinking water to affected households from outside. Short term consequences of the issue is that the initial cost of providing water and regular maintenance of the project as the residents are claiming that they should not pay for water as they had free water from their owned domestic sources. At the same time, instead of drinking water, impact of pollutant on agriculture is also questionable.

Other visible feature according to the data in the table is the existence of raw/slum houses in these urban areas. This problem should be reckoned with urban housing policy and programmes. Apart from the type of the house, condition of the physical unit depends on the materials used. Tables 9.9 and 9.10 briefly illustrate the type of material used for wall and roof of houses in the country and the districts of the Western province.

Table 9.9 *Type of material used for wall of houses in the country and districts in the Western province*

Region	*% of Types of materials use for walls*		
	Permanent (stone/ cement blocks/ bricks)	*Semi-permanent cabook/soil brick*	*Mud/kadjan/palmyra/ plank/metal sheet*
Sri Lanka	87.0	5.1	7.9
Colombo	90.8	5.7	3.5
Gampaha	89.7	4.3	6.0
Kalutara	79.3	15.4	5.3

Source: Authors compiled the table using the data of the Department of Census and Statistics, Sri Lanka, 2012.

According to the figures, it is very clear that 13 per cent of the national housing stock is built with semi-permanent/low quality or temporary materials. The problem is that the situation in highly resourceful urban areas of the country is also the same in this aspect. It also highlighted the fact that material used for the roof of housing units in the country and the three districts in the Western province is substandard. Similar percentage of houses uses higher quality material for roofing. Those who used low quality materials for wall may have used metal sheet or other low quality roofing materials for their houses.

Table 9.10 *Type of material used for roof of houses in the country and districts in the Western province*

Region	*% of types of materials use for roof*		
	Tile/asbestos/concrete	*Aluminum/metal sheet*	*Straw/kadjan/palmyra*
Sri Lanka	86.5	11.1	2.4
Colombo	94.7	5.0	0.3
Gampaha	94.3	5.1	0.6
Kalutara	93.4	6.2	0.4

Source: Authors compiled the table using the data of the Department of Census and Statistics, Sri Lanka, 2012.

Drinking water and availability of electricity and toilet are other key services needed for quality livelihood in a housing unit. The following three tables separately include statistics as discovered by the 2012 Census data.

Table 9.11 *Sources of drinking water in the country and districts in the Western province*

Region	*% of sources*			
	Well	*Tap born*	*Irrigation projects*	*Irregular sources*
Sri Lanka	50.8	30.5	12.7	6.0
Colombo	25.1	70.9	3.4	0.6
Gampaha	63.3	27.1	8.7	0.9
Kalutara	64.0	24.8	9.1	2.1

Source: Authors compiled the table using the data of the Department of Census and Statistics, Sri Lanka, 2012.

For more than 50 per cent of houses in the country and other districts, excluding Colombo, well-water is the source of water. Even in Colombo this source is popular as 25 per cent of houses find water from well. Therefore, well water-related problems should be thoroughly considered by authorities. Water quality and security of residence may be direct issues. Availability of adequate water in drought is another problem. A serious problem is as single houses are more in urban areas, construction of the sewerage system, drain system and other waste disposal mechanism should be seriously supervised by relevant authorities. Crime and other social issues are other aspects to be looked into; especially in complex urban areas and industrial areas.

Availability of electricity in the country is considerable and major urban areas situation is better than the national level. As it is evident by table 9.12, in Colombo city, nearly 98 per cent of houses are provided with electricity facility. Two other districts are also recorded as more than 95 per cent of houses are having electricity. It is able to reduce the 2–5 per cent of houses in Western province that do not have electricity as these are comparatively higher resources as well as less expensive for provision than rural areas.

Table 9.12 *Sources of energy for lighting in the country and districts in the Western province*

Region	*% of sources*	
	Electricity	*Other*
Sri Lanka	87.7	12.3
Colombo	97.9	2.1
Gampaha	96.7	3.2
Kalutara	94.3	5.6

Source: Authors compiled the table using the data of the Department of Census and Statistics, Sri Lanka, 2012.

Table 9.13 *Toilet facilities in the country and districts in the Western province*

Region	*% of sources*		
	Own toilets	*Sharing others'*	*No toilets*
Sri Lanka	95.1	3.2	1.7
Colombo	95.8	4.1	0.1
Gampaha	98.2	1.7	0.1
Kalutara	98.0	1.8	0.2

Source: Authors compiled the table using the data of the Department of Census and Statistics, Sri Lanka, 2012.

The Way the Housing Problem is Currently Being Addressed

Throughout the history, country's efforts on addressing the urban low income housing problem cannot be merely criticized. However, it seems that different socio-cultural issues as well as policy and the philosophical issues have been huge hurdles in finding effective solution for the urban low income housing problems of the country. Hence, it is important to discuss how the country is working towards a better situation.

It is noted that the current largest national housing programme which is called 'Jana Sevana', launched by the NHDA under the Ministry of Construction, Engineering Services, Housing and Common Amenities, have planned to address the housing issue in a holistic way, including the housing for the urban poor. The official website of the National Housing Development Authority has described the concept of Jana Sevana as,

> 'Jana Sevana' is a living concept, although, priority is given for construction of houses, Jana Sevana is not merely a programme for housing. The Jana Sevana Housing and Settlement Development Drive for one million housing was formulated at the end of 30 year prolong bloody war, making Sri Lanka towards a proud independent and sovereign state by providing housing facilities to all homeless families in the Island. (www.nhda.gov.lk accessed on 22.02.2013)

It seems that the current national housing policy aims at overall national development. It has realized housing as not a physical entity but a 'housing facility'. This programme is strengthened with some specific features as well. This programme has identified housing as a broad concept, which has links with all facets of the society and the macro environment. Therefore, it has incorporated following philosophical features:

- It is aiming towards building a 'self-reliance nation' through providing housing facilities. This means that the programme has a broader aim.
- It encourages only 'eco-friendly' development programme. The programme concerns the environment aspects.
- It concerns 'power and energy saving'.
- It expects 'safety and the self-reliance' of the society.
- It also expects that the society should become as the true partner of the development. This programme expects enabled households.
- Producing real partners of development through house own society. This is not merely provision of housing.
- It believes that the ultimate goal of creating a better society is not possible by merely providing a housing unit with four walls and a roof.
- Good communication by working with community as a guider without bureaucratic differences is an adopted practice which seems to be a strong strategic device of the programme.

As the housing problem is severe and complex, it should be addressed by comprehended and holistic approaches and strategies. According to the way that the current approaches have been documented, it seems that better outcomes may be possible. Yet the proposed holistic approaches do not clearly state about the housing for the urban poor, which is severer in the country. Hence, it can be suggested that two important aspects must be considered by policy makers as to *'how strategically the proposed holistic actions are taken for housing of urban poor'* and *'how wisely the previously learnt lessons are applied in new approaches in connection with the housing for urban poor'*.

Notes

1. As cited by Sivam, *et al.* 2001.
2. Sri Lanka is comparatively a small country. Its land extent is about 65,000 square kilometres and population is around 20 million according to the 2012 Census.
3. Former Minister of Housing and Common Amenities, Sri Lanka.
4. 2011 census did not cover the North and East provinces due to the situation of those areas not being normal then.
5. As cited by Abeywickrama (in http://www.lth.se/fileadmin/hdm/alumni/papers as accessed on 10.03.2010)

References

Abeywickrama, H.W.D.P. (Date is not available), 'Common Spaces as a Better Living Environment in Low Income Housing – Sri Lanka: Modifications in Urban Housing Scheme and their Relationship for User Modification', as available in http://www.lth.se/fileadmin/hdm/alumni/papers

Adesoji, D.J. (2011). 'Urbanization Challenges and Housing Delivery in Nigeria: The Need for an Effective Policy Framework for Sustainable Development, *International Review of Social Sciences and Humanities*, 2(1) (2011), pp. 176–185, available in www.irssh.com accessed on 09.03.2013.

Anderson, J. (2001). 'Breaking the Cycle of Housing Stress: An Update of the Housing Needs Assessment for Gold Coast City', *Social Research Studies 13*, Sponsored and published by Gold Coast City Council, in conjunction with the Gold Coast Housing Network and Queensland Shelter, UK.

Ariyawansa, R.G. (2009). 'Housing for the Poor and Land for the City Development: A Case of Sustainable Township Program in the City of Colombo', Ranvinder Singh Sandhu, Jasmeet Sandhu and Balwinder Arora (eds), *Urban Poverty in Developing Countries: Issues and Strategies for Sustainable Cities*, New Delhi: Bookwell.

Ariyawansa, R.G. (2010). 'Study on Dwellers' Participation in Providing Houses for the Next Generation in Public Housing Schemes in Colombo', Unpublished report submitted to the University of Sri Jayewardenepura, under the University research grant (ASP/06/RE/2008/02)

Ashraff, F. (2007). 'The Mahinda Chinthana 'Vision of Sri Lanka' Made an Opportunity to Build Cities in Rural Areas', Speech made by the Minister of Housing and Common Amenities, addressing the 21st Governing Council session of UN-Habitat in Nairobi, Kenya on 17th April, in www.nhda.ac.lk accessed on 07.03.2010

Bandarage, A. (1983). 'Colonialism in Sri Lanka: The Political Economy of the Kandyan Highlands, 1833–1886', Colombo: Lake House Investment Ltd.

Barnabas, W. Don. (2006). 'Improving Access to Domestic Capital for Slum Upgrading and Low Income Housing Projects', *5th Slum Upgrading Facility Working Paper Development of A Sustainable Low-Income Housing Finance Programme in Sri Lanka, A Study For The UN-Habitat Slum Upgrading Facility*, Nairobi: UN-Habitat

Berner, E. (2000). 'Learning from Informal Markets: Innovative Approaches to Land and Housing Provision', *Development in Practice*, 11(2 and 3), pp. 292–308.

Central Bank of Sri Lanka in www.centralbank.ac.lk accessed on 07.03.2010

Claudio, A Jr. and H. Christopher. (2011). A Practical Guide for Conducting: Housing Profiles Supporting evidence-based housing policy and reform', Nairobi: UN-Habitat.

Conred de Tissera. (2006). in www.nhda.ac.lk accessed on 07.03.2010

David W. (1994). Community Participation and Empowerment: Putting Theory Into Practice, York: Joseph Rowntree Foundation, The Homestead, 40 Water End.

Department of Census and Statistics Sri Lanka. (2012). *Population of Sri Lanka by District: Census of Population and Housing 2011*, as in http://www.statistics.gov.lk/PopHouSat/CPH2011/index.php?fileName=CPH%202011_R1&gp=Activities&tpl=3, accessed on 21.02.2013.

Dolapihilla (2000). 'Public Sector Housing Development in Sri Lanka: With Special Reference to Urban Informal Resettlements in Colombo', as in http://www.lth.se/fileadmin/hdmalumni/papers accessed on 10.02.2010.

Erguden Selman. (2001). 'Low-cost Housing: Policies and Constrains in Developing Countries', Paper Presented for the International

Conference on Spatial Information for Sustainable Development, 22 October, Nairobi.

Fernando, D. (date is not available), 'Sustainable Housing for Urban Poor: Design of a Preventive Maintenance and Management Mechanism for Public Urban Housing Schemes', as in http://www.lth.se/fileadmin/hdmalumni/papers accessed on 10.02.2010

Ganepola, GAPH. (date is not available), 'Direct Housing Construction Programme in Sri Lanka: Construction Management Aspects', in www.hdm.lth.se/alumni/al, accessed on 10.03.2010

http://www.hnz.co.nz/hnzc/web/research-&-policy/strategy-publications/nzhs/online-version/area-1 – sustainable-housing-supply.htm accessed on 12.06.2009

http://www.hud.gov/offices/cpd/affordablehousing/index.cfm#shop accessed on 10.03.2010

http://www.unhabitat.org/content.asp?cid=5234&catid=534&typeid=8&subMenuId=

Jayaratna, K.A. (2002). *Poverty Profile: City of Colombo*, Sevanatha Urban resource Centre.

Joan, C. (2011). 'The Foreword', *A Practical Guide for Conducting: Housing Profiles Supporting Evidence-Based Housing Policy and Reform*', Nairobi: UN-Habitat.

Mirihagalle, L. (date is not available),'Unauthorized Alterations in Condominium Housing in Sri Lanka Mechanism for Beneficiary Participation in the Design and Development Process', as in http://www.lth.se/fileadmin/hdmalumni/papers accessed on 10.02.2010

National Housing Development Authority. (2008). Database, as cited by M.S.V. Vipulaguna, *Community Participation in the Development of Walk-up Apartments Formal Sector Lower-middle Income Housing in Sri Lanka*, as in www.hdm.lth.se/alumni/al, accessed on 10.03.2010

Norman, R.J. (2000). 'How People Power Brings Sustainable Benefits to Communities, USDA Rural Development Office of Community Development.

Parnwell, M. (1993). *Population Movements and the Third World*, London: Routledge.

Rajapaksa, G. (2010). 'Development Plans for the City of Colombo', as in http://www.sundayobserver.lk/2010/12/26/fea02.asp accessed 20.10.2011

Ramadasa, S.K., *Energy Conscious Design in Hot and Humid Climates Design Guidelines on the Use of Natural Lighting and Natural Ventilation in Housing in Sri Lanka*, as in http://www.lth.se/fileadmin/hdm/alumni/papers

Samaranayake, C. (date is not available), *Accessibility Towards Sustainability … Providing a Habitable Environment for Differently-able People in Sri Lanka*, as in http://www.lth.se/fileadmin/hdm/alumni/papers accessed on 12.02.2009)

Sandhu, K. (2008). 'Growth Dynamics and Challenges in an Infant Metropolis: The Case of Amritsar City', *Sri Lankan Journal of Real Estate*, 01, pp. 49–64.

Sarkissian, W. (2002). 'What is Community Participation?, Theorists are Talking about Equity and Representativeness', *Adapted from Chapter 1 of New Directions, a Community Participation in Practice publication, as* in http://sarkissian.com.au/ downloads/Sarkissian%20Associates%20Planners/What_is_community_participation.pdf

Sepani. S.N. Zainudeen and C Weddikkara. (2006). 'Factors Affecting Condominium Development in Sri Lanka', *Built Environment Sri Lanka*, 7(1), pp. 23–28.

Siriwardana, S. (1999). Sri Lanka Housing Standards Study, Colombo, Sri Lanka.

Sivam, A. (2002). Constrains Resisted the Urban Land Market in Developing Countries: Case study of India', *Habitat International*, 26, pp. 523–537

Sivam A. (2003). 'Viewpoint: Housing Supply in Delhi', *Cities,* 20(2), pp. 135–141.

Sivam A. et al., (2000), 'An Approach to Improved Housing Delivery System in Large Cities in Less Developed Countries', *Habitat International*, 25, pp. 49–113.

Urban Development Authority. (1998). *Colombo Metropolitan Regional Structure Plan (CMRSP)* Vol. 1, Colombo: Ministry of Housing and Urban Development.

Urban Development Authority, Ministry of Urban Development, Construction and Public Utilities, (1998), A Best Practice from the City of Colombo: Sustainable Township Programme, Sri Lanka.

Wakely P. (2008). 'Land Tenure in Under-Served Settlements in Colombo Urban Poverty and Environment (UPE)', *Report Series* 6, IDRC, Canada

Wijewardena, D.H. 'Designing Homes for the Urban Poor: Professional Intervention – Experience in Public Sector Housing Schemes in Colombo', as in http://www.lth. se/fileadmin/hdm alumni/papers accessed on 10.02.2010

www.nhda.ac.lk accessed on 07.03.2010

www.nhda.ac.lk accessed on 07.03.2010

www.indexmundi.com/facts/sri-lanka/urbanaccessed on 09.03.2013 www.indexmundi.com/sri_lanka/demographics_profile.html in Sri Lanka Demographics Profile 2012 accessed on 09.03.2013.

10

Housing for the Urban Poor in India

Emerging Trends and Issues

Manoj Kumar Teotia

'We shape our dwellings, and afterwards our dwellings shape us.'

–Sir Winston Churchill

India is the second largest urban system after China and housing is emerging as a major problem in urban India. The housing shortage in urban areas is growing and the situation seems to be worsening for the urban poor who either reside in slums or squatters. It has become a serious problem in the wake of rapid urbanization, commodification of land and housing, distortion in land market and the weakening of public sector housing provision in the post-liberalization period in India. The onset of liberal regimes in promoting development of real estate markets, beginning of low interest home loans, etc. seems to have made land and housing in urban areas a commodity for speculation. The private sector real estate builders, property dealers and rich individuals seem to have taken maximum benefit of the liberal housing markets, leaving no or negligible scope for the urban poor to buy a decent house in urban areas. Housing and urban development for the low income population seems to be neglected in urban policy planning over successive planning eras.

The world is urbanizing and in 2008, a turning point was achieved in human history when the number of people living in cities exceeded those in the countryside. Between 2007 and 2050, the world population is projected to increase from 6.7 to 9.2 billion and most of this growth will occur in the urban areas of less developed countries. Urbanization *per se* is often a positive development, as urban areas tend to be more productive than rural areas ... yet rapid urbanization can outreach the capacities of cities to absorb and cater for an ever growing number of inhabitants (Matuschke, 2009). The south is urbanizing even faster. It has been projected that level of urbanization in Africa and Asia will be 52 per cent and 54 per cent respectively, by the year 2030. The cities of developing world are spectacularly ill prepared for the explosion in urban living (Van Ginkel, 2008).

Almost without exception, the political and urban authorities in developing nations were simply not ready to house so many migrants in such a short space of time. The consequence has been a large shortage of housing and the growth of slums and squatter settlements (Aldrich and Sandhu, 1995).

Housing is one of the major problems developing cities are facing today. Migrants who cannot afford proper housing are forced to build temporary housing without proper utilities. These settlements are known as slums and squatters. The total number of slum dwellers in the world stood at about 924 million people in 2001. This represents about 32 per cent of the world's total urban population. At that time, 4 per cent of the combined urban populations of all developing regions lived in slums, while 78.2 per cent of the urban population in least developed countries were slum dwellers (UN-Habitat, 2003). According to UN-Habitat (2010) more than 30 per cent of world's urban population are either living in poor housing conditions in slums or are homeless.

Slums and urban poverty are not just a manifestation of a population explosion and demographic change, or even of the vast impersonal forces of globalization but a result of a failure of housing policies, laws and delivery systems, as well as national and urban policies (UN-Habitat, 2003).

India is not an exception to the emerging urban scenario. With its huge urban population residing in 7,935 towns (Census of India, 2011), the country's urban population has grown to over 377 million (31.16%). India is urbanizing. This transition will see India's urban population reach a figure close to 600 million by 2031. The scarcity of affordable housing drives the poor and some non-poor to slums and most of these settlements lack even basic water and sanitation facilities. Even though the urban poverty ratio has declined by half over the 30-year period since 1973–74, there were still 80.8 million persons in urban India in 2004–05 who were officially defined as 'poor', increasing from 76.3 million in 1993–94 (HPEC, 2011). In India the estimates of inadequate housing of the urban population run as high as 20 to 25 per cent (Nagpaul, 1988). Urbanization and the housing shortage in India seem to go together and substandard housing and slums seem to have close linkages as housing shortage is more acute in slums. The presence of slums and squatter settlements in a society is a clear indication of the failure of a society and government to provide adequate habitat for human development. The amount of squatter housing is one indication of the extent of housing poverty in a society (Aldrich and Sandhu, 1995). The slums and squatter settlements are growing in urban India with serious deficiencies in housing, basic amenities and livelihood. Whereas more than 23 per cent of the urban population resides in slums (Census, 2001), a much higher proportion of the urban population of metropolitan cities lives in slums; it is estimated that 55 per cent of the population of Mumbai lives in slums (NUHHP, 2007). The National Sample Survey 65th Round (July 2008 – June 2009) shows about 49,000 slums in India. The lack of adequate access to basic services, sanitation and livelihood in slum settlements makes housing one of the most crucial urban social problems in the country.

It is in this context that this chapter is an effort to look into the emerging trends and issues in housing for the urban poor in India. An effort has been made to look into the data pertaining to housing situation in India, housing trends, housing shortages, housing poverty, access to basic infrastructure, land, services and low cost building material to the poor, linkages between housing, urban development, poverty and slums, investment patterns, national, state and city-level housing and habitat policies, five-year plans, schemes for Economically Weaker Sections (EWS) and Low Income Groups (LIG), initiatives for housing to the poor, slum rehabilitation programmes, legal, institutional and financial mechanism for housing, public and private sector housing, home loans for the target groups, security of tenure, low cost rental housing, and the future of housing for the poor.

Housing Situation in India: Housing Trends and Shortages

The housing shortage in urban India is growing and the situation is worsening for the poor. The housing stock in 2001 was 50.95 million for 55.8 million urban households. According to the Tenth Five-Year Plan, urban housing shortage at the beginning of the Tenth Plan has been assessed to be 8.89 million units. As much of 90 per cent of the shortfall pertains to the urban poor, and is attributable (among other reasons) to ... (non) provision of housing to slum dwellers. According to the report of the Technical Group on estimation of housing shortage constituted in the context of formulation of the Eleventh Five-Year Plan, the housing shortage is estimated to be around 24.71 million. About 99 per cent of such households are from the Economically Weaker Section (EWS) and low income groups (LIG). During the Eleventh Plan period, total housing requirement, including the backlog, is estimated at 26.53 million. But according to an Asian Development Bank study (ADB, 2007) India's housing shortage is as high as 40 million units and more than 200 million people are living in chronically poor housing conditions. The high shortage of houses in the low income segment constitutes a large proportion of total shortage of housing in India.

India faces the mammoth task of providing affordable homes to an estimated 38 million households by 2030 which will not be able to afford a market-priced house. India has chronically underinvested in its cities for many years, and the results are plain to see – gridlock, slums, poor provision of public services, and subpar urban economic growth (McKinsey Global Institute, 2010).

On the basis of past trends, housing shortages might have further increased in last decade. The housing shortage seems to be resulting in homelessness as the number of homeless people has been growing. According to the NHB the number of houseless people has increased from 1.95 lakhs in 1961 to 7.89 lakhs in 2001. Although NHB figures do not seem to convey a real picture of housing shortage, Sandhu (2000) calculated the housing shortage in urban India at 15.92 million in 1991 which have gone up with rapid urbanization during last two decades as pointed by the Eleventh Five-Year Plan. The *Report of the Technical Group on Urban Housing Shortage* (MoHUPA, 2012) shows the urban housing shortage of 18.78 millions comprising 10.55 million (56.18%) for Economically Weaker Sections (EWS Households having income up to ₹ 5,000 p.m.), 7.41 million (39.44%) for Low Income Groups (LIG HHs with income between ₹ 5,001 and ₹ 10,000 p.m.), and 0.82 million (4.38%) for Middle Income Groups (MIG and above categories HHs). The major shortage of housing is in EWS and LIG categories and congestion in living conditions is a crucial dimension of the housing problem in the LIG categories.

Non-affordability of housing by economically weaker sections of society and low income families in urban areas is directly linked with the magnitude of urban poverty. One-fourth of the country's total urban population, numbering 80.7 million persons is below the poverty line (NUHHP, 2007).

The labour is shifting to urban areas. At the onset of the 21st century (2001), 32 per cent of the total workforce resided in urban areas. According to the 2001 census, 29 per cent of the urban workforce falls in the category of 'main workers' and the balance in the category of 'marginal workers'. Further, it is of critical significance that 79 per cent of the new jobs totalling 19.3 million between 1991–2001 were generated in urban areas and only 5 million jobs were generated in rural areas (NUHHP, 2007). The poor workers cannot afford the costlier rentals and, hence, move to settle in slum areas in temporary settlements in illegal manner.

The issue of 'housing poverty' seems to be larger than income poverty. To a large extent, shelter poverty is the result of the heavily distorted land markets, a highly inadequate regulatory regime of protecting property rights, and absence of a well-crafted strategy for inclusion of economically and socially weaker sections in urban planning.

Housing in Slums: The Case of Multiple Deprivations

'Slums and pavement dwellers are the most visible manifestation of shelter poverty in urban India. In 1991, 21.3 per cent of the total urban population lived in slums. In 2001, 23.5 per cent of the total urban population living in 1,743 cities and town lived in slums' (Report on Indian Urban Infrastructure and Services, 2011). According to (Census, 2001) India had about 42.6 million slum dwellers in the country (640 cities/towns in 26 states/union territories reported slum population). This constitutes 15 per cent of the total urban population of the country and about 23.5 per cent of the urban population of the states/union territories reporting slums. More than 11 million of the total slum population of the country are in Maharashtra followed by Andhra Pradesh 5.2, Uttar Pradesh 4.4 and West Bengal 4.1 million. Andhra Pradesh has the largest number of towns (77) reporting slums followed by Uttar Pradesh (69), Tamil Nadu (63) and Maharashtra (61). There has been very high concentration of slum population in metropolis and class I towns. A slum population of 17.7 million was reported in the 27 cities with a million-plus population. Greater Mumbai Municipal Corporation with 6.5 million slum dwellers has the highest slum population among all the cities followed by Delhi Municipal Corporation (1.9 million), Kolkata (1.5 million) and

Chennai (0.8 million). Although the Census of India 2011 indicates a declining trend in slum population, some larger towns have very high levels of slum populations. In 2011, about 1.37 crore households or 17.4 per cent of urban Indian households (about 68 million people) lived in slums in 4,041 statutory towns. The slum population of Vishakhapatnam was 44.1 per cent, Mumbai 41.3 per cent, Kolkata 29.6 per cent, Chennai 28.5 per cent and Delhi 14.6 per cent in 2011.

Slums are environmentally sensitive human settlements in urban areas. According to The National Sample Survey 65th Round (July 2008 – June 2009), 24 per cent of slums were located along *nallahs* and drains and 12 per cent along railway lines, 57 per cent were built on public land, 64 per cent were notified, about 48 per cent of slums were affected by water logging. 'Most of the slum settlements lack water and sanitation systems and are often located in high-risk areas of cities. Not all slum dwellers are poor, however. Some non-poor live in slums because rent control laws have created extreme scarcity of housing for low income groups. All this has profound implications not only for environmental degradation but also for the productivity of those who live in slums with huge under provision of basic urban services' (Report on Indian Urban Infrastructure and Services, 2011). 'The scarcity of affordable housing drives the poor and some non-poor to slums and most of these settlements lack even basic water and sanitation facilities' (Nagpaul, 1988).

The majority of slum dwellers also belong to socially marginalized groups. According to Census of India 2001, 7.4 million (17.4%) of the total slum population belong to the Scheduled Castes and one million (2.4%) to the Scheduled Tribes, both historically underprivileged populations. Slum areas presented lower sex ratio (876) in comparison to the non-slum areas (905). A huge population of children i.e. 6 million (in the age group 0–6) were enumerated in slums. Similarly literacy rate in slum areas was reported at 73.1 per cent with 80.7 per cent male and 64.4 per cent female literacy against overall non-slum urban literacy rates of 81 per cent for total, 87.2 per cent for males and 74.2 for females in the states reporting slums. The work participation was also reported on the lower side and very low for the women; 32.9 per cent slum population was reported as workers. While male work participation rate was 51.3 per cent, female work participation rate was only 11.9 per cent. Therefore, slums have high level of dependant population; 91.1 per cent workers in the slum population are 'other workers' and only 5 per cent have been counted as 'household industry workers'.

Land Availability, Security of Tenure and Land Reforms

Access to land and legal security of tenure are strategic prerequisites for the provision of adequate shelter for all and for the development of sustainable urban human settlements. Inadequate availability of serviced land in the urban areas is becoming a major constraining factor in taking up housing projects for the poor. Teotia (2008) emphasizes that the high cost and non-availability of adequate vacant lands in the industrial city of Ludhiana are major constraints keeping local authorities from providing adequate housing for slum dwellers. Similarly, a recent study of the planned city of Chandigarh (Teotia, 2012) highlights that land is not available in central areas of the city and hence all the slum rehabilitation sites are being developed in fringe or peri-urban areas. The main aim of the Urban Land (Ceiling and Regulation Act), 1976 (hereafter ULCRA), to facilitate the availability and affordability of urban land by increasing its supply in the market, has not been fulfilled and hence it was repealed by passing the Urban Land (Ceiling and Regulation) Repeal Act, 1999. Many states subsequently repealed the act except Andhra Pradesh, Assam, Bihar and West Bengal. Even repeal of ULCRA which resulted in release of excess land by the states has not helped much in terms of availability of land for the urban poor. Similarly, the provision of earmarking of 20–25 per cent land for the poor in housing projects under JNNURM has not made any change in the housing scenario for the poor.

As far as security of tenure for the poor is concerned, until 1970s, there was no particular mention of it in any of the policy documents. The Model Slum Areas (Improvement and Clearance) Act of 1956 provided secure tenure indirectly by notifying areas as slums although tenure regularization was not a part of the Act. This implied that residents of slums cannot be evicted without the approval of the competent authority. It was in the year 1972, that the Environmental Improvement of Urban Slums (EIUS) Scheme was launched for providing basic services in the notified slums under the Slum Areas Act 1956. It was jointly funded by the central and state governments. Indirectly, this scheme also provided security to slums from eviction for a period of 10 years as one of the criteria for funding was to obtain a certificate from the municipality declaring that the slum would not be evicted for at least ten years. During 1980s and 1990s, security of tenure has been the subject of attention in India after a report in 1983 by the task force which recommended legal tenure for slums. This is evident in the recent housing policies and Five-Year Plans but the policies and programmes aimed at providing security of tenure to the poor were short termed and were not designed for a long-term approach with institutional rigour. The National Slum Policy, 2001 was considered a good step towards the provision of the tenure and provision of basic services in slums. However, the policy is still in its draft stage and has not yet come into effect.

Basic Services for the Urban Poor

Basic services such as water, sewerage, sanitation, health, education and livelihood are important in the context of housing and their access is highly skewed in favour of higher income groups. 'While the available evidence points out an overall improvement in the income of the urban people, the incidence of poverty in urban areas has been quite a disturbing phenomenon. Evidence shows that other manifestation of poverty in terms of access to housing and basic services is equally serious' (Sivaramakrishnan and Singh, 2004). 'The urban poor have limited access to basic services. According to the 2001 census, there is a 9 per cent deficiency in drinking water, 26 per cent in toilets and 23 per cent in drainage. It is quite understandable that most of this shortage pertains to Slums' (NUHHP, 2007).

NSS data on the characteristics of 49,000 urban slums (2008–09) shows a very grim picture of basic amenities in slums. Housing has deficiencies. In 64 per cent of notified slums, a majority of the dwellings were *pucca*; the corresponding percentage for the non-notified ones being 50 per cent. The major source of drinking water was either tap or tubewell in 95 per cent slums. The availability of electricity in slums is better but access to individual connections is an issue; 1 per cent notified and 7 per cent non-notified slums did not have electricity connection. About 22 per cent of notified slums and 43 per cent of the non-notified slums do not have a *pucca* road inside the slum. About 27 per cent notified and 42 per cent non-notified slums had a motorable approach road. About 48 per cent of the slums were usually affected by water logging during monsoon, 32 per cent with inside of slum waterlogged as well as approach road to the slum, 7 per cent where the slum was waterlogged but not the approach road, and 9 per cent where only the approach road was waterlogged in the monsoon. Future urbanization in India 'would generate a heavy demand for better quality infrastructure in urban areas; especially water, sewerage, public transport and low cost housing' (Planning Commission, 2011).

The sanitary conditions in the slums in terms of latrine facility showed that latrines with septic tanks (or similar facility) were available in 68 per cent notified and 47 per cent non-notified slums. At the other extreme, 10 per cent notified and 20 per cent non-notified slums did not have any latrine facility at all. About 10 per cent notified and 23 per cent non-notified slums did not have any drainage facility. Underground drainage systems or drainage systems constructed of *pucca* materials existed in about 39 per cent notified slums and 24 per cent non-notified slums. Underground sewerage existed in about 33 per cent notified slums and 19 per cent non-notified slums. Government agencies were collecting garbage from 75 per cent notified and 55 per cent non-notified slums. About 10 per cent notified and 23 per cent non-notified slums did not have any regular mechanism for garbage disposal.

A study of health and living conditions in eight large Indian cities – Chennai, Delhi, Hyderabad, Indore, Kolkata, Meerut, Mumbai, and Nagpur – based on data from India's National Family Health Survey (NFHS–3 – 2005–06) shows that slums have much poorer housing conditions than non-slum areas whether we consider construction material, residential crowding, or ventilation of the dwelling. However, the poor have the worst housing conditions on all counts (Gupta et al., 2009).

Investment Requirements for Housing and Basic Services

The investment requirement for meeting the housing backlog is huge and growing. According to the NHHP (2007), 'The total estimated investment for meeting the housing requirement up to 2012 was estimated to be of the order of ₹ 3,61,318.10 crores consisting of ₹ 1,47,195 crores for mitigating housing shortage at the beginning of 11th Plan and ₹ 2,14,123.10 crores for new additions to be made during the 11th Plan period (this includes construction of *pucca* houses and upgradation of semi-*pucca* and *kutcha* housing units)'. It seems continued gaps and the huge need of investments in housing and basic services in cities have outshined the positive role of urbanization.

Similarly the need of investments for augmenting basic services is huge. The Eleventh Five-Year Plan of India (2007–2012) has estimated that the total fund requirement for implementation of the Plan target in respect to urban water supply, sewerage and sanitation, drainage and solid waste management is ₹ 12,92,370 million comprising ₹ 5,36,660 million for water supply, ₹ 5,31,680 million for sewerage and sewage treatment, ₹ 2,01,730 million for drainage, ₹ 22,120 million for solid waste management, ₹ 80 million for Management Information System (MIS), ₹ 100 million for R&D and PHE training, etc. The Working Group Report on Urban Transport for the Eleventh Five-Year Plan has estimated an investment requirement of ₹ 13,25,900 million (including modern buses) for improving the transport system (Vaidya, 2009). Since the gaps in terms of coverage and quality of basic urban infrastructure and services in slum areas are more evident, it is assumed that they need a major share of these funds.

Affordable Housing for the Poor

Affordability is a relative concept. It is difficult to define affordability as it varies in different contexts. In India, MoHUPA defines affordable housing on the basis of size category of the minimum/maximum built up area and carpet area such as for EWS-minimum of 300 sq ft super built-up area and 269 sq ft or 25 sq m carpet area, for LIG minimum of 500 sq ft super built-up area and maximum of 517 sq ft or 48 sqm carpet area and for MIG 600–1,200 sq ft super built-up area and maximum of 861 sq ft or 80 sqm carpet area. In addition the EMI/Rent of the unit should not exceed 30–40 per cent of the gross monthly income of the buyer. The housing sector policy paper of the World Bank observes that housing 'typically constitutes 15 per cent to 20 per cent of household expenditure. Investment in housing represents up to 20 per cent to 30 per cent of fixed capital formation in countries with vigorous housing programmes' (cited from Odeyar D. Heggade, 1998).

From primary exploration of the situation and a review of literature, it appears that public and private sources of housing finance have failed in addressing the funding requirements of the poor for affordable housing. Consequently, they look for other informal sources of housing finance. The financial arrangements for financing the affordable housing are not pro poor and banking institutions resort to all kind of conditions and practices which could be termed 'anti poor' in the context of financing affordable housing. Peer Smets (2004) in his book on 'Housing Finance and the Urban Poor' highlights that 'at least 50 per cent of the households in many developing countries, and 80 per cent in India, are dependent on finance from wages, employers, the wider family, friends, ship networks, and agents in the 'informal' financial sector to help them construct homes. This suggests that the poor are a large part of middle-income families which cannot afford 'formal' housing finance (Pugh, 1990)'.

The higher costs of land, building material, basic services, etc. are making it difficult for the poor to afford housing units. The low cost material is not easily available and the locations of cheaper houses are in the periphery or very far away from the work places of the poor. The means of transport are inadequate and costly. The poor have little or no surplus income to afford the EMI or rental for a decent house. The rules for Floor Space Index (FSI) are not pro poor and buildings by-laws are not clear. Similarly, the Rent Control Act hinders free flow of housing into the rental market and, hence, a high percentage of housing units are found vacant. Lack of access to adequate external commercial borrowings (ECBs) for affordable and low income housing until the recent past was due to the high rate of withholding tax on interest payments. It can also be one of the reasons for inadequate private sector initiatives for affordable housing for the urban poor.

Initiatives for Housing to the Poor: Policies, Five-Year Plans and Schemes

Housing and urban development seem to be neglected in urban policy planning over successive planning eras. The cities are increasingly becoming centres of economic growth but at the same time they continue to experience serious deficiencies in housing in terms of quantity as well as quality, etc. Since independence, the Government of India through various Five-Year Plans, has tried to tackle the problem of housing and basic services to the poor by creating various institutions/organizations and ministries, schemes and housing and habitat policies. These include the formation of the Ministry of Works and Housing, the National Building Organisation (NBO) and the Town and Country Planning Organisation (TCPO), the introduction of Industrial Housing Scheme and Subsidy Scheme and the creation of the new town of Chandigarh during the First Five-Year Plan (1951–56); widening of the Industrial Housing Scheme to cover all workers, introduction of Rural Housing, Slum Clearance and Sweepers Housing schemes and beginning of preparation of Master Plans during the Second Plan (1956–61); widening of the scope of needs of the Low Income Groups during Third Plan (1961–66); establishment of Housing and Urban Development Corporation (HUDCO) to finance the housing and urban development programmes, and introduction of Environmental Improvement for Urban Slums (EIUS) during Fourth Plan (1969–74); setting up a Task Force for development of small and medium towns, enactment of Urban Land

(Ceiling and Regulation) Act during Fifth Plan (1974–79); introduction of Integrated Development of Small and Medium Towns (IDSMT) during the Sixth Plan (1980–85); setting up of National Housing Bank and National Commission of Urbanization, reconstitution of NBO into the Building Material Technology Promotion Council (BMTPC), launching of Urban Basic Services for the Poor (UBSP) and National Housing Policy (NHP) during Seventh Plan (1985–90); revision of NHP to tune with the New Economic Policy of India and attract FDI in housing sector during Eighth Plan (1992–97); modification of the NHP as 'National Housing and Habitat Policy 1998' during Ninth Plan (1997–2002); introduction of JNNURM and promotion of housing and basic services to the poor through BSUP and IHSDP, launching of the National Urban Housing and Habitat Policy 2007 (NUHHP, 2007) for realizing the goal of 'Affordable Housing for All' during Tenth Plan (2002–2007); introduction of Rajiv Awas Yojana (RAY) to meet the housing shortage through slum-free planning during Eleventh Plan (2007–2012) have been some of the important developments during last six decades.

The Government of India implemented Jawaharlal Nehru National Urban Renewal Mission (JNNURM) in 2005 for providing affordable housing to urban poor under Basic Services to the Urban Poor (BSUP). JNNURM has completed about seven years and has ended. It has faced a number of criticisms i.e. it was able to utilize only about 60 per cent of the grants, planning process was poor, failed to adopt service benchmarks, lacked capacity, one size fit all does not work and incomplete reforms, etc. It is also argued that it did not adequately integrate housing and infrastructure delivery to the extent required. The fate of Twenty Point Programme (launched in 1975, revised in 1982, 1986 and 2006) approved by the Indian Cabinet in 2006 in conformity with the priorities contained in the National Common Minimum Programme (NCMP), the Millennium Development Goals (MDGs) of the United Nations and the SAARC Social Charter had a similar fate. The *Garibi Hatao* (poverty eradication), *Subke Liye Awas* (Housing for All) and *Basti Sudhar* (Improvement of Slums) are three crucial points in the context. But data indicates that interlinked problems of poverty, slums and housing are continuing and the condition of the poor is becoming even more miserable due to socio-economic and political marginalization and social exclusion.

In the last Union Budget, the rate of withholding tax on interest payments for External Commercial Borrowings (ECB) has been reduced from 20 per cent to 5 per cent to mobilize low cost borrowing for affordable housing. The government is likely to extend the debt to developers who would reserve 70–90 per cent units of their housing projects for the EWS and LIG. It is expected that with this policy change, more capital will flow for the low cost affordable housing projects and the small developers will be able to avail themselves of the facility to construct small housing projects.

National Housing and Habitat Policy

The National Housing and Habitat Policy provides the basic framework for achieving the objective of 'shelter for all'. The policy was first evolved in 1998 with the long-term goal of eradicating houselessness, improving the housing conditions of the inadequately housed, and providing a minimum level of basic services and amenities to all. It was formulated to address the issues of sustainable development, infrastructure development, and for strong Purchasing Power Parity (PPPs) for shelter delivery with the objective of creating surpluses in housing stock and facilitating construction of two million dwelling units each year in pursuance of the National Agenda for Governance. However, the housing sector has witnessed several changes since then. The 1998 National Housing Policy has been replaced by a National Urban Housing and Habitat Policy 2007 (NUHHP, 2007) with land and the development of civic amenities to make land habitable as its two critical elements. NUHHP (2007) seeks to provide 'Affordable Housing for All' particularly the EWSs and LIGs. The policy advocates equitable supply of land, shelter and services at affordable prices to all sections of society. The impact of this policy also seems to be negligible on the plight of houseless urban poor.

It seems that not much has been achieved to translate the housing policies and programmes into reality. A recent study of 10 towns in Gujarat under IHSDP on housing for the urban poor (UNNATI, 2009) shows that 'the present design is simply inadequate to address the ever increasing need for affordable and appropriate housing for the urban poor and is unfriendly to the poorest among the urban poor. The cost of housing units and the cost share by the beneficiary are too high and appropriate financing schemes are absent. It is also not able to be sufficiently focused on improving the conditions in the slums'.

Legal, Institutional and Financial Mechanism

Legal, institutional and financial mechanism for affordable housing in India seem not to be working as most of the public sector funding and banking institutions and legal instruments have been unable to achieve the desirable results during the last 60 years. In the First Five-Year Plan (1951–56) a separate Ministry of Works and Housing and the National Buildings Organisation (NBO) were established. The National Housing Bank (NHB) offered refinance assistance to Housing Finance Companies (HFCs) in respect of their loans given to individuals for housing. In the Second Plan (1956–61), the Central Government decided to support State governments for providing affordable housing to the people by creating State Housing Boards. In the Fourth Five-Year Plan (1969–74), need was felt to provide housing finance to low-income groups and therefore in 1970 the Government set up the Housing and Urban Development Corporation (HUDCO). In the Fifth Plan (1974–79), the Government passed the Urban Land (Ceiling and Regulation) Act (ULCRA) to make more land available to the landless and houseless urban population. A housing finance company, i.e. the Housing Development Finance Corporation (HDFC), was also set up in 1977 to provide housing finance. In the Sixth Plan (1980–85), few more private companies entered in to housing finance. But it was the Seventh Plan (1985–90) which changed the government policies. Instead of public sector, housing construction and financing was overtaken by the private sector. The Government framed a draft National Housing Policy in 1988 and formed the National Housing Bank (NHB) and the Building Materials and Technology Promotion Council (BMTPC). The mixed economy approach adopted by the Government during pre-liberalization planning era did not prove to be effective for addressing the problem of housing the poor.

The Government liberalized the economy in early 1990s after the economic crises which subsequently resulted in changes in the institutional mechanisms and the role of government in housing for the poor. The government's role in housing for the poor (EWS and LIGs) was drastically reduced in the Eighth Plan (1992–97) despite the formulation of first National Housing Policy (1994). The trend seems to have continued during subsequent plans, i.e. Ninth Plan (1997–2002) and Tenth Plan (2002–2007). The government became the facilitator and encouraged the housing mortgage market by leaving the role of provider to the market (private sector). The pro market reforms were initiated to attract private capital into the housing market. A revised National Housing Policy in 1998 was also adopted and ULCRA was repealed in 1999. The Ninth and Tenth Plans promoted commercial housing finance which increased considerably. The 'planned investment proposed total investment in housing has soared from ₹ 11.5 billion under the First Plan to ₹ 7.26 trillion (USD 0.15 trillion) in the Tenth Plan. However, the proportion of housing in the total capital expenditure under the plans has declined due to the shift in the government's emphasis from provider to facilitator' (Garg, 1998 cited in UN-Habitat, 2008). The same trend continued under Eleventh Plan (2002–12). It was projected that the ambitious mission of JNNURM will completely change the housing scenario in the country although it also proved to be a missed opportunity. The Twelfth Plan (2012–17) emphasizes an inclusive approach and dreams of a slum-free urban India through an ambitious scheme of Rajiv Awas Yojana (RAY) to solve the problem of housing for the poor.

Some recent and prospective housing policy reforms fall largely within the new political economy (NPE) model (Pugh, 1995) which provides the legislative, institutional and financial framework whereby entrepreneurship in the private sector, in communities and among individuals can effectively develop the urban housing sector. The NPE has both macro-economic orthodoxy associated with IMF and World Bank loan programmes for stabilization and adjustments and an acceptance of markets in micro-economics in which improvement has to be sought across all fronts, i.e. in markets, NGOs, self-help in households and public administration. Under the NPE, according to Pugh, housing subsidies can be better targeted for anti-poverty purposes, and infrastructure can be developed within joint ventures, NGOs and organized self-help groups. But it seems that not all is well with the World Bank's model which after its implementation in the post-liberalization period in India has miserably failed to provide housing to the poor.

The legal mechanism for housing for the poor seems to be insufficient and ineffective in case of providing adequate housing to the poor. Most of the acts, housing policies, schemes, and recently mission mode programme of JNNURM have not yielded the desirable results. The aim of The Urban Land (Ceiling and Regulation) Act, 1976 (ULCRA), was to release the additional land. After reaching the ceiling on the land, a person (individual, a family, firm, company or association) can only own between 500 to 2000 sq metres. 'However, the act failed to achieve these objectives and has had many adverse side effects. In all, an estimated 19,200 hectares were procured and much land was locked up in litigation' (UN-Habitat, 2008). The excess amount of land after ULCRA, therefore, could not be used for housing for the urban poor. The legal framework for raising home loans for the low income and BPL segment is very stringent as financial institutions see this type of funding riskier from the perspective of Non Performing Assets (NPAs).

The institutional mechanism for providing affordable housing to the poor has various deficiencies. The existing institutions have failed in solving the growing problem of housing for the poor. The public sector housing institutions have been gradually withdrawing from the responsibility of providing housing to the poor. They are unable to cope with the growing challenge of providing affordable housing to the poor. The private sector housing companies and real estate developers seem to have taken over the housing sector. Most of the Housing Boards, Improvements Trusts and Urban Development Authorities created for addressing the concerns of the housing have been behaving in the same fashion as the private sector housing and real estate developers. The cost of the land and housing units provided by them are very high and beyond the affordability of the low income groups and poor.

Summing Up

Housing for the urban poor in India, particularly for EWS and LIG households, is emerging as a major problem caused by forces within and outside the political economic system. The problem of housing for the poor has been observed in the form of inadequate housing in terms of poor quality of housing stock, insecurity of tenure, lack of privacy in terms of no separate rooms, high level of congestion, absence of separate kitchens, toilets, bath facilities, etc. due to shortage of space and poor income levels, as well as infrastructure and basic service inadequacies due to lack of institutional support. The housing problem among slum dwellers seems to be magnified due to various factors such as continuous inflow of poor migrants from other states, inadequate housing supply to them, commodification of land and housing, poor livelihood and income levels of the poor. The continuation of the housing problem for many decades will keep the level of social, economic and human development low as slums have poor literacy, poor skills, informal employments, negligible incomes, and poor quality of life. The settlements segregated due to housing poverty seem to be detrimental to the social and environmental fabric of the city.

The cities are increasingly becoming centres of economic growth but at the same time they continue to experience serious deficiencies in housing in terms of quantity as well as quality. Another crucial dimension of the housing problem is the illegality of the large number of human settlements in the cities. It seems to be due to the reason that housing policies, planning norms and minimum standards have been set unrealistically high, resulting in the growth of illegal housing.

The housing crisis is more visible in larger towns where slums have grown rapidly. Despite efforts made by the government in containing the number of slum dwellers, the sprouting of slums and housing problems is ever increasing and the situation is worsening with the passage of time (Census of India, 2001) in the wake of rapid urbanization, commodification of land and housing, distortion in land market and weakening of public sector housing provision in post-liberalization period in India. The onset of liberal regimes resulted in change in legal, institutional and financial mechanism for the housing. The liberalization agenda also resulted in development of real estate markets, beginning of low interest home loans, etc. which seem to have made land and housing in urban areas commodity for speculation. The private sector real estate builders, property dealers and rich individuals seem to have taken maximum benefit of the liberal housing markets leaving no or negligible scope for the urban poor to buy a decent house in urban areas.

The financing of affordable housing for the poor is becoming a crucial issue. The urban poor are not in position to pay for a dwelling unit out of their own pocket and they mainly depend on external financial sources outside the banking sector to finance the construction of their dwelling. In addition, they find difficulty in fulfilment of specific terms and conditions. The problem is going from bad to worse for them due to the limited supply of public sector housing and land within the city limits, lengthy procedure of getting formal housing, meagre funds and their misallocation and diversion towards the higher income groups.

The future of affordable housing for the poor needs a different approach. While the private sector may be incentivized for taking up the projects promoting low cost housing, a greater allocations of public sector investment is required to tackle the growing problem. The development and application of low cost material and technology are a must. The use of mix of prefabricated technology and low cost material involving less time in construction and low cost may be used in affordable residential projects. This could be one of the options available for promoting affordable housing. The strict regulation of private sector housing to see the provisions for the affordable housing is necessary as most of the private builders tend to avoid earmarking of land and housing for the poor due to inadequate profit and pressure of high income groups. The existing public institutions such as NHB and HUDCO need to upscale their efforts and achieve the targets set from time to time for providing housing to the poor.

There is an urgent need to speed up social housing programmes to include all the slum dwellers and homeless people suffering due to housing poverty. Housing affordability is a major issue and effective repayment capacity of the poor for better housing is very poor. Any social housing programme based on beneficiaries' contribution will have to look on the repayment capacity. Last but not the least, a strong political will is needed at central, state and local levels to address the problem of housing for the poor.

References

Aldrich, Brian C. and Ranvinder S. Sandhu (eds). (1995). *Housing the Urban Poor: Policy and Practice in Developing Countries*, London: Zed Books.

Asian Development Bank. (2007). Housing Finance II (HUDCO). http://www.adb.org/Documents/Profiles/LOAN/30204013.ASP

Census of India 2001 and 2011. New Delhi: Office of the Registrar General and Census Commissioner, India (ORGI).

Gupta, Kamla, Fred Arnold, and H. Lhungdim. (2009). *Health and Living Conditions in Eight Indian Cities*, National Family Health Survey (NFHS-3), India, 2005–06. Mumbai: International Institute for Population Sciences; Calverton, Maryland, USA: ICF Macro.

Heggade, Odeyar D. (1998). *Urban Development in India: Problems, Policies and Programmes*, New Delhi: Mohit Publications.

Matuschke, Ira. (2009). 'Rapid Urbanization and Food Security: Using Food Density Maps to identify Future Food Security Hotspots', Contributed paper prepared for presentation at the *International Association of Agricultural Economists Conference,* August 16–22. Beijing.

Ministry of Housing and Urban Poverty Alleviation. (2012). *The Report of the Technical Group on Urban Housing Shortage*, New Delhi: Government of India.

Nagpaul, Hans. (1988). 'India's Giant Cities', in M. Dogan and J. Kasarda (eds) *A Word of Giant Cities*. CA, Newbury Park: Sage. pp. 252–90.

National Urban Housing and Habitat Policy. (2007). Ministry of Urban Development. Government of India. New Delhi: Government of India.

Peer Smets. (2004). *Housing Finance and the Urban Poor,* Jaipur and New Delhi: Rawat Publications.

Planning Commission. (2011). *Faster, Sustainable and More Inclusive Growth: An Approach to the Twelfth Five-Year Plan*, New Delhi: Government of India.

Pugh, Cedric. (1990). *Housing and Urbanisation: A Study of India*, New Delhi: Sage.

Pugh, Cedric. (1995). 'The Role of World Bank in Housing', in Brian C. Aldrich and Ranvinder S. Sandhu (eds) *Housing the Urban Poor: Policy and Practice in Developing Countries*, London: Zed Books. pp. 34–92.

Report of the Task Force on Urban Governance and Financing (2001). New Delhi: Ministry of Urban Development, Government of India.

Sandhu, Ranvinder Singh. (2000). 'Housing Poverty in Urban India'. *Social Change,* March–June. 30(1&2).

Sivaramakrishnan, K.C. and B.N. Singh. (2004). 'Urbanisation', in R.K. Sinha, (ed.), *India 2025: Social, Economic and Political Stability*. Delhi: Shipra Publications.

Teotia, Manoj Kumar. (2008). Urban Poverty Reduction Strategy for the City of Ludhiana, An Unpublished Report submitted to NIUA, New Delhi under GOI-UNDP Project on National Urban Poverty Reduction Strategy. Chandigarh: CRRID.

Teotia, Manoj Kumar. (2012). Planning for the Urban Poor in Northwestern India: Emerging Policies, Practices and Issues (A Case Study of Chandigarh). An Unpublished Study submitted to HUDCO under HUDCO Research Grant. Chandigarh: CRRID.

The High Powered Expert Committee (HPEC) (2011). for Estimating the Investment Requirements for Urban Infrastructure Services. New Delhi: Ministry of Urban Development, Government of India.

The National Sample Survey 65th Round. (July 2008-June 2009). *Some Characteristics of Urban Slums*. The National Sample Survey Office. National Statistical Organisation. New Delhi: The Ministry of Statistics and Programme Implementation.

The Mckinsey Global Institute (MGI). (2010). *India's Urban Awakening: Building Inclusive Cities, Sustaining Economic Growth,* The Mckinsey& Company April (http://www.mckinsey.com/mgi/reports/freepass_pdfs/india_urbanization/MGI_india_urbanization_fullreport.pdf).

UN-Habitat. (2003). *Global Report on Human Settlements 2003: The Challenge of Slums*, London: Earthscan Publications.

UN-Habitat. (2008). *Housing Finance Mechanisms in India*, Nairobi: UN-Habitat.

UN-Habitat. (2010). *State of World's Cities 2010/11'*. Nairobi: UN-Habitat.

UNNATI. (2009). *Housing for the Urban Poor: A Study of Ten Towns under IHSDP in Gujarat*, Ahmedabad: UNNATI Organization for Development and Education.

Vaidya, Chetan. (2009). 'Urban Issues, Reforms and Way Forward In India. Department of Economic Affairs', Ministry of Finance, Government of India. Working Paper No.4/2009-DEA (http://finmin.nic.in/workingpaper/urbanissues_reforms.pdf.Viewed on May 23, 2013).

Van Ginkel, H. 2008. 'Urban Future'. *Nature.* 456 (October), pp. 32–33.

PART III

Comparative Housing Policies

11

Low-Income Housing and Market-Driven Urban Development in Asian Cities

Yap Kioe Sheng

In his 1976 book *Housing by People: Towards Autonomy in Building Environments*, Turner argued that occupants appreciate their house not just for its exchange value, the price it can fetch in the market ('what it is'), but for the use they can make of it ('what it does'). He compares the formal-sector ('oppressive') house built for the urban poor family with the informal-sector ('supportive') house built by the urban poor family. While the exchange value of the formal house is much higher that of the informal house, its use value to the occupants is lower, because it is small and unsuitable for income generation; it is located away from employment opportunities; and it requires regular utility payments from an irregular income.

Turner stresses the need for autonomy in housing to ensure that a house is useful for its occupants, as the urban poor know better than middle-class architects what they need and can afford. If houses are designed and built by large, centralized organizations, any form of autonomy is denied, because their products are standardized types of housing. Only if owner-occupants can control its design and development, will the house match their needs, priorities and conditions. Turner notes that informal (unregulated) settlements provide people with a freedom to build, making those settlements a solution to the low-income housing problem rather than the problem itself.

These ideas led housing activists to call on governments (a) to regularize informal settlements and to provide what the urban poor are unable to obtain on their own (i.e. security of land tenure and network infrastructure), and (b) to develop sites-and-services schemes which emulate informal settlement development in a planned manner. Despite the support for these approaches from the United Nations and the World Bank during the 1970s, the idea of freedom to build and, by implication, of incremental housing development never caught on with policy-makers and politicians.

The politically powerful landed class objected to the regularization of land tenure in informal settlements, because it perceived squatters as trespassers and illegal occupants. Politicians objected to the initially low quality of housing in sites-and-services schemes and regularized squatter settlements and to the long gestation period before the poor develop a 'complete' house that meets middle-class expectations. Politicians do not want to take responsibility for government-endorsed slum-like settlements, but prefer to be seen inaugurating multi-storey buildings designed by architects and engineers and constructed by large construction companies.

Any attempt to supply housing through a centralized, standardized approach is complicated by the wide variety in housing needs across the urban population. The rich design and build their own house to ensure that it meets their specific needs. Middle-income families accept pre-designed houses, but the market ensures the required variety and the middle-income family makes trade-offs to meet their housing needs as much as possible. The poor design builds and improves their informal housing according to their needs and resources, ignoring regulations that would make the house unaffordable. In public-sector housing projects, the poor must accept what has been designed and built for them.

The construction of medium-rise buildings with small low-rent apartments has proven time and again to be ineffective and too expensive to address the low-income housing problem. Such housing has to be subsidized to be affordable for the urban poor, but this makes it unaffordable for the government given the magnitude of the needs for low-income housing. Because many urban poor for whom the housing is intended consider it unsuitable to their needs, they are quite willing to sell the unit or the right to its occupancy. Highly subsidized housing becomes an easy prey for middle-income families who are equally desperate to find adequate housing. Without a suitable alternative, the urban poor families return to their informal housing.

The only exception to the above is Singapore where the government after independence decided to resettle the kampung population in multi-storey apartment buildings. Because it attached high priority to an adequately housed population, it took radical measures such as land expropriation, involuntary resettlement, integration of housing and public transport into urban planning and the use of a central provident fund for housing financing. Singapore's conditions are, however, unique: it is a small city-state without a rural hinterland; it has an elected, but authoritarian government that has been in power for five decades, allowing it to implement long-term policies; and it has accumulated the wealth to finance housing.

In most countries, the default policy became a benign (or sometimes not so benign) neglect: informal settlements were tolerated, because the government had no realistic alternative. Sometimes, informal settlements were provided with basic infrastructure services for humanitarian reasons or due to popular pressure on local politicians and municipal officials. More often, the settlement's population had to look after itself and take charge by organizing into community-based organizations (CBO) to improve the settlement's conditions as much as they were capable of. Sometimes, the CBO could reach an agreement with local government that it would take charge of the internal development of the settlement, while the local government would be responsible for connecting the settlement's self-built infrastructure to the municipal network.

As time went by, the policy of benign neglect led to a perception of increased security of land tenure among the population who felt that it would be difficult for the authorities to evict long-term residents. Once squatter settlements had been accepted as a housing delivery system, the terminology for the settlements also changed. The problem was not so much about land tenure security, but its crowded conditions ('overcrowded settlement'), its lack of infrastructure services ('underserved settlement') and the poverty of the residents ('urban poor communities'). Given the wide variety of conditions in and among the settlements, no single term describes its exact nature. Although it is not very precise, this article will use the term 'informal settlements'.

While politically land tenure security improved, legally it remained rather low throughout this period of benign neglect. Evictions still occurred, if a landowner wanted to develop his or her land or the government decided to expand infrastructure and chose a trajectory through an informal settlement rather than through a formal neighbourhood. Evictions occurred mostly in times of rapid urban economic growth when land prices skyrocketed and calls for investment in infrastructure were strong.

Enabling Housing Strategies

In the late 1980s, the World Bank and UNCHS (now UN-Habitat) shifted their position with regard to housing policy and started to persuade governments that the public sector had no direct role to play in housing development (UNCHS, 1991; World Bank, 1993). They argued that government should act as a facilitator and enabler for non-governmental actors, the private sector in particular, to supply housing. Private-sector housing would benefit not only middle-income families, but also the urban poor, as any form of low-income housing would inevitably be captured by middle-income families without an adequate supply of middle-income housing. With the private sector taking care of middle-income housing, government could focus its attention on the development and application of innovative approaches to low-income housing.

Many governments were eager to adopt the enabling approach as politicians felt more comfortable working with private real estate developers on middle-income housing than with housing activists and community organizers on informal settlements and sites-and-services schemes. Moreover, politicians and senior government officials in many countries were closely connected to real estate developers, landowners, construction companies and building material producers through class, kinship and economic interests. Developers and politicians in Mumbai are known to maintain long-standing links that are mediated by the underworld (Mahadevia and Narayanan, 2008: 31).

Enabling housing policies have been quite effective in many cities of Asia, resulting in the supply of large numbers of affordable middle-income housing. Its success cannot, however, be attributed to the enabling housing policies only; other factors also played a role. During the same period, cities in developing Asia became the recipients of massive foreign direct investments (FDI) from private companies in developed economies. FDI turned many cities of Asia into the factories and workshops of the world. The resulting economic growth expanded the urban middle-class which had money to spend and the aspiration to buy quality housing.

Under these circumstances, housing finance became more interesting for banks and, thus, more widely available to private developers and middle-income families. It made housing affordable to ever-larger sections of the urban population. Private developers became more experienced and were able to undertake large projects at a relatively low cost per unit. Some low-income families were able to move up into the middle-class and to improve their housing conditions, but the enabling policies did little for the low-income population in the informal settlements; neglect simply continued.

The enabling housing policies did not come alone, but were part of a package of neoliberal urban policies which shifted the attention from stand-alone housing projects to institutional reform of the housing sector, from low-income housing to the housing sector as a whole and from housing as such to urban management. Urban managers had the responsibility to mobilize public and private resources to ensure that rapid urbanization was matched by the development of urban infrastructure services. The underlying assumption was that better managed cities would enable land and housing markets to perform more efficiently and that this would eventually benefit everyone, including the urban poor. Gradually, the focus of local governments shifted from improving the quality of life of the population to stimulating urban economic growth through city promotion.

Competitive Cities

In the globalized economy, a city cannot take for granted that it is and will remain attractive for investors, as cities anywhere in the world are now trying to divert investments in their direction through city marketing. The availability of low-cost labour, an initial determinant for attraction, is no longer sufficient, as many cities in Asia and elsewhere can supply low-cost labour. Cities must be competitive in terms of the infrastructure (roads, ports, airports, power supply) and services (ranging from the protection of property rights to international banking facilities). Investors are increasingly seeking places with universities and research centres of global reputation and an environment that encourages creativity and innovation. If it lacks high-skilled workers, a city will try to enhance the 'quality of place' to attract them as they are footloose and can work anywhere in the world (OECD, 2005: 5).

Singapore which has an aging population is actively attracting young scientists. It hosted the first Global Young Scientists Summit in 2013. Besides attending presentations by renowned scientists, the participants will '*visit the universities, research centres and other research and technology landmarks of Singapore in the final two days of the* [five-day]

Summit. Cultural events will also be organized for visitors to appreciate the sights, sounds and tastes of multicultural Singapore' (NRF, 2012). Over the last 20 years, the government also spent more than a billion dollars on new museums and cultural institutions with the goal of turning Singapore into a 'global arts city' by 2015 (*New York Times*, 10 June 2011).

The need to compete in the global economy has shifted the agenda of local governments from 'managerialism' to 'entrepreneurialism' (Harvey, 1989), from a concern with service delivery to citizens to a focus on economic growth. The entrepreneurial local government is characterized by pro-economic-growth strategies, city marketing and city branding and an interest to cooperate closely with the business sector. Many local governments in Asia now believe that it is essential for their city to become 'world-class' in order to prosper in the globalized economy, as a world-class city has the conditions and resources to attract investors, highly skilled professionals, tourists and other visitors.

The organization of international meetings, incentives, conferences and events is seen as a major opportunity to beautify and showcase the city. The proof of being a world-class city is being selected to organize a mega-event: the Olympic Games, the World Championship Football, a World Expo or a large international conference. The justification for the high costs of organizing such an event is that it will bring income, generate employment and benefit the entire population. Singapore (Asia's shopping paradise and trading centre) and Shanghai (where the World Expo was held in 2010) are examples of what other cities, like Mumbai and Colombo, want to emulate.

With 20 million inhabitants, Mumbai is India's largest city and its financial and commercial centre, but that is no longer sufficient. Most political parties agree that Mumbai should be a world-class city on par with Shanghai so that it can lead India into the global economy. Bombay First, established by the private sector in 1995, took as its vision: '*Transforming Mumbai into a world class city with a vibrant economy and a globally comparable quality of life for its citizens*' (Bombay First, 2010). In a brochure, Bombay First (2009: 2) stated that it wants '*To enhance the quality of life of the citizens of Mumbai and improve the economic and social fabric of the city. In short, to turn Mumbai into a world-class city, one of the best places in which to do business.*'

Many have criticized the entrepreneurial agenda of local governments and their efforts to develop world-class cities. Harvey (1989: 7–8) notes that world-class city events often divert attention and resources from broader urban problems. Hasan (2009: 3–4) observes that the repercussions of an entrepreneurial agenda are 'a growing influence by global capital over the physical and social forms of the city and a focus on land values rather than social and environmental concerns in urban planning.' Fainstein (2010: 36) writes that urban policies under the control of pro-growth governments favour the well-off over the disadvantaged rather than being economically, politically, socially and spatially redistributive.

Local government and the private sector often join forces to organize events and market a city as 'world-class', but in such public-private partnerships the public sector may end up paying the costs, while the private sector reaps the profits. It is undoubtedly difficult to design an agreement that accommodates the public interest represented by the government and the profit orientation of the private company. However, some public-private partnerships look more like collusions by public officials and business circles for their personal advancement.

A mega-event may be an opportunity to beautify the city, but it is also used as the justification to evict urban poor communities and demolish their settlements. The number of people evicted for the Olympic Games in Beijing will probably never be known, but COHRE (2008: 7) reports that 1.5 million people were displaced. In 2008, the Lao government agreed to lease 20 km^2 of wetlands – home to 17 village communities, 20 species of fish and rice paddies – to a Chinese-led joint venture in exchange for the construction of a new sports complex for the 2009 Southeast Asia Games (Reuters, 7 April 2008). NGOs estimate that preparations for the Commonwealth Games in Delhi in 2010 resulted in the eviction of 2,00,000 urban poor (HLRN, 2011: 4).

Despite the upheaval in the global economy, some in East Asia are becoming richer and richer. Moving money into stock markets, bonds or savings accounts is not very attractive. For many, the preferred investment is real estate. So, over the past years, the Asia-Pacific region has become the second largest region (after Europe, but before North America) in real estate invested stock, i.e. commercial real estate held by investors (DTZ, 2012). As foreign investors search for the most profitable locations and have little sensitivity for local impacts, their investments in real estate often lead to large-scale evictions. Given the limited supply of centrally located urban land, urban development is a zero-sum game with the investors as the winners and the urban poor as losers.

As more and more urban poor communities have to move in order to beautify the city, make way for the construction of infrastructure, or the development of middle-income housing, hotels, offices, shopping centres and casinos, space for informal housing for the urban poor is becoming scarce. Pure squatting (i.e. the unauthorized occupation of vacant land) has been almost impossible since a long time and much of the new informal housing consists of infill in existing settlements. Rental housing is replacing home ownership in urban poor settlements, while sharing is a common pattern. The result is increased population densities in informal settlements and worsening living conditions.

As pressures to develop urban land commercially rise, the regularization of informal settlements through the provision of long-term land tenure security is increasingly unlikely. It raises the questions: Is the era of informal settlements coming to an end? Will the outcome be '*cities without slums*', i.e. cities without housing for the poor?

Buying a Place in the City

Some approaches have emerged that take into account these circumstances: one is a compromise solution called 'land sharing'; the other takes the dominance of the market for granted and aims at empowering community-based organizations of the urban poor to acquire urban land through buying or leasing.

The government-sponsored Baan Mankong programme in Thailand aims at empowering urban poor communities to negotiate with landowners and local governments for the acquisition of the land which the community has occupied for an extended period of time. Empowerment in this respect means that families in an urban poor settlement organize into a savings-and-loans group which develops into a CBO, and establish a network of CBOs in the city or town. This citywide network supports each of the communities in its negotiations with the landowner and will help identify affordable alternative land in the proximity, if negotiations fail. Baan Mankong provides loans and grants to buy land, to develop infrastructure and to build or improve houses. Since 2003, Baan Mankong has supported some 90,000 households (CODI, 2012).

Reliance on the market to acquire land rather than claiming the right to adequate housing, while more pragmatic, also has its limitations. The approach is effective if land prices are not too high, landowners are willing to sell or lease land at a discounted rate and affordable alternative land is available nearby. These conditions may be met in smaller cities and towns, where development pressure on the land is low and distances are manageable. Landowners may be willing to sell or lease land at a discount, if they have a strong sense of corporate social responsibility;

the Crown Property Bureau in Thailand is an example. Where these conditions are not met, it is difficult to negotiate an affordable deal with landowners or to find affordable alternative land.

To limit market penetration in the settlement, Baan Mankong insists that the acquired land is collectively owned or leased, and that house owners ask for permission from the community to sell their house. This should prevent higher-income outsiders from buying property in the neighbourhood and disrupting the sense of community. Baan Mankong stresses the importance of strong and cohesive communities to ensure that even the poorest can benefit from the project through mutual support. The risk is that the very poor are drawn into a project that is beyond their means, accept a loan they cannot afford and become dependent on community leaders and better-off families for their continued stay in the neighbourhood. With clientelism widespread in Thailand, it could make the poorest less, rather than more, empowered.

Land Sharing

Attempts to regularize land tenure in informal settlements or to evict urban poor communities from land they occupy without the owner's consent can result in a stalemate: the community refuses to move from the land it occupies, while the landowner insists on having the land back that he or she legally owns. Land sharing tries to break this stalemate by dividing the land between the landowner and the urban poor community. The commercially most interesting part of the land is returned to the landowner for development; the urban poor community buys or leases the other part, preferably at a subsidized rate.

The main advantage for the community is that it can continue to live at more or less the same location and can keep its social and economic network intact. It has, nevertheless, to demolish and rebuild all the houses in the settlement, as they will have to relocate onto a smaller portion of the original plot of land. For the landowner, land sharing is also a compromise: only part of the land is returned, but that is still better than losing the entire plot or having to go to court for a protracted and possibly expensive court case. There is also the negative publicity, if the police is called to evict poor families and demolish their houses. However, landowners recognized that it would be easier to pay the families a financial compensation, while the community recognized that the compensation could never buy them housing in a similarly suitable location. So, a new stalemate emerged and a new solution had to be found.

A new form of land sharing developed: a tripartite public-private partnership between the government, a private developer and the urban poor community. The government declares the land occupied with informal housing a redevelopment area and invites private developers to bid for the redevelopment project. In exchange for permission to develop the land, the private developer agrees to provide housing (usually apartments) within the project to the affected families, often free of charge. This looks like an attractive solution for the poor, as they can continue to live in the same location and will have formal housing at no cost to them (or to the government).

Many local governments see redevelopment of land occupied by an urban poor community not only as a financially attractive approach to improve the housing conditions of the urban poor, but also (or perhaps primarily) as an effective way to optimize land uses, raise property values and build a world-class city (without slums). The experiences with this redevelopment approach are, however, not encouraging from the perspective of the urban poor.

Sahaspura, Colombo

On the investment page of its website, the Urban Development Authority of Sri Lanka states its vision for its urban renewal projects in Colombo:

'To eliminate shanties, slums and other dilapidated housing from the city of Colombo by resettlement of the families presently living under unhygienic and poor environmental conditions in such housing in new housing schemes of internationally recognized standards and in doing so to make the City of Colombo the most attractive city in South Asia' (www.uda.lk/investment_ relocation.html).

In 1997, the president of Sri Lanka asked a task force to draft a new approach to address, amongst others, the country's housing problems, while keeping in mind the government's goal of making Colombo the financial and commercial hub of South Asia in the 21st century. The task force recommended the adoption of an enabling approach for housing in general, but a provider approach for Colombo's under-served settlements in order to release prime urban land for commercial and economic development.

One of the results of the task force's work was the Sustainable Townships Programme (STP), aimed at resettling the urban poor in high-rise buildings in order to improve their quality of life and free 'underutilized' land for urban development. The STP developed a plan for townships with high-rise condominium buildings in the Colombo Metropolitan Region. The urban poor would be invited to exchange their plot for an apartment in one of the buildings. The construction of the buildings would be financed from the proceeds of the redevelopment of the vacated land by private developers. To manage this process, the STP created a company called Real Estate Exchange Limited (REEL) with equity partners comprising the relevant land-owning government agencies.

The initial idea was to invite private developers to propose building designs for a number of sites in the city simultaneously in order to allow the urban poor to choose their preferred site and design from several alternatives. However, REEL could, with some difficulty, identify only one piece of government land for resettlement housing: one hectare of land near Colombo's oldest and largest underserved settlement. The obvious reason was that none of the landowning public agencies was willing to contribute valuable land to resettle poor families. Consequently, the urban could only choose a building design, not the site. REEL completed the project, called Sahaspura, with a 14-storey building and a total floor area of almost 3,000 m^2 in 2001.

The STP had identified around 850 families in 14 underserved settlements for resettlement in Sahaspura. Initially, many residents were not interested to be resettled in a high-rise building and 'social marketing' was necessary to convince them (Wickrema, 2005). Out of the more than 850 families, 651 families actually moved to Sahaspura, 52 families were relocated elsewhere and 161 families refused to move. By 2010, some 100–150 families had sold their new apartment and moved to the suburbs or back to their original settlement (Wijayasinghe, 2010). Because some families had refused to move and others returned, the original sites (except two) could not be cleared and utilized for redevelopment, jeopardizing the financial arrangements of the programme.

A survey of resettled families found that many were satisfied with their new housing which they considered much better than the housing in the slum and shanty settlements. Families with a higher income and/or a regular job were more satisfied. However, there were also complaints: about the house design which was insensitive to cultural norms, the available space which made it difficult to run a home-based enterprise, the impossibility to expand the house when more space was needed, the constraints of high-rise living which made it impossible to use firewood and paddy husk as fuel, problems with the elevators, the refusal of the banks to accept the title deed as collateral, the additional costs of utilities, and the inadequate maintenance of the building (Wijayasinghe, 2010).

Borei Keila, Phnom Penh

Borei Keila Sports Village was built in 1966 and includes eight three-storey apartment blocks and other buildings. After the fall of the Khmer Rouge, many people moved into the empty apartments, making it one of the most conspicuous and populous slums in the city. The authorities claimed that the site was state land, but most residents claimed possession rights under the 2001 Land Law. Repeated efforts to evict the 1,800 families failed. In 2003, Borei Keila became the first land sharing project in Phnom Penh, when the government accepted a proposal by a private company to subdivide the land in two parts: 2 hectares for 10 six-storey buildings with walk-up apartments for the original residents, 2.6 hectares for commercial development (Rabé, 2010: 9–10).

According to Rabé (2010: 11), the project had serious flaws which caused problems once the project had started. The contract was awarded to the developer in a non-transparent manner. There was insufficient consultation with the residents about the land sharing arrangement and the building design. There were widespread irregularities in the identification of eligible beneficiaries and in the allocation of housing units. It had been agreed that the allottees could sell their unit only after five years of continuous occupancy, but 40 per cent of the families had sold their unit by late 2011 (Cambodia Daily, 23–12–2011). Moreover, stories are circulating about allottees who assumed two or more identities to claim additional units and about outsiders who bought the identity of original allottees, with support from local government officials, to obtain a unit in the project.

The problems accumulated when the private company announced that it would build only eight (rather than 10) buildings for the affected families due to a lack of funds. The government simply accepted this change of plans, which left almost 400 families homeless, in addition to the 300 families who had never been allocated a unit (apparently, because they had HIV/AIDS-positive family members). In early 2012, riots broke out in the area, as government officials, police and security guards tried to force the remaining residents off the portion of the land which the company was expected to redevelop commercially. The families who were still living there had been offered plots in resettlement sites in the province which they had refused. Eventually, the police managed to clear the area and to disperse the people. However, protests continued.

Dharavi, Mumbai

Bombay First believes that turning Mumbai into a world-class city is not possible as long as the city is full of slums which house an estimated half of the city's population. An example is Dharavi, perhaps Asia's most populous agglomeration of informal settlements, with a population of 0.6 to 1 million. Besides people, it houses recycling enterprises and industries that produce garments, leather goods, pottery, soap, cutlery and food. To remove the slums, the government worked to attract the interest of the local and international private sector in a redevelopment of the site, with the objective of improving the living conditions of all residents at no cost to the government (Patel and Arputham, 2007).

A plan was prepared for one sector of Dharavi that houses 57,000 families. Each house owner would receive a 30-m^2 apartment for free in a multi-storey building to be maintained by the developer for 15 years. However, renters would not be compensated and there would be a cut-off date (first, 1995; later, 2000) for residents to be eligible for re-housing. Business owners would receive 25 m^2 of space for free and have to pay for additional space. The private developer would have to provide 3 million m^2 of housing, schools, parks and roads for the current population, and could build 40 million m^2 of houses and offices for sale in return (Ramanathan, 2007).

Not everyone supports the plan (Giridharadas, 2006). Critics expect that the developers will try to minimize the space and costs of accommodating current residents and enterprises, and to maximize the space they can sell. They also worry that high-rise living will disrupt the livelihoods of vendors, shop keepers and fishermen, whose work requires them to live in ground-level homes where they can store their boat or supervise their store. In brief, there is concern that the plans and designs of the government and the private developers will not match the urban poor's way of live and their social and economic conditions.

This has already become clear in subsequent surveys. A survey in one of Dharavi's sectors found that 31 per cent of the families had moved to Dharavi in 2000 or later and, thus, were ineligible for free housing. It also found that the sale of housing is a regular feature: around one-third of the houses in the sector had changed hands since 2000, and house prices were rising rapidly in anticipation of the redevelopment (*Hindustan Times*, 22 Junary 2011). The implications of these findings are that many current residents will not be rehoused in the project, but rather made homeless, and that the occupants of the redeveloped housing may not all belong to the original Dharavi residents. In view of these findings, it is unclear how the scheme can proceed.

Housing the Poor or Real Estate Development?

Politicians will be pleased to point to the buildings of Borei Keila, Sahaspura and, in the future, Dharavi and proclaim that they made a major contribution to the solution of the low-income housing problem. However, the challenge is not to produce buildings, but to improve the living conditions of the urban poor. This will not have been achieved, if the original target group did not live in the buildings or if living in those buildings had actually worsened their conditions. This is not to say that the urban poor should never live in medium or high-rise buildings. Some will be very happy to do so; others will not. The question is: Has it improved the living conditions or not?

In this respect, it is useful to look at policies for resettlement. The World Bank and the Asian Development Bank developed resettlement policy frameworks with principles that should guide any involuntary displacement and resettlement as the result of a development project which they finance. Its core principle is: when a project is undertaken to improve the well-being of the population, it is unacceptable that the people most immediately affected by the project because of their involuntary resettlement do not have their well-being improved and often see it deteriorate. From this, three principles follow (ADB, 2007: 3–4):

1. Compensation for loss of assets should be such that the economic and social future of the affected persons will not be worsened (and preferably better) than without the resettlement.
2. The absence of a formal legal title to land by the affected persons should not be a bar to compensation.
3. Affected persons should be consulted about the compensation and should have basic access to mechanisms to enforce their entitlement to just compensation.

Application of these principles to the redevelopment projects of Dharavi, Sahaspura and Borei Keila implies that it is insufficient to compare the market (exchange) values of the housing before and after the resettlement, as the government and the private developer like to do. The market value of the new formal housing unit is undoubtedly higher than that of the lost informal housing unit, but market value cannot be the only yardstick. It is the use value of the new housing that determines to a large extent the social and economic future of the affected families. If the new housing unit is not as functional as the old one, in terms of income generation, a size and shape that can accommodate the larger household, and its adaptability to changing needs, it will have a low use value for its occupants.

Someone who works in Dharavi, was quoted by the *New York Times* (28 December 2011) as saying: '*People who come to Dharavi or other slum areas – their priority is not health,*' '*their priority is earning*'. Many low-income families require space for income generating activities; it can be a store, a workshop or a small production unit. Informal settlements have a multitude of convenience stores which are difficult to replicate in a high-rise building, because there is no space, the public road is far away and any production or repair work will disturb the neighbours. Real estate managers may actually prohibit the use of the home for income-generating activities, as the separation of home and work is the (middle-class) norm. This disadvantages women, as they tend to work more at home, because it allows them to look after their small children.

Inclusion in the project is usually limited to those who can show that they lost property as a result of redevelopment, even if it is part of an unauthorized settlement and lacks a proper title. Many low-income families are renters or live rent-free in the house of a friend or relative. Renters, who are often poorer than homeowners and may depend on their social networks for survival are rarely compensated and resettled in the redevelopment project, despite their loss of housing. Some renters do not want to become homeowners, but rather remain renters, because the high transaction costs of home-ownership tie them down, if employment opportunities require them to move. An inclusive housing policy would ensure that the housing needs of all families affected by the project are met, not only homeowners.

Determining the eligibility of the residents is difficult. The population of an informal settlement is never stable, as people move in and out for employment or family reasons. Cut-off dates make sense from the point of view of the project managers as a means to keep speculators out, but for the urban poor a cut-off date is very artificial, as if life and work can be frozen in place. Moreover, the market value of the housing unit which is given free of charge makes it into a likely target for corruption by government officials and community leaders. As the cases of Borei Keila and Sahaspura show that many families sell their occupancy right or their identity, voluntarily or involuntarily, to persons outside the target population.

The construction of new houses as part of the redevelopment project will take time and the original residents will need to relocate temporarily. The relocation site may be close to the original settlement or further away, but whatever its location, the temporary resettlement is likely to disturb the economic and social networks of the family. Because they have seen promises broken so often in the past, many affected persons will also be worried that the developer will not keep his promise and that resettlement will never happen. That makes them more inclined to sell rather than to wait and find out that they have been cheated or that the promised housing is not what they expected. For the developers, this may actually not be a bad development, as the replacement of low-income by middle-income families will probably increase the value of the property.

When building middle-income housing, private-sector developers conduct market research to determine what kind of housing will sell. In a redevelopment project, the private developer is unlikely to consult the prospective residents, as time is limited and their demands are in any case too diverse to be met. There may be one or a few standardized designs to minimize costs. For government officials, the design of housing units for the urban poor is also an opportunity to force the poor to live in an urban middle-class type of house and teach them a 'better', modern lifestyle. However, the adoption of middle-class housing standards and designs will only facilitate the replacement of low-income by middle-income families.

The problems that emerged in the above public-private partnerships are similar to those observed by Turner 50 years earlier. A difference is perhaps that in Turner's time governments made serious, though flawed, attempts to house the urban poor, while today's redevelopment projects have low-income housing merely as a sideshow to efforts to optimize urban land use, raise property values and promote economic growth. The inhabitants of Dharavi are well aware that the redevelopment is not aimed at improving their situation. 'People from all over the city, and the politicians, are making hue and cry that Dharavi must be developed,' [a businessman in Dharavi] said. 'But they are not developing it for the people of Dharavi. They will provide office buildings and shopping for the richer class.' (*New York Times*, 28 December 2011).

As Fainstein (2010: 170) observes, urban planning and policy have increasingly adopted a single-minded focus on economic growth through public-private partnerships, without trying to distribute the benefits as widely as possible. In this respect, the definition of urban competitiveness by Lever and Turok (1999: 792) is relevant: 'the degree to which cities can produce goods and services which meet the test of wider regional, national and international markets, while simultaneously increasing real incomes, improving the quality of life for citizens and promoting development in a manner which is sustainable.' (emphasis added)

Neither the government nor the private developer seems to be particularly interested to know what the original population which was resettled to make way for the redevelopment project thinks about the project and what happens to them afterwards. Available information (like in the case of Borei Keila) is mostly of anecdotal or journalistic nature and does not give insights into the long-term dynamics of a redevelopment project. Ex-post facto evaluations of such projects are hard to find. An assessment of the effectiveness of a resettlement project or approach will not be easy as it requires a measurement of the socio-economic conditions of the affected families before and after. Affected families are not only those who are currently (say, 5–10 years after the resettlement) living in the buildings, but also includes families who were never resettled and families who were resettled, but have left since. Knowing their fate is critical to determine whether the project was inclusive.

There are many reasons why a family may have left before or after the resettlement project; some of the reasons can be considered positive, others should be considered negative. Not all families living in informal housing are poor, and some families may simply have owned or found alternative housing elsewhere. Some families may not have wanted or could not afford to become involved in the complex process of resettlement with its negotiations and its uncertainty. Others may have realized immediately that the type of housing being offered would not suit them. Finally, there may have been families who did not want to move and did not plan to move, but waited for a housing to be allocated to them and then sold their right to someone else, hopefully at a price that would allow them to build or buy alternative housing elsewhere. A study of a resettlement project in Bangkok gives insight into the complexities and dynamics of urban poor communities

Suwan Prasid 2, Bangkok

In 1988, the State Railways of Thailand leased 1,376 ha of land along Rama IX Road to a private company to build a shopping area, a hotel and houses. As a result, 110 households in three informal settlements came under the threat of eviction. The developer offered each household a compensation of Baht 8,500 (US$340). Some accepted and left; they were said to have ended up living under a nearby bridge. Most households rejected the offer. As negotiations went on, the developer paid one of the community leaders to abandon his community which fell apart and dispersed. Through his connections with other urban poor communities, another community leader found a relatively cheap plot of land for sale in a fringe area of Bangkok.

The National Housing Authority (NHA) provided loans at a subsidized rate so the remaining households could buy the land. They called the settlement *Suwan Prasid*. The NHA divided the land into 100 plots to house 100 households, but only 44 households from Rama IX Road ('Rama IX allottees') had moved by the end of 1989. Others simply did not want or could not participate in the project, because the new site was too far from their place of work. So, the NHA decided to allocate the remaining plots to evicted households from other settlements ('allottees from elsewhere').

Suwan Prasid was revisited in 2011 to study the changes after 20 years (Leerutanawisut, 2011). A survey found that only 38 households from the original 100 households in 1990 still owned a plot; many others had sold their property and left and had been replaced by others ('newcomers'). The newcomers tended to have a higher income and better houses than the original allottees. In addition, there were six squatter houses in the neighbourhood; one of them was occupied by an original allottee who had lost her plot to a moneylender.

Table 11.1 *Plot distribution in Suwan Prasid (1990, 1992, 2011)*

Type of owner	*Plot allocation in 1990*	*Plot occupancy*	
		1992	*2011*
Rama IX allottee	44	35	27
Allottee from elsewhere	56	28	11
Newcomer	–	–	54
Unknown (empty plot or locked house)	–	37	8
Squatter house	–	–	6
Total	100	100	106

It was difficult to find out why some of the original allottees had left and what had happened to them. A partial reconstruction showed that some had sold their right to a plot before they had actually occupied it or had returned the plot to the National Housing Authority, because it was too far from their place of employment. Others had lost their plot when they had taken out a loan from a moneylender and had been unable to repay the loan.

Table 11.2 *Circumstances of the plot originally occupied by an allottee*

Plots	*No.*
Plot still with original owner	22
Plot inherited from original owner	5
Plot sold after the death of original owner	1
Plot sold right-to-plot to someone else	5
Plot returned to NHA due to distance to job	1
Plot sold when owner was unable to repay loan	5
Plot sold and owner returned to the province (reason unknown)	5
Total	44

Some people had become legal owners of the land by repaying their loan to the NHA, but lost it in times of financial problems. Respondent A: *'I repaid my loan and the land belonged to me. When my son went to the jail because of drugs, I wanted to help him. I used my land to borrow money. I could not borrow from the bank, because I did not have stable income. I borrowed from a moneylender at 10 per cent interest per month, very high compared to the bank. I had no choice but to borrow from her. When I could not pay back, I lost my property.'*

De Soto has argued that plot-owners can use their land title as collateral to borrow from a bank to improve their house or start a business, but that is not always possible. Respondent B: *'To improve our house, we wanted to borrow money from the bank, but the bank did not accept our land as collateral, because we did not have a stable job. The Government Housing Bank which is supposed to help people buy or improve their house had the same criteria as commercial banks. So, we could not improve our house.'*

When the original settlers arrived in 1989, the area was in a remote corner of Bangkok, with limited employment opportunities and long, expensive commutes to the centre. By 2011, the area had become an integral part of the city, and a six-lane road gives direct access to *Suwan Prasid*. Land prices have increased. An adjacent urban poor community was evicted to develop a middle-income housing scheme. Some residents had received attractive offers for their plot of land.

Conclusions

The redevelopment projects have found an innovative way of financing low-income housing: public-private partnership. However, to meet the variety in housing needs (location, type and design) of the urban poor, the government needs to make sure that the affected families have a range of options to choose from. It is unlikely that a private developer would be able to provide a wide range of low-income housing options within a single redevelopment project. The original plan for resettlement housing in Colombo envisaged citywide approach with development of several sites for low-income housing by different private developers. This proved difficult to execute.

Apartment units in a redevelopment project are a valuable contribution to the low-income housing stock, but other housing options also have to be made available to accommodate low-income families with different housing needs. Since the private sector is unlikely to be involved in sites-and-services projects, core-housing schemes and low-rent housing due to the low profit margin, public-sector agencies and/or civil society organizations may have to take care of this type of low-income housing. Some will argue that detached housing will not achieve the densities required in urban areas, but this is still being debated.

The Sri Lanka approach also assumed that public-sector agencies would be willing to provide urban land for housing the poor, but this always proves difficult as well. Here, the Singapore government set the example: it expropriated the land it needed to resettle families. The current focus on optimization of urban land use cannot be the only objective; an equally important objective has to be the improvement of the housing conditions of the population affected by any redevelopment project, including renters and other marginal groups, with the enforcement of the principles of resettlement (equal or, preferably, better socio-economic and physical conditions after the resettlement).

References

Giridharadas, A. (2006). 'Not Everyone is Grateful as Investors Build Free Apartments in Mumbai Slums', *The New York Times*, 15 December.

Harvey, D. (1989). 'From Managerialism to Entrepreneurialism: The Transformation in Urban Governance in Late Capitalism', *GeografiskaAnnaler, Series B, Human Geography*, 71(1), pp. 3–17.

Hasan, A. (2009). 'The World Class City Concept and its Repercussions on Urban Planning for Cities in the Asia Pacific Region', Paper prepared for the *IAPSCSDE Network Symposia on Culture, Space and Revitalization*, Istanbul: Turkey, 12–16 October.

HLRN – Housing and Land Rights Network. (2011). *Planned Dispossession: Forced Evictions and the 2010 Commonwealth Games*, Housing and Land Rights Network, Delhi.

Leerutanawisut, K. (2011). *Tenure Security and Housing Improvement in Resettlement Projects: A Case Study of Suwan Prasid 2*, Bangkok, Thailand. Unpublished M.Sc. Thesis, Erasmus University, Rotterdam.

Lever, William F. and Ivan Turok. (1999). 'Competitive Cities: Introduction to the Review', *Urban Studies'*, 36(5–6), pp. 791–793.

Mahadevia, D. and H. Narayanan. (2008). *Shanghaing Mumbai: Politics of Evictions and Resistance in Slum Settlements*, Ahmedabad: Centre for Development Alternatives.

Patel, S. and J. Arputham. (2007). 'An Offer of Partnership or a Promise of Conflict in Dharavi, Mumbai?', *Environment and Urbanization*, 19(2) pp. 501–508.

Rabé, P. (2010). 'Land Sharing in Phnom Penh and Bangkok: Lessons from Four Decades of Innovative Slum Redevelopment Projects in Two Southeast Asian Boom Towns', Paper for the Policy Workshop *'Places We Live: Slums and Urban Poverty in the Developing World'*. Washington DC, 30 April.

Ramanathan, G. (2007). 'Dharavi Redevelopment Plan is Robbing Us of Space: Residents', *Hindustan Times*, 5 September.

Turner, John F.C. (1976). *Housing by People: Towards Autonomy in Building Environments*, London: Marion Boyars.

UNCHS – United Nations Centre for Human Settlements – Habitat (1991), *Global Strategy for Shelter to the Year 2000: Implementation of the First Phase*, Nairobi: UN Habitat.

World Bank. (1993). *Housing: Enabling Markets to Work, with Technical Supplements*, A World Bank Policy Paper, Washington DC: World Bank.

12

Urban Land Planning and Management for Affordable Housing

Experiences in Countries in Ibero-America and their Implications for Mexico

Guillermo Olivera, Carla Narciso and Julio Guadarrama

In a historical context where urban governance is characterized by the implementation of an entrepreneurial style, and where the production of urban spaces has been shaped by the markets (Harvey, 1989, 2008 and 2010; Theodore, Peck and Brenner, 2009), we should ask ourselves whether local governments still have the ability to meet the land and housing needs of the more disadvantaged social groups, with these needs often not met by the private sector. Looking at Mexico's experience, the answer to this research question would be 'no', due to the combination of two key elements: the weakness and neglect of local governments to drive the growth of cities in relation to real estate capital, and the *sui generis* character of the social property regime that remains a major obstacle to the creation of urban land. However, the experiences of Portugal, Brazil and Colombia allow a slightly more positive answer to the initial question, as they have developed some relatively successful land management tools that have adaptations in their general legal frameworks and the strengthening of local governments as a common reference. This chapter is divided into four parts. The first defines the limited and interrupted attention that has been given to the housing needs of the poor in Mexico. This is followed by a review of the situation in Lisbon and Porto, the two major Portuguese cities, where there are specific relocation and leasing programmes.

Then we look at the case of Natal, a medium-sized city in Brazil that pioneered the implementation of the Municipal Master Plan from which the Special Areas of Social Interest[1] tool was derived. For Colombia, the case of Bogota is reviewed; in particular the different land management models for social housing that have been developed by *Metrovivienda*, a public company established by the city council. Finally, there will be some reflections on the meaning and potential implications these experiences may have for Mexico.

The Mexican Situation

The limited and interrupted attention to the housing needs of the poor. Schematically, the evolution of institutional urban, housing and land policies covers two periods: from the early 1970[2] to 1992 in the 20th century and from 1992 to 2012. The first period coincides with the later stages of the interventionist state in economic development (state promotion of housing), and the second[3] coincides with the stage of trade liberalization (liberalization of housing production).

During the first period the State was responsible for providing land, channelling funds and coordinating the construction of homes, their locations and their allocation through credit, all through the national housing organizations (ONAVIS)[4], with a social approach that served at least two thirds of demand from employees on lower incomes. In the second period, from 1992, the ONAVIS were transformed into a kind of mortgage bank, limited to financing the construction of housing and allocating mortgages, while they assigned land acquisition, construction and location of housing to private housing construction and development companies who, as expected, put profit maximization before producing an accessible social benefit for the poor of the city. In this case, even more housing was built, but only for those who could afford to pay for it (workers earning more than four times the minimum wage, but mainly for those on over six times the minimum wage) (Schteingart, 1989 and Puebla, 2006).

As shown, during the aforementioned periods, the national housing policy has been aimed at building housing for employees in the formal economic sector, and has only secondarily conducted programmes for sectors of the population not in formal employment. This means that the population working in the informal sector[5] in Mexico, equivalent to 60 per cent of all workers in 2012 according to the International Labour Organization, does not qualify for housing credit. This is also because 50 per cent of urban growth in Mexican cities occurs in slum settlements (Fundación Centro de Investigación y Documentación de la Casa y Sociedad Hipotecaria Federal, 2012). Additionally, 57.7 million inhabitants, of a total of 112 million in 2010, are living in poverty; few needs for suitable housing are met. The current federal government (2013) estimates that there is a deficit of 9 million households to cover until 2030.

To meet the housing needs of people on low incomes, the National Trust Fund for Low-Cost Housing in Mexico (FONHAPO) was created in 1981, with its history going back to 1954. Its aim has been to finance housing for the population not in formal employment and with income below two times the national minimum wage. Unlike the ONAVIS, who devote most of their resources to the development of new housing, FONHAPO's work is to fund the acquisition of urban land, housing construction in stages (progressive), and home improvement. It, therefore, focuses on unfinished housing, which nevertheless solved part of the housing problem of the poor, particularly in medium-sized cities and rural areas, which was a success.

FONHAPO had its best performance between 1983 and 1988 when, with only 4.2 per cent of its total financial resources for housing nationwide, it carried out 17.5 per cent of all activity of the public sector housing programme (Sedue, 1989 and Connolly, 2006). Fiscal resources (some of them non-recoverable) and World Bank loans were used. At the time a 50 per cent subsidy was provided to the beneficiaries, explaining the favourable results. The decentralization of credit management to state governments and some city councils also proved successful, as did the collective allocation of credits, rather than individual allocation, to organized social groups (Ortiz, 1996).

It has been recognized that land availability was critical to the success of FONHAPO in the 1980s. This land availability had been expropriated and inherited by the Institute of Community Development, defunct in 1981, to the state governments (Connolly, 2006). In the subsequent absence of land, FONHAPO's activities declined in the 1990s when some of its actions were also centralized to a federal level at the Secretariat of Social Development (SEDESOL), as part of its social policy. With the commercial reorientation of the national housing policy, came the interruption of a learning process of social and self-managing production of housing and local habitat, the aim being to recover this in the second decade of the 21st century. In fact, one of the objectives of the Housing Act 2006 is to support people on low incomes through the Social Housing Production scheme, as the original FONHAPO scheme is called, for which federal funds and loans from the Inter-American Development bank will be provided through subsidies. The results will be seen in several years and with the participation of other institutions, because the changes at FONHAPO since 2001 have modified their original functions.

What is attractive about the way housing is produced through subsidies is that it seems viable to recover at least the investment; the housing needs of the poor are effectively met; and land located within the established urban area is occupied. The key is, therefore, the social focus of housing policy and urban land management, which at the time was limited to the administration of land reserves obtained through purchase and expropriation. Since then, progress has only been made in the privatization of public land, which is a form of collective ownership present in Mexico, but not in the imposition of charges to property, that could fund social housing production.

The Social Function of Land and Planning: Under-used or Wasted?

In Latin America, Mexico had, before Colombia and Brazil, a legal framework that established the principle of the social function of property. This was stated in Article 27 of the constitution in 1976, when it was amended to indicate that the 'Nation' could impose limits on the property:

'The Nation shall have ... the right to impose on private property such limitations as the public interest may demand, as well as the right to regulate the utilization of natural resources which are susceptible of appropriation, in order to conserve them and to ensure a more equitable distribution of public wealth ...'

In the same reform it is stated that it is the responsibility of the State 'to plan and regulate' human settlements, a function that is reinforced in Articles 25 and 26 of the Constitution. Planning, as a tool to realize the social function of property, is also supported by Article 73 of the Constitution, which states the possibility that federal, state and municipal governments will work together on human settlements, particularly in metropolitan affairs (conurbated areas). Article 115 of the Constitution, which had three major reforms in 1973, 1976 and 1999, also recognizes the autonomy of the municipality as a level of government and describes its functions and sources of resources, in addition to establishing its responsibility for driving urban development through planning.

Finally, 1976 also saw the publication of the General Human Settlements Act, which is the framework law that regulates matters relating to human settlements in the country.

What tools stem from this institutional framework to give validity to the social function of property? Basically, there are two groups: those involved in planning as the main regulatory activity, and those involved in the instrumental part of imposing charges on urban land along with the 'new' forms of incorporation of public land into urban development, or privatization, as introduced by a new amendment to Article 27 of the Constitution in 1992, in line with the recommendations of the International Monetary Fund and the World Bank in full decline of the promoter state. The reform was undoubtedly necessary, although it was restricted to the privatization of public land, without providing further options to governments to obtain resources from land management, except for existing mechanisms for the regularization of squatting, and it maintained property taxes, such as council tax, as they were, offering insignificant resources.

Regarding the first group, Mexico has a national planning system on three levels: the federal government, state governments and the municipal governments. Municipal governments, through municipal urban development plans, are responsible for the regulation of land use, as well as the granting of building permits. And even though it is the product of a long process of political and administrative decentralization and democratization of the State, there are many doubts about the advisability of local governments being the only suitable body to deal with all types of problems faced by cities, and in particular, being able to advise on urban development. In this regard, it is clear that in many cities, city councils have been unable to cope with the pressures of large real estate companies who have managed to adapt the plans to their investment needs, benefitting from the regulation of land use, with the resulting urban sprawl. In short, urban planning is experiencing one of its worst periods by not asserting its social function.

With regard to the incorporation of land to urban development, sufficient progress has not been made for the fulfilment of the social function of property and for public interest to prevail. Until 1992, there were basically only expropriation tools available, in addition to the purchase of private property, to create land reserves and to regularise irregular settlements. After this time what was achieved was to privatize public land through a main procedure that is the 'adoption of freehold title', which involves the end of the public land regime, which was not possible beforehand. This introduced a potential 50 per cent more land around Mexican cities that had lost their agricultural function to the urban land market.

Other procedures, with less impact on the privatization of public land, are the regularization of urban sites and public housing associations, although they are not relevant mechanisms for the creation of urban land reserves. There is, however, a procedure in the General Human Settlements Act called 'pre-emptive rights', which would allow state and local governments to buy the land 'included in the declaration of reserves, when such properties are put up for sale or, through any legal act, will be the subject of transfer of ownership'. Unfortunately, this is not used; the decision was made to waive the crystallization of the social function of land, not only for this particular tool, but because others have been created with this aim.

By contrast, other flexible land management tools have emerged, and these aim to facilitate investment in large cities, such as selective planning mechanisms. For example, this applies to the Special Development Zones (ZEDECs) in the 1980s in Mexico City, instead of the application of the 'Master Plan'. The 'Development Potential Transfer System' in the 1990s, to transfer surplus building rights strength from an owner to a third party, if permitted in the recipient area. Once into the new millennium, 'Investment and Development Corridors' (CIDs) were desirable areas for economic growth, such as *Avenida Reforma* in Mexico City (Parnreiter, 2011), among others.

In short, Mexico requires original urban land management tools in order to meet the housing needs of the poor in its cities. In the following paragraphs, various tools developed in some cities in Portugal, Brazil and Colombia are shown, affirming that local governments in other countries have been much more active and creative in meeting the land and housing needs of the more disadvantaged strata of the population.

The Portuguese Experience

The Contributions of the Democratic Interventionist Regime to Social Housing

Housing policies in Portugal designed from the late 19th and early 20th centuries were interrupted by the *Estado Novo* under a dictatorship, whose public intervention coincided with a low rate of urban development in the country, so housing did not have much priority on the political agenda. The 'affordable housing programme' and 'housing for poor families' were unable to help families in uncertain situations, and, although by then there were at least 15 types of affordable housing and dozens of regulations in the field, only 5 per cent of the total housing stock was produced with state support between 1953 and 1962. Among the main initiatives in Lisbon are the ones in *Alvalade* (1949–1955), *Olivais Sul* (1955–1958), *Olivais Norte* (1964–1966), and the one in the *Camarários* neighbourhoods[6] in the city of Porto (1956–1959). In this context of isolated initiatives, a national housing deficit of between 4,60,000 and 6,00,000 households had accumulated in 1960.

At the beginning of the 1960s, and because of late industrialization, there was a surge in migration to major cities, which was shown by the proliferation of illegal shantytowns, especially on agricultural land. This phenomenon showed the limitations of the housing production system in Portugal, especially in metropolitan areas (Instituto de Habitação e Requalificação Urbana, 2008). Therefore, since 1965 the State gave to private initiatives the responsibility to offer urban land, transferring control of its production. But this concession resulted in dysfunctional growth of urban space, with no order or consistency with city and neighbourhood plans.

In 1970, the first Land Act was ordered (Diário da República Portuguesa, Decreto de Lei No. 576/70, 1970) and systematic expropriation was established. This law allowed the local government to acquire land through expropriation, without the need to defend a public purpose. The government could expropriate to develop social housing programmes, but it set the criteria itself, and no effect was made to use all the land for that purpose. This feature of the law caused the majority of the land expropriated by the government to cover equipment shortages, so there was not really a land acquisition policy for housing.

After the revolution of 25 April 1974, and the establishment of a democratic regime, the State took more interventionist measures in 1976 by reformulating the previous Land Act (Diário da República Portuguesa, Decreto de Lei No. 794/76, 1976) that is still in force to date. This law passed the Expropriation Code (Diário da República Portuguesa, Decreto de Lei No. 845/76, 1976) and established the legal framework for housing development and construction.

The return migration of former Portuguese colonies pressured the State to give continuity to the policy of 'social housing', using models of mass construction similar to those in other European countries, thus creating the 'Direct Promotion' programme that was implemented for land acquired by expropriation. According to Vilaça (2001), the land reserve formed in this way was the State's last major intervention, and the available land continues to be used to this day. Then came the establishment of indirect promotion programmes to build social housing, such as 'Municipal Promotion', 'Cooperative Promotion' and 'Home Development Contracts (CDH)', with the promoters being the councils, housing cooperatives and construction companies. Two important aspects of the housing policy were sector decentralisation and the inclusion of social participation. The Building Refurbishment Support Programmes also began, with lines of credit to finance the recovery of run-down housing.

From 1980 there was an increase in investment in housing construction, driven by the promotion of construction companies and easier access to home ownership through credit systems, which later led to many families having debt overhang. At the same time, in some low-income social sectors overcrowding and deteriorating housing was taking place, especially in historic centres, as an unexpected effect of the Leasing Act.[7]

In 1984, the National Housing Institute (INH) was created, now called the Institute of Housing and Urban Redevelopment (IHRU). It is a public body that invests its own equity in the promotion of social housing (or Low-Cost Housing, as it is now called) of three types: municipal, cooperative[8] and private companies. Between 1984 and 2004, this institute built over 1,26,000 units in the three categories of low-cost housing, of which approximately 47 per cent were for rent and the rest for sale (Portal da Habitação, 2013).

Later, in 1990, the Municipal Master Plan[9] arose as a land management tool that manages all city council land all over the country.

However, a reflection on the analysis of the Land Act and the municipal master plans is that, while they do contain lines of intervention, safeguarding and restrictions in urban areas, there is no legal tool that makes it obligatory to construct social housing. As an option, however, this should not be ignored. Meanwhile, on a more positive note, councils are endowed with a strong autonomy and legal mechanisms to promote social housing, as well as the power to join state programmes in the same field.

The experience of Portugal, although with shortcomings and problems, is important because according to the 2011 census, there are

2,98,242 people living in 1,18,750 houses classed as 'social housing'; in addition, 95.2 per cent of those homes are occupied on a lease basis (and will eventually be bought), hence the importance of the procedure for access to housing. In the Lisbon Metropolitan Area (with a population of 2.8 million), there are 52,119 households classed as 'social housing', of which 95.3 per cent are rented; and in the Porto Metropolitan Area (with 1.6 million inhabitants), there are 32,684 social housing units, of which 95.9 per cent are rented (Portal da Habitação, 2013).

Because of its relevance as a form of land management for social housing, we then developed the experience of the Special Relocation Programme in Lisbon and Porto.[10]

In 1987, a relocation programme was established in Portugal to eradicate shantytowns, but its poor results led to restructuring and 1993 saw the creation of the Special Relocation Programme (PER), operated through the IHRU, with impact mainly in the metropolitan areas of Lisbon and Porto.[11] The aim of the programme was to relocate people living in shantytowns into affordable housing. This involved providing resources to local councils for the construction, sale or lease of houses for families living in these shantytowns. Other options were the refurbishment of run-down houses or buildings at the request of beneficiary organizations, and the acquisition of defunct buildings or houses for renovation, providing that they were used for the relocation of families participating in the programme.

In addition to the specific relocation programme in the Lisbon and Porto areas, it is also possible for other towns and cities in Portugal to run relocation activities for social housing, either constructed or bought with financial support from the central government and banking institutions to grant funding for this purpose.

This policy was significant for relocation programmes: with all the errors that are indicated, with or without reason, they eradicated around 35,000 shacks (huts or similar) throughout Portugal in the period of 10–12 years. Significant public investment was a deciding factor in this, along with state resources and councils' access to credit from the Bank (Vilaça, 2001). Vilaça himself refers to Lisbon as a paradigmatic case, since it substantially increased housing for relocation. IHRU figures (available on its website www.ihru.pt) confirm this, because according to this institution some 60,000 houses were built for relocation purposes from 1984 to 2004. However, as of 2004 direct state promotion decreased and the relocation processes ended, redirecting housing policy toward urban redevelopment and leasing.

The Experience in Natal, Brazil

Planning and the Concept of Social Interest in Affordable Housing Actions

The city of Natal is the capital of Rio Grande del Norte state, situated in Northeast Brazil. It has a population of approximately 8,00,000 and is considered to be fully urbanized, so it does not have a land reserve policy. As in almost all Latin American cities, one of the serious problems it is faced with is that of poor settlements (shantytowns and favelas in the case of Brazil).

Natal had an unsuitable housing situation characterized by a large deficit, legal inconsistencies and a lack of basic infrastructure and environmental clean-up, resulting in people living in dangerous areas (on hillsides or near high-voltage lines) and environmental protection areas.

The first urban projects were in the late 1960s and were headed by the National Housing Bank (BNH). The bank helped to promote the process of urban development and to define the current boundaries of the city through social housing programmes, for sectors of the population with low incomes. In addition to this, it oversaw the construction of more than 32,000 residential units up to 1983. While at the beginning of the 1960s Natal had a population of 1,62,215, it had more than doubled by 1980, reaching 4,16,898. A significant part of that contingent of the population benefitted from BNH projects, occupying housing complexes located on the edge of the city, which later became notable urbanized areas on the outskirts of the city. Another part of the population, without the required income to access such programmes, was excluded from the process, causing a significant increase in slums (by over 60%) in the same period (Ataide, 1997).

The first actions of urban regulation and production occurred until the 1980s, when the city adopted its first urban planning tool to control the city production process: the Master Plan of 1984. For the first time, this plan defined the concept of Special Areas of Social Interest (AEIS), which included 70 favelas, 2,217 small villages and 118 housing estates that housed 15,233 families on incomes of up to three times the minimum wage and a population of 65,122 inhabitants. Along with the Master Plan, the Municipal Social Housing System (SMHIS) is assigned to the task of implementing the social housing policy for the city of Natal. The SMHIS is made up of an administrative unit, its management and control agency, the Social Housing Board (CONHABIN – responsible for land regulation), the legislative support, the supply of new housing, management actions, and monitoring of the AEIS and risk areas. It also approves the budget proposal by the Urban Development Fund (FURB) and the allocation of resources by the Social Housing Fund (FUNHABIN – its economic tool), which gives assistance and financial support to social housing programmes in cities. The main responsibility of the SMHIS is to ensure that public resources are subsidized to those earning the equivalent of three times the minimum wage or less, so it is decentralized but has the participation of the three levels of government, and engages private initiatives and organizations from society.[12]

The 1984 Master Plan was updated in 1994 and 2007. In each version identifications are made, although differently, of specific mechanisms to regulate access to housing. For example, the 1994 Master Plan recognized the concept of social interest in the different forms of housing production, whether formal or informal, legal or illegal, or regulated or not by the so-called formal urban space production market; it also considered the links between urban planning and housing policies, and introduced the concept of Social Housing (HIS). In turn, the current 2007 Master Plan created a new housing board, CONCIDADES, which is more equally representative and deliberative.

In Natal, there are different levels of intervention. The first includes social housing as part of the AEIS and its main objective (probably because most of them are already consolidated areas) is to improve living conditions and land regulation, although in certain cases it may also include relocation of parts of the population, preferably to adjacent areas. This type of housing is for people with an income level defined by the AEIS themselves. However, there is also social housing for people with a slightly higher salary range, granted through the rent of new or refurbished buildings. In this case, the council can build in publicly-owned vacant areas, obtained by expropriation or by the creation of a real estate consortium. Private initiatives can also participate in these processes, respecting the regulations as defined in the Master Plan. Let us briefly consider these two forms of access to social housing.

Special Areas of Social Interest (AEIS)

With regard to the AEIS, the prefecture may expropriate any land adjacent to the areas of intervention necessary to relocate and keep people close to their habitual place of residence. The council has its own resources (from other sources of funding) to intervene in these areas; this is the case of the Urban Development Fund (*FURB*), created by Ley Complementaria n° 7, de 5 de agosto de 1994, which, according to the master plan, applies to infrastructure works, expropriation payments and other urban projects or to purchase new buildings for the *AEIS*, in compliance with the Social Housing Policy for the city of Natal. Likewise, the city may purchase properties through 'pre-emptive rights', with some of the following purposes: land regulation and urban regulation programmes, execution of social housing programmes and projects, and the creation of land reserves, among others. The city or the owner of the property located in the Special Area of Social Interest may require the establishment of a Real Estate Consortium as a way of enabling a development plan, or to recover the property built for social housing purposes.[13] These interventions are defined by the Master Plan as the Urban Consortium Operation (*OUC*). As a minimum, each Urban Consortium Operation should consider benefits for a AEIS, among other things.

A relevant social housing development in Natal was built in an area that includes the communities of Passo de la Pátria, Areado and Pantanal, all included in the Special Areas of Social Support. The core elements of this project were land legalization,[14] urban development of the area, addressing environmental issues, construction and improvement of housing units, as well as social work for programme sustainability. This type of development also provides for prototype homes, which vary from individual units (households) to collective buildings (apartments). This project included the participation of all the public bodies of the prefecture of Natal and also had the participation of the public. However, it was not finished and had to be taken up by the current Secretariat of Housing, SEHARPE. Generally, the regulatory process for the AEIS has been a slow one, experiencing particular difficulty in having effective land regulation mechanisms and the participation of society in compliance with the criteria defined by the Master Plan planning system.

On the subject of land reserves and the policy aimed at constructing low-cost social housing, the legislation is still vague and general, although in terms of construction, the homes can be built in dense areas defined in the Master Plan or in the AEIS programme, sponsored by the public or private sectors and, in the latter case, favoured by construction rates and rules. For example, the Federal Savings Bank (*Caixa Econômica*) provides financing to private agents wishing to build social housing, although they must build properties with a minimum of 30m^2, ensuring that the funding is for people with income equivalent to up to six times the minimum wage. The City Social Housing Board must approve these projects (Secretaria Municipal de Meio Ambiente e Urbanismo (SEMURB): www.natal.rn.gov.br).

Low-cost Housing for Rent

The prefecture of Natal has endeavoured to provide more affordable housing on a rental basis. To do this, institutional policies and council efforts have adopted preventive actions in terms of progress on the legislation front, as is the case with the master plan (providing for the revision of the AEIS concept so they can accommodate a larger number of low-density areas). This is also the case with the work code and the supply of new homes through programmes such as the Residential Leasing Programme (PAR), the Social Housing Programme (PSH), the Residential Social Housing Programme (PRSH) and the Special Housing Programme (PEH). PAR is a programme subsidized by the federal government, exclusively for housing for people on low incomes in major urban areas, making monthly payments as if the property were for rent. The PAR works with an income ranging from three to six times the minimum wage and at the end of the contract, which is 15 years, the interested party has the option to purchase the property.[15]

The Experience in Bogota, Colombia

Like the great cities of Mexico and Brazil, the housing shortage in Bogota affects the low-income population and is caused by the lack of developed land, equipped with infrastructure and public service networks, at affordable prices. This is a result of the high cost of housing and the difficulties for this sector of the population to access financing mechanisms offered by the market. This has given rise to two patterns of production of affordable housing: an informal one and a formal one, comprising social housing.

The informal market has satisfied the needs of low earners through self-build processes in illegal developments, which generally do not meet suitable living conditions. In 1998, for example, 1,433 informal settlements made up 23 per cent of the 30,000 urban hectares in the city and 38 per cent of its population (Aristazabal and Ortiz, n.a., 2–3).

Formal urban development has also had an impact on the urban growth of the outskirts of Bogota since the early 1990s, when the State made the decision to subsidize demand based on market mechanisms, thus changing its role from promoter to facilitator of supply and demand. According to Aristazabal and Ortiz (n.a., 2–3), Bogota required an average of 50,000 new social housing homes per year in the 10 years from 1998; and another estimate for 2005 showed that the housing shortage in the city was 5,27,269 units, and that approximately 7,600 hectares of land would be required in order to build them.

Interest in halting informal construction in the city and in alleviating the high costs generated by this phenomenon gave rise to some policies and tools that would allow the planning and management of land and housing in the 1970s and 1980s, although it was not until the early 1990s that the most significant amendments were made to the general legal framework (Arteaga, 2008). The first one was the new Colombian Constitution of 1991, which involved a significant change in urban planning and housing production for those on low incomes, by establishing the right to public services of water, sewerage and electricity, regardless of proprietary rights, as a fundamental right for all Colombian citizens (Aristazabal and Ortiz, n.a., 4–5).

Subsequently, Act 388 of 1997 set new guidelines for urban planning in Colombia by introducing new management tools and bolstering local governments' ability to manage the land. One of the most notable accomplishments in connection with the law was the Plan for Territorial Organisation (POT) of Bogota, adopted through Order in Council 619 of 2000 and amended by Order in Council 469 of 2003. The POT defined a city model, with different intervention levels and priorities; it incorporated the concept of sustainability and proposed compact urban growth. It also considered public space as a structuring element of the city; this issue was addressed using ecology, urban facilities and the road system.

These modifications to the general legal framework did not pay off immediately, as some authors like Ceballos (2005) warn that Bogota's experience of urban planning and its legislation for affordable housing production up to the 1990s allowed one to appreciate favourable developments for the economic interests of urban developers, but unfavourable developments for those seeking this type of housing. In fact, it was not until the first decade of the new millennium that Colombia launched several innovative experiences in this area, particularly in the cities of Bogota, Medellin and Pereira (Torres and Garcia, 2010). We cannot review all of those experiences here, nor can we assess the impact they have had on the structure and dynamics of those cities, so we will refer only to the creation of the public company

Metrovivienda, the most successful tool to break the traditional way of managing urban land for social housing (Gallo, 2010).

Metrovivienda: A Successful Land Management Tool for Social Housing

Metrovivienda is a public company created by Bogota city council in December 1998. Its main objectives are to promote the mass supply of urban land to facilitate the implementation of Integrated Social Housing Projects; to develop the functions of land banks or real estate banks in relation to buildings set aside for implementation of any urban projects that take into account the provision of Priority Social Housing; and to promote community organization of low-income families to enable their access to land earmarked for priority social housing[16] (Alcaldía Mayor de Bogota, 1998: www.metrovivienda.gov.co)..

In the history of this company, three land management models stand out. The first, implemented between 1999 and 2003, was designed to curb informal urban development through its land bank and housing development functions, and had two courses of action. On the one hand, there are the *direct intervention,* or first generation projects, where land is acquired through voluntary or judicial expropriation, given primary urban development and sold to construction companies. This method was applied to projects in Ciudadela El Recreo and Ciudadela El Porvenir de las Americas, situated in the town of Bosa. On the other hand, in *associative,* or second generation projects, the owner provides the land and *Metrovivienda* provides capital for investments in primary urban development in order to then sell the blocks to construction companies; this system saw the development of the projects Ciudadela Nuevo Usme, to the southeast of the city, and Ciudadela Campo Verde, in the town of Bosa. The four quoted projects provided 381 hectares of raw land, of which 181.6 hectares are usable area with a potential for 35,809 homes. In the first stage, *Metrovivienda* financed 141.5 hectares, marketed 31.9 hectares and promoted the construction of 4,607 single-family priority houses. The main results of this management model are as follows:

It slowed down illegal expansion in Bosa, and partly in Usme. It also streamlined and legitimized the legal priority housing market (VIP) in the city, and facilitated coordination between housing system components: provision of land, housing construction, environment and community facilities, as well as channelling subsidies, savings and loans.

The promotion of 4,067 VIP properties benefitted a segment of the population earning over the equivalent of twice the minimum wage in the formal job market, affiliated to Family Welfare Financial Institutions. This aspect is observed in the results of the homes built, as part of the *Metrovivienda* projects, of which 8.9 per cent are housing type 1 and 91.1 per cent are type 2.96.7 per cent of the commercialized area was bought by private construction companies and the remaining 3.3 per cent by popular housing organizations (OPVs). A considerable amount of the supply of private firms was progressive (Casasfranco and Arcos, 2007: 19–21).

In line with housing targets that were set in the development plan Bogota Without Indifference (*Bogotá sin Indiferencia*), drawn up by the Mayor's Office of Bogota in 2004, a second land management model was implemented to emphasize popular housing organizations (OPVs) versus market operation, in order to benefit citizens earning less than the equivalent of twice the minimum wage. It also sought to reduce housing costs through organized community involvement. The plan set a goal of building 70,000 new homes, of which 50 per cent were to be contributed by the private sector, and the other half were to be provided by *Metrovivienda*, through land management in ongoing projects. The main results of this management model are:

High participation on the part of OPVs and their access to urban land sold in *Metrovivienda* projects: in 2004 the OPVs obtained 68,972m^2, compared with 30,204m^2 from private firms, and the participation of private firms fell from 96.7 per cent in 2000–2003, to 41 per cent in 2004–2005.

However, OPVs encountered administrative difficulties in managing the resources of their partners (savings, subsidies and loans) and projects had significant delays both in construction time and legal registration of single-family homes. Because of this, the performance of private firms contrasts with that of OPVs, because while the former legally registered 5,388 homes (83.5%) in 2004–2006, the OPVs legally registered just 1,067 homes (16.5%) (2007: 22–25).

Finally, between 2005 and 2007, a third land management model came into operation, comprising a more dynamic land bank with the consolidation of VIP programme objectives. *Metrovivienda* sped up the process of urban development of available land in the projects El Recreo and El Porvenir de las Americas, and adjusted the marketing scheme in order to encourage more competition among developers for the land available, and increased speed in the promotion of priority housing. The most important results of this model are:

In the period 2004–2007 (September), 74 blocks over a total area of 45.3 hectares were sold, while in 2001–2003, 32 blocks over an area of 30.2 hectares were sold.

Reduction in the time, from 18 to 15 months, given to builders to comply with their housing construction and registration obligations, meant greater dynamics in the rate of housing construction. A higher number of housing units promoted every year, and more homes sold: 7,528 units in 2004–2007, compared to 4,607 in 2001–2003.

The combination of the variables of land shortages, high demand for developed land for VIPs by large construction companies and high housing shortages in the city led to *Metrovivienda* promoting greater use of land in the projects El Recreo and El Porvenir de las Americas, encouraging the construction of high-rise blocks of flats (up to six floors). This initiative involved a substantial change in the potential of land use and more homes and families benefitted, unlike the trend during the first years that favoured the construction of single-family homes. The shift towards intensive land use is as follows: from 2001 to 2007, 71 per cent of the usable area was earmarked for single-family homes and 29 per cent for blocks of flats.

In accordance with the housing policy established in the development plan Bogota Without Indifference 2004–2008 (*Bogotá sin Indiferencia,* 2004–2008), which proposed to benefit the lower-income segments of the population, *Metrovivienda* directed its actions towards increasing the amount of type 1 housing. During the first two years of management in the organization, all houses sold were type 2. In 2003, in projects in the organization, 408 type 1 housing units were legally registered for the first time (27.3% of 1,495 registered that year). The share of type 1 homes has increased significantly, compared to type 2 housing, so that 2006 saw 2,759 type 1 homes registered (97.5% of total registrations), showing the political strategy of going further into the niche market of the poor earning less than two times the minimum wage. The balance sheet for 2001–2007 shows a balance in strata diversification, so that at the end of 2007, 51.3 per cent of households were type 1 and 48.7 per cent were type 2 (2007: 26–32).

Conclusion: Main Implications of Ibero American Experiences for Mexico.

In studying the cases of Portugal, Brazil, Colombia and Mexico, it is clear that in all cases the respective national governments face the challenge of providing the poor in their cities with housing alternatives or developed land. The information shows that this is only possible through public policies with a social orientation, although such policies have to make way for the standardized housing policies regulated by the market, and they are prevailing. We also observed that, in order for policies to translate into specific land and housing programmes, at least three conditions are essential:

The first is the existence of a legal and institutional framework to provide different levels of government with means to impose 'public interest' on ownership and various economic figures, requiring proper intergovernmental coordination to address real estate capital and regulate it. The urban policy framework must provide legal instruments for local councils to acquire land at low cost, as well as develop it, build affordable housing and allocate it to those living in poverty. Naturally, this goes hand-in-hand with the availability of financial resources, but part of them have to come from suitable land management, while the correct use of subsidies should be assessed positively.

The second condition is the decentralization of land and housing management to local governments, since it is specifically at this level that the applications from the population in poverty are made. In this area, the attention of organized groups of housing applicants seems a better option in terms of social housing policy and implementing the right to housing, in comparison to individual lending.

Third, planning systems and urban regulations are the means by which it is possible to regulate the actions of private bodies (individuals or companies) on city territory, and allocate appropriate uses and purposes of the various spaces for best performance.

The case of Mexico is representative of a country whose housing policy has a market orientation that, although it can be considered a relevant case from a commercial standpoint by creating an average of 7,00,000 homes per year between 2000 and 2012 from a housing needs perspective for the poor, is an unsuccessful case. The reasons for this are the lack of investment in this sector of the population, and the lack of legal resources for land management.

From the experiences of the other three countries reviewed, thought could be given to the possibility of adopting some tools or programmes to the situation in Mexico, with the appropriate modifications. For example, to relocate informal, risk area settlements, the relocation programmes as in Portugal, as well as urban redevelopment programmes, could be considered.

The cases of Brazil and Colombia show the importance of joining housing policies with urban development policies, an omission that has been heavily criticized in Mexico, resulting in expansive urban growth and with very low population density. More specifically, this can refer to the designation of Special Areas of Social Interest (AEIS) or the lease-based, low-cost housing scheme in Natal, as well as the effective use of the 'pre-emptive rights', or the creation of real estate consortia. In the city of Bogota, the land bank schemes for the provision of VIPs, or the direct intervention projects (first generation) and associative projects (second generation) are all worthy of mention, among others that were not considered due to lack of space.

With the specificities of each country, there are some very valuable elements to consider from the Ibero American countries reviewed here, in order to enrich the management tools and urban development planning in Mexico.

Notes

1. The concept of social interest in Mexico and Latin America, associated with the topic of housing, is equivalent to the concept of social housing in English. And so it is used throughout the text.
2. For housing, the first period began in 1972 when national housing agencies were created, and for land and urban development it began in 1976, when the General Human Settlements Act was made public. However, in both areas there is a history of programmes and policies dating back to the 1940s, among which, in the case of housing, the Housing Finance Programme stands out.
3. To be exact, 1986 is the year that is considered to be representative of the change in the development model in Mexico, as it is the date the nation joined the General Agreement on Tariffs and Trade (GATT), the predecessor to the World Trade Organization. The year 1992 is quoted because this is when reforms were made to housing organizations and to Article 27 of the Constitution, which led to the privatization of social land in the country.
4. The national housing organizations (ONAVIS) are the Mexican Federal Institute for Workers' Housing (INFONAVIT), the Housing Fund at the Institute for Social Security and Services for State Workers (FOVISSSTE) and the Military Housing Fund (FOVIMI-ISSFAM), the first two being the most important. They were created in 1972 because Article 123 of the Constitution established the obligation of the employer to provide its workers with housing. Their resources came from the mandatory contributions made by employers, equivalent to 5 per cent of workers' salaries. This is important, because they are not Federal Government resources.
5. National Institute for Statistics and Geography [www.inegi.org.mx].
6. The term *Camarários* refers to neighbourhoods with affordable housing built by the council for people with low salaries.

7. The Leasing Act No. 6/2006, which approved the new Urban Leasing Regime (NRAU), establishes a special regime of old rents, and alters the Civil Code, the Civil Procedure Code, Order in Council 287/2003 of 12 November, the Council Tax Code for Property and the Property Registration Code.
8. This type of production is based on cooperativism and aims to construct, maintain and purchase low-cost housing for its members.
9. The Municipal Master Plan is a planning tool 'that sets the spatial structure model of the municipal territory, constituting a synthesis of local development and management strategy, integrating national regional options with impact on the respective area of intervention'. Order in Council 380/99.
10. Although the Special Relocation Programme has been relevant, it should also be noted that there has been little attention to the construction of housing for people living outside the slums, whose socio-economic conditions are equally precarious.
11. Order in Council 163/93 of 7 May that led to the Special Relocation Programme for the metropolitan areas of Lisbon and Porto (PER). Order in Council 79/96 of 20 June on the Partnerships Grant Scheme to support the purchase or refurbishment of housing for families covered by the Special Relocation Programme in the metropolitan areas of Lisbon and Porto (Special Relocation Programme for Families, an extension of the Special Relocation Programme).
12. Secretaria Municipal de Meio Ambiente e Urbanismo (SEMURB): www.natal.rn.gov.br.
13. Natal Master Plan. Complementary Act No. 082 of 21 June 2007. Chapter VI: The Real Estate Consortium, Article 82.
14. Land legalization anticipates specific considerations on the type of subdivision and land occupancy that is practiced in a given area, in the specific case of each Special Area of Social Support.
15. Secretaria Municipal de Meio Ambiente e Urbanismo (SEMURB): www.natal.rn.gov.br
16. By Priority Social Housing we understand a housing solution of which the sale price does not exceed the sum of 1,50,00,000 Colombian pesos (COP), an amount that will change monthly, from the time the Agreement is signed by the Mayor, based on the national consumer price index of the respective month, in accordance with reports issued by the Office for National Statistics in Colombia; any developers of urban projects may not increase the selling price set in this Article (Agreement 15, 1998: Article 3). Updates to this figure for 2005 produced a price of 1,90,00,000 Colombian pesos, equivalent to 50 times the legal monthly minimum wage (*Metrovivienda*, n.a.).

References

Aristizabal, Nora and y Ortiz, Andrés (sf) *Aproximación Innovativa a la Tenencia de la Tierra Para los Pobres Urbanos en Bogotá.* Lincoln Institute of Land Policy.

Arteaga Arredondo, Isabel. (2008). Del Perímetro al Centro. Procesos de Construcción y Transformación de la Periferia Consolidada en Bogotá'. Paper presented at the IV Simposio Internacional Territorios y Sociedades en un Mundo en Cambio. Miradas Contrastadas en Iberoamérica, Barcelona.

Ataide, Ruth. (1997). *Habitação de Interesse Social nos Planos Diretores de Natal – 1984/1994: O Desafio Para Incluir, a Exclusão que Permanece.* Dissertação de Mestrado em Ciências Sociais, Universidade Federal do Rio Grande do Norte, Natal, Brazil.

Casasfranco, María Virginia y Arcos, Oscar. (2007). *10 Años De Metrovivienda. Modelos de Gestión del Suelo, Vivienda y Hábitat.* Bogota: United Nations Development Programme, UN-Habitat, Metrovivienda y Alcaldía Mayor de Bogotá.

Ceballos Ramos, Olga Lucía. (2005). La legislación Urbanística Para la Producción de Vivienda de Bajo Costo. La Experiencia de Bogotá, *Scripta Nova. Revista Electrónica de Geografía y Ciencias Sociales.* 9(194), p. 25. [Online edition: www.ub.es/geocrit/sn/sn-194–25.htm].

Connolly, Priscilla. (2006). El Financiamiento de Vivienda en México (unpublished manuscript).

Diário da República Portuguesa. Decreto de Lei No. 576/70. Lei de Solos, 1970.

——. Decreto de Lei No. 794/76. Reformulação da Lei de Solos de 1976.

——. Decreto de Lei No. 845/76. Código das Expropriações, 1976.

Fundación Centro de Investigación y Documentación de la Casa (CIDOC) y Sociedad Hipotecaria Federal (SHF) (2012) *Estado Actual de la Vivienda en México,* Mexico.

Gallo, Ignacio. (2010). 'El Recreo y Nuevo Usme: Gestión del Suelo Para la Vivienda Social en Bogotá', in Torres, Patricia y García, María Constanza (eds) *Ciudades del Mañana. Gestión del Suelo Urbano en Colombia.* Washington, DC: Interamerican Bank of Development, pp. 103–134.

Harvey, David. (1989). 'From Managerialism to Entrepreneurialism: The Transformation in Urban Governance in Late Capitalism', *Geografiska Annaler. Series B, Human Geography,* 71(1), pp. 3–17.

——. (2008). 'El derecho a la Ciudad', *New Left Review,* 53, pp. 23–39.

——. (2010). 'La ciudad Neoliberal', in M. Alfie, I. Azuara, C. Bueno, M. Pérez Negrete y S. Tamayo (eds) *Sistema Mundial y Nuevas Geografías.* Mexico: Universidad Autónoma Metropolitana Azcapotzalco y Universidad Iberoaméricana.

Instituto de Habitaçâo e Requalificação Urbana [www.ihru.pt] (2008)

Metrovivienda [www.metrovivienda.gov.co]

Ortíz, Enrique. (1996). FONHAPO. Gestión y Desarrollo de un Fondo Público en Apoyo de la Producción Social de Vivienda. Mexico: Habitat International Coalition.

Parnreiter, Christof. (2011). Formación de la Ciudad Global, Economía Inmobiliaria y Transnacionalización de Espacios Urbanos, *Revista EURE,* 37 (111): 15–24 [Online edition: www.scielo.cl/scielo.php?script=sci_issuetoc&pid=0250-716120110002&lng=es&nrm=iso].

Plano Diretor de Natal (1994) Ley Complementaria N° 7, de 5 de agosto de 1994.

Portal da Habitação [www.portaldahabitacao.pt] 2013

Puebla, Claudia. (2006). Las Instituciones Públicas de Vivienda en México, in Centro de Estudios Sociales y de Opinión Pública, *La vivienda en México: Construyendo Análisis Y Propuestas,* pp. 135–148.

Schteingart, Martha. (1989). Los Productores del Espacio Habitable. Estado, Empresa y Sociedad en la ciudad de México. Mexico: El Colegio de México.

Secretaria Municipal de Meio Ambiente e Urbanismo (SEMURB) [www.natal.rn.gov.br]

Sedue. (1989). Estadística Básica de Vivienda, 1989–1992. Mexico: Secretaría de Desarrollo Urbano y Ecología.

Torres, Patricia y García, María Constanza (eds). (2010). *Ciudades Del Mañana. Gestión del Suelo Urbano en Colombia.* Washington, DC: Interamerican Bank of Development.

Theodore, Nik, Peck, Jamie y Brenner, Neil. (2009). Urbanismo Neoliberal: la Ciudad y el Imperio de los Mercados, *Temas Sociales,* (66): 1–11 [Online edition: www.sitiosur.cl/publicacionescatalogodetalle.php?PID=3532&doc=&lib=Y&rev=Y&art=Y&doc1=Y&vid=Y&autor=&coleccion=Temas%20Sociales&tipo=ALL&nunico=3532].

Vilaça, Eduardo. (2001). 'O 'Estado da Habitação' medidas sem politica num País Adiado, *Revista Cidades, Comunidades e Territorios,* 3, pp. 83–92.

PART IV

Conclusion: Challenges for the Future

13

Conclusion

Challenges for the Future

Brian C. Aldrich and Ranvinder S. Sandhu

World population increases and the associated population shifts from rural to urban areas will continue to add to the numbers of urban poor and housing shortages in developing countries. While these trends will add more potential workers to the urban labour force and provide a growing market for the expanding neoliberal market economies, there is little or no indication that housing and related services will keep up with the rising demand. The analysis reported in the above chapters has highlighted the responses of selected cities and societies to urbanization and houselessness. These cases describe the new context of housing for the urban poor as policies and conditions have changed over the decades from 1990s. They can be summarized under the following four points:

1. The World Bank, followed by other international organizations, moved from a policy of supporting specific projects for low income housing to requiring states to integrating low income housing needs into the housing market and other sectors of the economy.
2. The varying support for social housing.
3. An increase in the range of skills required to implement the enabling policies called for by the World Bank.
4. The recognition of the 'use value' of housing for the urban poor rather than the 'exchange value'.

The analysis of housing for the urban poor at the programme, societal and international levels provides a clearer understanding of these changes and their consequences for the housing of the urban poor in developing countries.

Free Market Housing

The limiting case in regard to the emergence of a free market in housing, is the Cambodian case reported by Yap and Brauch in Chapter 1. They assert that the government '... lacks the institutional capacity (including policies, laws, regulations and procedures) and the political will to regulate urban development ...' (p. 2). Outside political pressure from the German government and the UN Human Rights Commission had to be applied to the government to get it to support a system of land registration in Cambodia. In order to preserve the land rights of those who occupied the Boeung Kak Lake area, the Cambodian central government promulgated Circular 03. It was an ad hoc, that is, temporary, settlement regarding squatter settlements in Cambodia.

The Egyptian government, in the midst of the 'Arab Spring', was not able to control new land invasions under conditions of poor security. Ahmed M. Soliman points out the lack of a free market approach in government policies regarding informal housing in Chapter 7. He describes the demobilization, participatory, manipulative, cost-recovery and transitional socio-economic and political modes the Egyptian government has tried over the last ninety years up to the present (p. 3). He concludes that a programme of development via the civil society, as opposed to the government or the market, would be more efficient. He recognizes that none of the previous modes have succeeded in solving the problem of lack of housing for the poor.

At the other end of the free market scale are the case studies of China and Turkey. The Chinese shift to a state-driven market economy, including the housing sector, is an example of an unrestrained market in housing with major social consequences. On-Kwok Lai, in Chapter 6, states that this '... pro-market continued reform has been creating new urban poverty of various forms: not only the increasing number of those low income people who cannot catch up with the rise of housing and commodity prices, but the dis-enfranchised and underprivileged groups created by property-development ...'. The middle class, new university graduates, the unregistered workers migrating in from the rural areas and those sharing property through marriage, are all at risk by the unfettered housing market. Included in the list of consequences of the new policy is environmental pollution and disasters forced upon China and neighbouring countries.

Asuman Türkün, presenting the case of Turkey in Chapter 2, describes an authoritarian form of urban-oriented capitalism which has had negative consequences for the beneficiaries of previous rehousing programmes for squatters in Istanbul. She reports that Article 73 of *Municipal Law* (Law No. 5393) '... gave the responsibility to take decisions on urban development ... to local government ...' for a variety of purposes including restoring the older parts of the city, creating new housing area, industrial and commercial and social facilities, as well as areas subject to the dangers of earthquakes (p. 8). This law puts all of the power to take and redevelop areas into the hands of the government without recourse to citizen review. This approach has resulted in large scale protests due to the lack of public participation in the decisions made about housing development by the government. Included in this top-down approach is the taking of the green space around and within the older resettlement areas for former squatters and the relocation of residents to the periphery to facilitate the gentrification of older, central city neighbourhoods under pressure from the market.

The government of India has accepted the more open market model. Manoj Kumar Teotia, in Chapter 10, lists all the different programmes and policies which have been implemented to attempt to stem the tide of the need for housing the urban poor – in the face of strong and continued urbanization. Among these, he lists '... initiatives for housing the poor, slum rehabilitation programmes, legal, institutional and financial mechanisms for housing, public and private sector housing, home loans for the target groups, security of tenure, low cost rental housing ...' (p. 2). He concludes that there is still a long list of problems regarding the provision of housing for the poor, including '... poor quality of housing stock, insecurity of tenure, lack of privacy ... high level of congestion, absence of separate kitchens, toilets, bath facilities ... infrastructure and basic services inadequacies ...' (p. 10). The housing of the poor continues to be a challenge for the Indian government.

Social Housing for Low Income Families

Suzana Pasternak and Camila D'Ottaviano place the history and the latest modes of intervention into the political context of Sao Paulo, Brazil in Chapter 8. They review the political history from removal of squatter areas to the current holistic approach under the guise of the

Worker's Party in Sao Paulo. Current projects have been developed with additional state support to integrate the residents of the favelas into the socio-economic life of the city – rather than in isolating project areas. In the early 1990s '... the idea that favela residents were poor workers who had a right to the city and to be integrated into the urban fabric had already consolidated itself' (p. 7). The Barrio Legal Programme became the basis for implementing a social housing policy in Sao Paulo. The programme is a good example of what the World Bank was calling for in its new emphasis: state enabling of housing for the poor was not to be just a matter of putting everything in the market, but a widespread, bottom-up integration of the favelas into the life of the city (p. 8).

The housing challenges under the new World Bank enabling policy are described in several Asian countries, including Sri Lanka, Cambodia, Singapore, India and Thailand by Yap Koie Sheng in Chapter 11. He describes the strategy of land sharing used in several of the major cities in these countries as a way to provide housing for the poor – squatters, etc. – while providing more land for commercial development in the heart of these cities. He maintains a focus on the reluctance of urban governments to provide land in the city for resettlement in public-private projects which provide housing and access to jobs for the urban poor. The market for urban land continues to emphasize the production of goods and services for the global marketplace at the expense of an improved quality of life for its citizens (p. 11).

Chapter 12 describes similar challenges to the provision of social housing for low income residents in Mexico, Portugal, Colombia and Brazil. Guillermo Olivera, Carla Narciso and Julio Guadarrama compare the social housing policies in the latter three countries with their lack in Mexico. The problem in Mexico, the authors state, is that there has been a shift to the privatization of public land, but no taxing of property which would help fund social housing (p. 3). Portugal has no legal tools to enforce social housing policies, but does have a strong municipal council tradition which supports it. In Natal, Brazil, the support for social housing is present but weak – especially in regard to the Master Plan (p. 9). In Bogota, Colombia, they find both informal housing and formal urban development providing housing for the poor. The latter is based upon a commitment by the State in the 1990s to '... subsidies demand based on market mechanisms, thus changing it role from promoter to facilitator of supply and demand' (p. 10). They conclude that the provision of housing for the poor '… is only possible through public policies with a social orientation …' (p. 13).

Skills for Enabling the Integration of Low Income Housing into the Market

The programme-level cases described by several of the researchers in the book indicate the new kinds of skills required by governments, civil organizations and private sector builders to effectively provide for housing for the poor in the new, market-based arena. Sheela Patel, a leading activist for the poor in India, in Chapter 3 describes in detail the difficulties of working with the government under the new, liberalized land market in India. Based upon a survey of several projects across India, she concludes with a long list beginning with the lack of participation by the poor in the housing provision process. The problems begin with the Community Development Proposals, then continue through Project Design and Planning, Institutional Capacity, Land issues, Finance Management and Community Participation. She concludes that the professionals involved in this process do not have the skills nor an orientation to the needs of the poor necessary to make the new policies a success (p. 11).

Brazil, at the other extreme from India, according to the research on almost a dozen different housing projects, has been more of a success under the new rules. Fernanda Magalhaes, in Chapter 4, presents a detailed list of how housing projects for the poor need to be skilfully integrated into the fabric of the city. She reports on the new legal framework (see also Chapter 8) '… which gave rise to a number of urban policy instruments: compulsory land parceling, utilization and building, progressive property tax, and expropriation-sanction arrangements … to combat property speculation …' (p. 3). The chapter reports, in considerable detail, all the different aspects of the process that need to be covered – and the professional orientation and skills required to do it.

R.G. Ariyawansa and M.A.N. Rasanjalee Perera, in the chapter on Colombo, Sri Lanka (Chapter 9), describe the extent of the housing problems for the poor and the several attempts to deal with the 50 per cent of the residents, most of them poor or displaced by civil war, who need housing. Reporting on a major study of transportation in Addis Ababa, Ethiopia, Belew Dagnew Bogale and Kiran Sandhu (Chapter 5) illustrates the importance of integrating other institutional sectors to the housing needs of the poor. They show how transportation can increase the lack of access of the poor to housing and jobs.

Use Value Versus Market Value

The shift to a market-based solution to housing for the poor in developing countries has generated a concern for ways to conceptualize the context of urbanization and housing for the urban poor. Several of the authors in this text have chosen to use the work and concepts of the Logan and Molotch book, *Urban Fortunes* (1987), and the related series of articles based upon this model of urban capitalism.

The authors make a distinction between the 'use value' of land and housing and its 'exchange value'. The former has to do with its intrinsic value to the householder; the latter has to do with its market value. So in the cases described in Istanbul, Turkey, for instance, the squatter resettlement areas have 'use' value because they are close to jobs, provide interactions with relatives and friends, give access to green space, etc. 'Exchange value' on the other hand, is what that same housing space would bring on the open market if sold to high salary service workers, tourists or others who would also like to be located close to jobs, the cultural activities of the central city, etc.

The distinction is really between the uses that different groups would put a housing area to, and the price they are willing to pay, the market value, for access to that area. Several groups may be in competition over the use to which housing in an area is put; one mechanism for determining who gets to use it in the market. The chapters in this book describe the powerful competition for a place in the large cities of the developing and developed countries. But they also show how it is possible for houseless squatters and residents of informal housing areas – barrios and favelas – to be included in the life of these cities. State support of social housing and skilled participants, along with the support of the civic organizations and activists, can help level up the playing field for the urban poor. The chapters in this book spell out in some detail, both the obstacles and the tools to bring this equality about.

Reference

Logan, J.R., and H.L. Molotch. (1987). *Urban Fortunes: The Political Economy of Place,* Berkeley, California: University of California Press.

Index